REVOLUTION IN TEACHING

A broad, comprehensive study of the far-reaching developments in contemporary American education.

"The pages of this book attest to the ferment that characterizes American education today. . . . New curricula have been devised in the sciences and mathematics, and new efforts at curriculum construction are under way in the social studies and humanities and in the study of languages and literature. Film, the book, the laboratory, the 'teaching machine'—all have come under close scrutiny in the effort to hasten and deepen the learning process. Indeed, to the outside observer it must seem as if we were preparing to embark upon a **permanent revolution in education.**"

from the Introduction by Jerome Bruner,
Harvard University

ALFRED DE GRAZIA, Associate Professor of Government at New York University, is editor and publisher of the **American Behavioral Scientist,** a monthly magazine of theory and research in the social sciences. Dr. De Grazia has written many articles and several books, including **The American Way of Government** and **The American Congress.**

DAVID A. SOHN, instructor of English in Middlesex Junior High School, Darien, Connecticut, is Chairman of the Committee for Programed Instruction for the Darien school system. Mr. Sohn is also Assistant Supervisor of Study Skills, the Study Skills Office, Yale University.

BANTAM MATRIX EDITIONS

is a series of original and reprint works in the fields of mathematics, history, education, biology, philosophy, literary criticism and the other major disciplines. They are selected for the enduring insights they offer into the nature of the conditions which shape the life of man.

Matrix Editions in the field of Education: THE STORY OF EDUCATION / PROGRAMS, TEACHERS, AND MACHINES / VITAL ISSUES IN AMERICAN EDUCATION / REVOLUTION IN TEACHING.

BANTAM MATRIX EDITIONS

revolution in teaching:

new theory, technology, and curricula

•

Edited by
Alfred de Grazia and David A. Sohn

•

with an Introduction by Jerome Bruner

BANTAM BOOKS
NEW YORK/TORONTO/LONDON

REVOLUTION IN TEACHING
Bantam Matrix edition published October 1964
2nd printing
3rd printing

ACKNOWLEDGMENTS

For permission to reprint the selections in this volume, grateful acknowledgment is made to the copyright holders, publishers and authors named:

THE AMERICAN BEHAVIORAL SCIENTIST, Vol. VI, No. 3, November 1962, © 1962 Metron, Inc., for: "The New Educational Technology," Jerome Bruner; "Take-off to Revolution," James D. Finn; "The Challenge of Automation to Education," Luther H. Evans; "Educational Television and Films," Stephen White; "Libraries and Information Retrieval," Henry J. Dubester; "Testing, Tests, and Testing Service Organizations," Henry Chauncey and Robert L. Ebel; "The Emerging English Curriculum," J. N. Hook; "Social Science and the New Curriculum," Franklin Patterson; "The New Curricula in Social Studies with Emphasis on History," Henry W. Bragdon.

Alvin C. Eurich, for "A Twenty-First-Century Look at Higher Education," originally published in the ATLANTIC MONTHLY.

Donald A. Cook, for "The New Technology and the Educational Decision," an address given in July 1963 to the American Association of Higher Education of the National Education Association.

Donald Ely, for "Facts and Fallacies about New Media in Education."

Edward J. Gordon, for "Conflicting Values in the Secondary School," a speech delivered on Parents' Day, Yale University, October 1962, Copyright, 1963, by YALE ALUMNI MAGAZINE.

DAEDALUS, Spring 1962, and Aldous Huxley, for "Education on the Non-verbal Level," Aldous Huxley.

Goodwin Watson and TEACHERS COLLEGE RECORD, 1960, 61, 253–257, for "What Do We Know about Learning?," originally titled "What Psychology Can We Feel Sure About?" Reprinted as a separate pamphlet under the title "What Psychology Can We Trust?" (New York: Bureau of Publications, Teachers College, Columbia University, 1961.)

Samuel Gould, for "The Educational Promise of Television."

REDBOOK magazine, September 1963, and Richard Margolis, for "Teaching Machines—Do They Really Teach?," also titled "Programed Instruction: Miracle or Menace?"

SCHOOLMAN'S WEEK, 49th Annual, "Education and the National Purpose," University of Pennsylvania Press, for "Team Teaching in the Elementary and Secondary Schools," Robert H. Anderson.

ALA BULLETIN, February 1961, for "Images of the Future for School Libraries," J. Lloyd Trump.

LIBRARY JOURNAL, January 15, 1963, for "The Cheap Paperback Is No Country Cousin," Vincent Richards.

Donald Klemer, for "Freedom for Creativity: Data Processing in the Schools."

THE SCHOOL REVIEW, Spring 1962, University of Chicago Press, for: "The New Mathematics Programs," Edwin Moise; "The Physical Science Study Committee," Gilbert C. Finlay; "Chemistry—An Experimental Science," J. A. Campbell; "Renascent Biology," A Report on the AIBS Biological Sciences Curriculum Study," Bentley Glass.

SCIENCE TEACHER, October 1962, National Science Teachers Association, for: "Forces Redirecting Science Teaching," Ralph W. Tyler.

Northeast Conference on the Teaching of Modern Languages Reports 1961 and TEACHER EDUCATION QUARTERLY, Fall 1962, for "Learning a Modern Language for Communication," Nelson Brooks.

Georges L. Brachfeld, for "The Language Laboratory."

James R. Squire, for "Tension on the Rope—English 1961."

THE ILLINOIS ENGLISH BULLETIN, October 1958, and the author, for "Grammar and Linguistics in the Teaching of English," Albert H. Marckwardt.

ELEMENTARY ENGLISH, March 1961, for "What Have We Accomplished in Reading?—A Review of the Past Fifty Years," Nila Banton Smith. Reprinted with the permission of the National Council of Teachers of English and Nila Banton Smith.

ANNALS OF THE ASSOCIATION OF AMERICAN GEOGRAPHERS, September 1962, for "Geography in the High School," William D. Pattison.

CONTENTS

Introduction: The New Educational Technology, Jerome Bruner   1

PART ONE

THEORY, CHALLENGE AND CHANGE

A TWENTY-FIRST-CENTURY LOOK AT HIGHER EDUCATION, Alvin C. Eurich   11

TAKE-OFF TO REVOLUTION, James D. Finn   23

THE NEW TECHNOLOGY AND THE EDUCATIONAL DECISION, Donald A. Cook   31

FACTS AND FALLACIES ABOUT NEW MEDIA IN EDUCATION, Donald Ely   42

CONFLICTING VALUES IN THE SECONDARY SCHOOL, Edward J. Gordon   51

THE CHALLENGE OF AUTOMATION TO EDUCATION, Luther H. Evans   58

EDUCATION ON THE NONVERBAL LEVEL, Aldous Huxley   67

WHAT DO WE KNOW ABOUT LEARNING?, Goodwin Watson   82

PART TWO

THE NEW TECHNOLOGY

THE EDUCATIONAL PROMISE OF TELEVISION, Samuel Gould   91

EDUCATIONAL TELEVISION AND FILMS, Stephen White   101

PROGRAMED INSTRUCTION: MIRACLE OR MENACE?, Richard Margolis   108

TEAM TEACHING IN THE ELEMENTARY AND SECONDARY SCHOOLS, Robert H. Anderson   121

LIBRARIES AND INFORMATION RETRIEVAL, Henry J. Dubester   132

IMAGES OF THE FUTURE FOR SCHOOL LIBRARIES, J. Lloyd Trump   141

THE CHEAP PAPERBACK IS NO COUNTRY COUSIN, Vincent Richards   145

FREEDOM FOR CREATIVITY: DATA PROCESSING IN THE SCHOOLS, Donald Klemer   151

TESTING, TESTS, AND TESTING SERVICE ORGANIZATIONS, Henry Chauncey and Robert L. Ebel   159

PART THREE

THE NEW CURRICULA

THE NEW MATHEMATICS PROGRAMS, Edwin Moise   171

FORCES REDIRECTING SCIENCE TEACHING, Ralph W. Tyler   187

THE PHYSICAL SCIENCE STUDY COMMITTEE, Gilbert C. Finlay   193

CHEMISTRY—AN EXPERIMENTAL SCIENCE, J. A. Campbell   209

RENASCENT BIOLOGY: A REPORT ON THE AIBS BIOLOGICAL SCIENCES CURRICULUM STUDY, Bentley Glass   219

LEARNING A MODERN LANGUAGE FOR COMMUNICATION, Nelson Brooks   233

THE LANGUAGE LABORATORY, Georges L. Brachfeld   238

THE EMERGING ENGLISH CURRICULUM, J. N. Hook   242

TENSION ON THE ROPE—ENGLISH 1961, James R. Squire   250

GRAMMAR AND LINGUISTICS IN THE TEACHING OF ENGLISH, Albert H. Marckwardt   264

WHAT HAVE WE ACCOMPLISHED IN READING?—A REVIEW OF THE PAST FIFTY YEARS, Nila Banton Smith   272

SOCIAL SCIENCE AND THE NEW CURRICULUM, Franklin Patterson   287

THE NEW CURRICULA IN SOCIAL STUDIES WITH EMPHASIS ON HISTORY, Henry W. Bragdon   297

GEOGRAPHY IN THE HIGH SCHOOL, William D. Pattison   303

REVOLUTION IN TEACHING

Introduction:

The New Educational Technology

JEROME BRUNER
Professor of Psychology,
Harvard University

The pages of this book attest to the ferment that character-izes American education today. More than ever before, we are concerned with the nature of the educational process, with the goals of education, with the impact of change—and, besides, with the techniques and devices that can be used in improv-ing the educational enterprise. There has been much inventive-ness. New curricula have been devised in the sciences and mathematics, and new efforts at curriculum construction are under way in the social studies and humanities and in the study of languages and literature. Film, the book, the labora-tory, the "teaching machine"—all have come under close scrutiny in the effort to hasten and deepen the learning process. Indeed, to the outside observer it must seem as if we were preparing to embark upon a permanent revolution in education. And I think we are entering just such a period.

What characterizes this period is a change both in the con-ception of the educational enterprise and in our view of the learning process. With respect to the enterprise—or the edu-cational Establishment—there is a quickened recognition that the educational profession must be far broader in scope than previously conceived. It is symbolized by the presence of Nobel laureates in physics devoting their talents and energies to the devising of school curricula in science. The underlying conception is that those who know a subject most deeply know best the great and simple structuring ideas in terms of which instruction must proceed. But the matter goes further than that. It also encompasses the application of the policy sciences to education. There has begun to dawn a recognition that "educational" administration and "educational" economics and "educational" architecture are not special fields, but parts of the more general fields from which they derive. The *ad hoc* administrative, economic, and architectural ideas that have been the currency of educational practice are being re-examined today in the light of the general principles that inform administrative theory, economics, and architecture. And we are asking whether an enterprise that spends less than one tenth of one per cent of its resources on research and development—as is the case in American public education—can indeed carry out this task with any effectiveness. One cannot help but compare this outlay with practices in such new industries as electronics and chemicals where the expenditure for research and development is as high as 20 per cent. Education, in short, is being brought into the mainstream of national life— both intellectually and from the point of view of the forming of policy.

The revolution in our view of the educational process itself is, I think, premised upon several new and startling conceptions. At least they are new in their application and they are certainly startling when put bluntly. One of them has to do with our conception of the child and his intellectual processes. Consider the working hypothesis that *any subject matter can be taught to anybody at any age in some form that is honest.* The question of "when to teach what" must, then, be premised upon some more discerning criterion than "readiness." As I observe the various efforts to construct curricula, I sense that this is indeed the prevailing doctrine. But interestingly enough, it is not a point of view that denies the striking differences between the mind of the child, of the adolescent, and of the adult. Rather, it is a recognition of the fact that, with sufficient effort and imagination, any topic can be rendered into an honest form that is appropriate to the level of comprehension of students at any age.

It is worth looking in some detail at what this implies. I shall postpone for a moment the question of how "true" the hypothesis is. For there are certain matters that must be made clear before we can understand how one would go about "proving" such a proposition. Consider first a famous theorem of Turing that is central to the theory of computation—the theory of "thinking machines," if you will. In simple form, it states that any problem that can be solved can be solved by simpler steps than those now employed. For the theory of computation, this implies that there are steps simple enough to be carried out by even a digital computer: steps as simple as "make a mark in a certain place," "move the mark next to another mark," "erase the mark," etc. Thanks to high speed devices that can swiftly run off a large number of these simple operations in a manner prescribed by its program, the machine is able to solve stunningly difficult problems in very short order—and if the program is interesting, to do so with a certain amount of originality. To be sure, the theorem applies only to well-formed problems amenable to a unique solution (although this includes approximation tasks based on the use of iterative operations).

Let me propose that Turing's theorem has a profound relevance for all problem solving—whether the work of human problem solvers or artificial ones. It implies that any complex problem can be restated in a manner such that it can be brought within reach of any solver, even though he has only a limited repertory of operations that he can bring to bear on the problem. The inventive task is to find the translation of the problem that is appropriate to the powers of the person being asked to master it.

The layman—and popular magazines—always appear to be astonished that eight-year-olds can be taught quadratic functions, or that first graders can be introduced with intellectual profit to set theory, or that the conservation laws in physics can be made clear to the ten-year-old. The achievement is not astonishing. What is astonishing is that the adult should believe that quadratic functions are obscure—a kind of arbitrary game played with equations in the form of $X^2 + 6X + 9 = (X + 3)^2 = X (X + 6) + 9$. He is projecting his own confusion, produced by bad teaching, on the child who has not yet been confused. To avoid such confusion, one begins teaching with some simple embodiment of the idea of the quadratic within the reach of even a young child—such as the geometrical or "ordinary" square. The properties of geometric squares are made clear by giving the child, first, a way of constructing them and then, a way of describing their constituting elements. In time, the language he has learned for dealing with geometrical squares is extended to other forms of the quadratic or mathematical square—such as the balance beam. And gradually a mathematician is formed. The object is not to produce mathematical geniuses, but simply to make mathematicians who think and talk mathematics and enjoy its beauty rather than merely cranking out rote computation.

II

It seems to me that the present approach to the conduct of education calls for a fundamental reformulation of the sciences supporting education. Perhaps it is best if I illustrate by reference to the field I know best—psychology. It has been argued in the past that a psychology of learning is central to any doctrine of education. A psychology of learning elucidates how the child learns and, besides, indicates what kind of past experience leads the child to be receptive to learning. I think that any close observer of the educational scene would admit that over the past forty years there has been little direct influence of *learning* theory on the actual conduct of education. Learning theory, a descriptive discipline, has described how learning occurs in certain circumscribed situations that have been studied because they related to theoretical issues within the theory of learning. The theoretical issues in question have had little to do with the concerns of the educator. They reflected, in the main, debates that centered around conceptions of the nervous system or conceptions about the growth of personality. Typical of the former category were such matters as the continuity or discontinuity of the acquisition of responses, the status of reinforcement as "confirmation" or "reward," whether the fundamental element in learning was a stimulus-response connection or some more superordinate structure, and so on. Typical of the latter concern, personality growth, was the study of the role of early anxiety as a factor in character structure or whether drive level had an effect upon the acquisition of a response or only upon its performance. These are lively issues and fundamental ones, but they are not directly to the educational point.

For they are all descriptive, all concerned with what happens when learning occurs. The psychology of learning has only been tangentially concerned, until very recently, with the optimal means of *causing learning to occur*. Very little of learning theory is given over to the designing of optimum orders of encounter for the learning of materials. In most theories of learning, it is assumed that encounter with what is to be learned is random. Indeed, we even utilize techniques of experimentation in the study of learning that randomize the order of presentation, and then use materials to be learned that have a minimum of structure or of structurability.

Such research, and it can easily be justified, does not preclude another kind of research, research that poses the question: how can material of a certain kind be so presented and so sequenced that it will be most readily and most transferably learned? The results of such research would provide a basis for a *theory of instruction* that is complementary to a *theory of learning.* There is every reason to believe that a theory of instruction would both broaden and enrich theories of learning. Not until we have developed a theory of instruction will we be able to test propositions about the best way of teaching something. It is just such a theory that is required for "proving" ideas about curriculum.

Without a theory of instruction, we are likely to accept uncritically some particular *description* of learning as a *prescription* for optimal learning. A case in point is the idea that, in programed instruction, "small steps and immediate reinforcement after each step" is the best practice. What is a small step? How should one choose a path up which the small steps lead? In short, what is the program of programed learning? The evidence on optimum program sequences is virtually nil.

A theory of instruction would probably have three aspects. The first would be concerned with the optimum experiences that predispose the learner to learn. The second would deal with the kinds of structures in terms of which information or knowledge is optimally organized by a learner. The third would inquire into the sequences of encounter with materials to be learned that would be optimal. It is quite plain that there is much work of a highly general nature that can be done in each of these areas. It is also clear that there is much *specialized* work that would also be required in order to translate a theory of instruction into a particular curriculum—whether Roman civilization or finite mathematics. But what seems most promising to me is that the eventual contact of a particular curriculum effort and learning theory would be better assured by the existence of a mediating theory of instruction.

Is there a comparable point to be made about the other sciences that contribute to educational theory and practice? I think there is, and the issue is quite parallel. The point is well illustrated by anthropology. Anthropologists, adept at describing the internal coherence and interdependence of the elements of a culture, have given us a theory of social change that, in effect, warns that change in one major feature of a culture will produce widespread, perhaps chaotic effects in the rest of the culture. The theory of culture has rarely addressed itself to determining how in fact cultures can be and are changed with minimal disruption or maximum predictiveness. It is a pity—and a predictable one—that anthropologists are absent from the council table when the issues of *how* to regulate socio-economic development in backward areas is up for discussion. But again, one senses a change and

today there is the beginning of theories of economic and social
development that are geared to the prescriptive task of regu-
lating the educational development of newly emerging states.

III

Changes in educational practice have more often reflected
the conceptual *atmosphere* of the behavioral sciences than
they have been based upon the conceptual propositions available in these sciences. The "history of the school chair" reflects
the "style" of prevailing theories of learning more than the
actual content of such theories. When the Thorndikean model
of association learning was at its height, chairs were ordered
in rows, fastened to the floor. The student was tacitly regarded as a recipient of materials to be associated or otherwise
stored away. Dewey's instrumentalism led schoolmen to un-
fasten the chairs from the floor, to group them according to
the projects at hand. The child-centered school produced a
circle of seated children surrounding the teacher. The new
emphasis on phenomenology and the experience of the child
—particularly his "social perception"—led to the semicircular
arrangement. Perhaps our emphasis upon the structuring of
information, the arrangement of optimum sequences for
learning, and the rest, reflects a new concern with the efficient
use of information in a period of exploding knowledge.
In the pages of this book there are accounts of how information retrieval can be used more effectively in libraries (more the expression of a hope than the statement
of a theory or practice), there are accounts of how to organize
groups to change the teaching of English (again, more in the
spirit of aspiration than of plan), and there are statements on
how testing may be improved so that more searching criteria
of achievement can be established. It is important, in view of
the notable gap that has existed in the past between "reflecting
the conception" and actually using the concepts, to sound a
note of caution. There is a long effort ahead. Present ideas
about automatic information retrieval, still primitive when
matched against our knowledge of the subtle requirements of
human memory organization, may leave us rather dreamily
satisfied. And, indeed, a few libraries of a specialized kind
may be recoded for retrieval by some such system as "key-
words-in-context." But the brute fact of the matter is that we
have not yet come to grips with the basic theoretical issues
involved in matching machine systems to human memory

needs. So too in the teaching of written English. There are interesting contending conceptions of grammar—finite state theories, transformational theories, and phrase-structure theories. A vast amount of empirical and theoretical work will be required before we can understand the implications of linguistic theories for the teaching of language.

A smattering of rule-of-thumb linguistics in our texts on grammar is no more explicit a recognition of the problem of how to teach English than is the decision to unbolt the chairs from the floor a recognition of the implications of an instrumentalist theory of learning. We are indeed on the edge of a great period of revolution. But it would be a great pity if our zeal were too easily assuaged by partial victories. We do well to recall that most revolutions have been lost precisely because they did not go far enough.

PART ONE

THEORY, CHALLENGE
AND CHANGE

A Twenty-First-Century Look at Higher Education

ALVIN C. EURICH

Vice President,
Fund for the Advancement of Education

PROLOGUE

Colleges and universities, it is commonly said, are approaching a period of explosive growth. An explosion, according to Webster, is "a violent expansion, accompanied by noise." We are certainly experiencing an expansion of our total population and, inevitably, an upsurge in our college enrollments. This has come upon us so suddenly, as social changes go, that the effects have been violent on all our major institutions: our cities, our schools, our colleges, our occupational structure, our political system. As for noise—there has surely been no dearth of noise. We have all heard many speeches which center on the problems of growth. And yet I wonder if we comprehend fully the explosive character of the coming expansion.

Striking as the increase in college enrollments has been up to the present, we are now poised on the brink of an expansion far, far greater than that of the past forty years. If we were to continue operating our colleges along conventional lines, we would need to construct more college facilities in the next fifteen years than we have built in all our history. Take Kansas as an example: from 1950–1960 the number of college-age youth, 18 to 24, actually decreased. But during this period, college and university enrollments increased about 50 per cent. By 1980, on the basis of birth records, the number of youngsters will not decline; on the contrary, it will almost double. Thus college enrollments are likely to soar, conservatively speaking, from 250 to 300 per cent.

Such explosive growth plagues us with a variety of critical problems. We obviously cannot accommodate such numbers within the conventional framework of our educational system. We are virtually forced to consider how we can use available resources more effectively and efficiently.

All our plans, moreover, must be made with the awareness that students entering college now will be in the prime of their

lives when we move into the twenty-first century. The world
will then be quite a different place. The changes of the next
40 years, we are told, will equal in significance those of the
last 400. Travel to Europe and other parts of the world will
be only a matter of an hour or so. Travel to other planets may
be commonplace. Television and radio will go into homes on a
world-wide basis, and receiving sets the size of a wrist watch
will be available. Computers will translate languages automatically; the language barrier will be a thing of the past.
This is only a fraction of the changes that are certainly coming. They will affect higher education profoundly. We must
be prepared to meet them intelligently.

Let us assume for a moment that the next 37 years have
become history. It is now 2000 A.D. From this vantage point,
let us cast a glance at the development of higher education in
the United States during the twentieth century.

LOOKING BACKWARD

I am happy to report that we were able to avoid a Third
World War during the twentieth century. Several times in the
1960's we came precariously close to a nuclear holocaust
which could have wiped out all mankind. Russia and the
United States were then the two major world powers. At one
point, it is true, an atomic bomb was accidentally detonated,
but fortunately the explosion occurred in the center of an un-
inhabited Alaskan polar region. The crater it formed is now
a major tourist attraction, and heavily laden helicopters hover
over the many miles of its base, showing sight-seers the geological wonders of the area.

Our population has expanded far beyond the estimates of
40 years ago, when we numbered only 186 million souls.
Today we are approaching 350 million and our post high
school enrollment in institutions of learning is almost 25
million.

During the first half of the twentieth century, we established universal elementary and secondary education. During
the second half we made higher education universal through
the junior college. In the process we restructured our educational system. Many of our former liberal arts colleges were
unable, for one reason or another, to solve their financial
problems. Since their facilities were still urgently needed,
local communities transformed them into junior colleges. The
result is that a junior college is now available for every young
man and woman within commuting distance from home.

During the quarter-century following World War II, teachers' colleges disappeared completely from the American scene. Their place has been taken by multipurpose institutions which, together with the strong liberal arts colleges and the universities, have discontinued the first two years, since these now come almost wholly within the province of the junior colleges. The transition took place with surprising smoothness. Once football, basketball, and other sports became completely professionalized and the social fraternities and sororities vanished from the scene, the need for the first two years of college abruptly ceased.

These new institutions now admit qualified graduates from the junior colleges and offer three-year programs culminating in the master's degree. During the last quarter of the century, there were heated debates at meetings of the Association of American Colleges on the question of whether the baccalaureate degree should be granted at the end of junior college work. The traditionalists won; the junior colleges continued to award the Associate of Arts or Associate of Science degree, while the baccalaureate of arts or science fell into disuse because students going beyond junior college pursued a program leading directly to the master's degree or a professional degree.

The largest universities, with their clusters of professional and graduate schools and research institutions, have now become virtually self-contained cities. Some, like New York University, enroll more than 200,000 students. We continue to wonder whether these institutions are getting too big.

During the past half-century, the content of education at all levels was profoundly strengthened in two ways: (1) we became much clearer about the objectives of education, and (2) leading university scholars from various disciplines became sufficiently alarmed about our soft education that they were forced to produce, in co-operation with school teachers and administrators, new curricula extending from the kindergarten through the graduate and professional schools.

On the matter of objectives, our economy of abundance and our better system of distributing goods have made us less concerned with the strictly professional or vocational aims of education. We have overcome the temptation, prevalent during the 1950's and 60's, to judge the value of a college degree by the additional earning power it confers. We now minimize the time spent on acquiring practical skills and factual knowledge. We no longer seek to produce the person "crammed full of knowledge" or, (as the old *New Yorker* magazine expressed it in a cartoon more than a half-century ago) the speaker who "knows nothing but facts." We now place much more emphasis on developing wisdom; on leading our young people to higher levels of maturity in dealing with the ideas that have made a difference in the progress of civilization. We also concentrate on instilling such ideals as those that help to make leisure time more satisfying than in the early days of the affluent society, when men were consumed to the point of boredom with strictly materialistic pleasures. We now recognize the truth expressed by Mark Van Doren 50 years ago: "Freedom to use the mind is the greatest happiness."

As part of this change, we have seen the resurgence of philosophy as a key academic discipline. Like other subjects in the curriculum it has had its ups and downs. During the early part of the last century it lost its vitality and degenerated into a study of philosophical systems and the microscopic analysis of language. After several decades, however, antiquarianism and logical positivism seemed equally sterile. No great philosophers emerged; the sciences dominated the college and university campuses.

Those were the days when physicists, chemists, biologists, and aeronautical engineers with a bent for research could get almost any amount of money to advance their projects. As a result, we added to our knowledge so rapidly that the accumulation shocked us into a realization that we were entirely aimless in our endeavors. For example, our geneticists and biochemists gave us the necessary knowledge and techniques to mold human beings to our specifications. We can now direct the evolution of mankind; it need no longer be left to chance. Over the years Nobel prizes have been awarded for these contributions to a long line of geneticists and biochemists beginning with Morgan, Muller, Ledkerberg, Kornberg, Beadle and Tatum.

With the genetic possibilities available, however, we found that we were completely devoid of ideas concerning the kinds of men we wanted to create, and the nature of the society we aspired to build. Our desire for two automobiles, a boat on a trailer, a helicopter, and a twenty-hour work week had long ago been satisfied. We had come to the point where we recognized the urgency of freeing some outstanding scholars to help shape new directions for mankind. Some of our ablest minds were encouraged with fellowships and grants to follow up promising leads. The consequence is that exciting ideas are beginning to emerge from our explorations, and at least a dozen brilliant young philosophers are cutting across subject-matter disciplines and showing signs of developing a new synthesis of knowledge.

We are now beginning to take seriously Ortega y Gasset's insight in his "Mission of the University," first set down 70 years ago: "The need to create sound syntheses and systematization of knowledge, to be taught in the Faculty of Culture, will call out a kind of scientific genius which hitherto has existed only as an aberration, the genius for integration."

The most prominent difference between today's colleges and those of fifty years ago, however, is not in the curriculum, but in the use of learning resources. We have introduced devices and techniques which were not even thought of prior to the mid-twentieth century. Curriculum has always been the subject of educational debate and reform. But the learning resources which our students now take for granted were developed for the first time in the 1950's and 60's. These enabled us to fulfill the psychologist's dreams of making the best teaching available to all students, and of truly adapting instruction to individual rates of learning.

Take television, for example. Its use as an educational medium in colleges developed steadily after it was introduced in the 1950's. But educators were typically slow to see that this revolutionary device, which in a decade had transformed the living habits of a nation, would inevitably have just as great an impact upon our schools and colleges. It was only in the 1960's that the use of television soared, as demonstration after demonstration rammed home the fact that televised instruction was educationally effective and economically feasible. As early as 1962, 300,000 courses were being given over television in the United States. But not until recently have colleges recognized that television has made the standard lecture obsolete and the conventional laboratory demonstration inadequate and costly.

One of the reasons that television made slow progress at first was the fear that the availability of outstanding lecturers on television would somehow displace the classroom teacher and make the individual college obsolete. In this regard, the objections were essentially the same as those raised at Oxford and Cambridge in the latter part of the nineteenth century. When the "university lectures" were proposed, the Oxbridge dons predicted that the innovation would reduce the separate colleges to mere appendages. What actually happened was that the individual colleges became more important when they were relieved of the responsibility for lecturing. They could devote themselves to probing the student's mind and spirit individually or in small groups. And the students benefited from the opportunity to hear the very best lecturers in each field.

Television has had a similar effect. The first glimmer of this came in 1958–59 when a basic college physics course was offered over a national network under the direction of Professor Harvey E. White of the University of California. During the year, seven Nobel prize winners and other distinguished scientists helped to teach the course. They represented an array of talent that no single university could possibly have offered its students. Other courses in chemistry, biology, government, economics, and the humanities followed in rapid succession, first on national networks and then, with the success of Telstar, across national boundaries.

Now, fortunately, exemplary lectures by some of the greatest scholars of the world on the basic substance of their fields are available on electronic tapes. Because it was not until the middle of the 1960's that we began systematically to record the leading scholars of the world, we missed many great men who were alive in this period. Think how effective our teaching could be today if we had available taped lectures by such figures as Socrates, Leonardo da Vinci, William Harvey, Sir Francis Bacon, Sir Thomas More, John Milton, and Johann Wolfgang von Goethe.

The television courses that are now available are used on virtually every campus in the country. Students everywhere are privileged to listen to the great men who advanced our culture in every field of learning. We have made incalculable progress since the days when our youngest college students were taught almost entirely by academic novices.

After the students have mastered the basic materials through these taped lectures, they can meet with senior faculty members who, having been spared the drudgery of repeating over and over the basic substance of their fields, are eager to work with students on advanced topics. Moreover, the students themselves feel that they have a firmer grasp of the subject matter, because they have studied the taped lectures at their own rate, reviewing them on kinescopes as needed. In addition, the superb organization and planning which has gone into each lesson has had its effect, and the consequence is better teaching and easier learning.

Television has, in short, provided us with the technology we needed to build a genuine system of mass education—one in which each student has an equal opportunity to learn, no matter where his college is located or what its resources are.

But we have also made enormous strides at the other end of the spectrum, in teaching individual students. Here the most exciting developments have been in independent study, honors work, programed learning, and language laboratories. Independent study has had a curious history. Although we adopted the English College and the German University, we failed to import a basic ingredient of both, namely, their emphasis on independent work in higher education. Instead, we projected into the colleges and universities the elementary and secondary school notions of compulsory class attendance. It took us an unconscionably long time to recognize that independent study was essential to a maturing mind.

Programed learning, so common today, was hardly known fifty years ago. This scheme of instruction has developed into one of the most effective resources for adjusting instruction to the individual student's rate of learning. Yet as early as 1962, after experiments at Harvard, Hamilton College, and numerous secondary schools throughout the nation, it was clearly demonstrated that students consistently learned about twice as fast with programed materials as they did from conventional texts and lectures.

Here the resistance was different from that which confronted television. Educators knew what television was, but, by and large, they refused to grasp its pedagogical implications. In the case of programed learning, on the other hand, most college teachers and administrators didn't even know what the new technique was—except that, largely because of its unfortunate linkage with "teaching machines," they didn't like it.

As we can now see so clearly, television and programed learning, both introduced into education in the 1950's, defined the limits of a spectrum of instructional resources. Television provided the medium for mass instruction; programed learning provided the ultimate in individualized instruction. Between these two, and other devices and procedures such as language laboratories and independent study, a new diversity was added to the educator's repertoire. Together, these techniques enabled us to break through the ancient framework which used to bind college education into a rigid pattern. No longer do we have to divide the day into fixed fifty-minute periods, no longer do we measure a student's progress by the number of credit hours he has "banked," no longer do we march all students along through the same series of lectures and classes.

Today, flexibility and adjustment to individual differences are axiomatic. Each student progresses at his own rate. He studies much of the time on his own, or with fellow students but always with instant access to the complete range of learning resources; taped lectures, programed course materials, language audio tapes, bibliographies, and original documents on microfilm.

As a result of this independent work by the students, a professor nowadays rarely lectures to a group of thirty or forty students, as he used to half a century ago. Rather, the professor meets with students individually or in small groups after they have mastered a given block of knowledge through the use of diverse learning resources. We now insist upon complete mastery rather than partial learning of the basic substance in the field. In other words, all students learn the same quantum of a subject; they vary only in the time it takes them to acquire it.

Our professors now do only what no text or other learning resource can ever accomplish; they develop the mind of the individual student through intimate give and take based on sound knowledge and understanding. Under this system the three-year colleges, far from becoming obsolete, have rediscovered their primary function in education. Instead of pretending to be microcosms of all human knowledge, the individual colleges can lean heavily on the use of learning resources to provide the base of their instructional programs. But this firm foundation enables them to build real understanding and creativity in their students, through their achievements in the higher reaches of teaching. Never before have they had such an opportunity.

Even more drastic are the changes in our libraries. As a result of research carried on, not only in the United States but also in Japan, India, Belgium, Holland, France, and England, we have revolutionized the techniques of storing and transmitting information. Most of our actual documents are now reduced to pinpoint size and stored on film in a miniature library. If we had not developed such procedures, some of our libraries would now be trying to store 100 million or more volumes. Instead, we have developed the National Research Library which, as John D. Kemeny of the Dartmouth

Mathematics Department predicted some years ago, has reached more than 300 million volumes in miniaturized form. The information in these volumes is retrievable by computer systems through a multichannel cable. We can instantly transmit information from these volumes to reading units on campuses throughout the country. The space which was previously used for storing books has been freed by our new information retrieval system for faculty study, reading rooms, and independent study.

Even the architecture of our campuses reflects the innovations in teaching techniques. For the lectures over television, students listen to portable television sets in their own dormitory rooms. These lectures are generally followed by small-group and individual discussions. The programed learning laboratories are open twenty-four hours every day, and the student may study whenever he desires to do so.

Along with the clarification of objectives, the upgrading and updating of the curriculum, the use of a variety of devices and procedures for learning, and our new library system, we have also vastly improved the process by which students are admitted to the institution, and the way in which they progress through the course of study. It is amusing now to read the hundreds of conference reports issued during the middle decades of the twentieth century dealing with the required courses in four years of liberal education. Like medieval theologians debating the number of souls which could be conveniently packed into a given corner of hell, educators of the 1950's seemed to have discussed endlessly the question of whether this or that course, in this or that order, should be included in the four-year program. They put things in, they took things out, they substituted one course for another.

Little progress was made, however, until educators began asking more fundamental questions. Why must the liberal arts curriculum fit into exactly four years? If students learn at different rates of speed, couldn't some of them achieve the goal in three years or two, while others worked at it for five or six? Would it not be wise to tell the student what is expected of him, what the end result of his liberal education should be—what kind of mastery he needs to earn his degree —and then let the student decide, in the light of his own personality, interests and abilities, how he can best make use of the university's resources to achieve that mastery? To do this, of course, the colleges had to define more precisely the goals they were striving for in the liberal education of students. Whereas formerly the administration could lean heavily on the accumulation of credit hours as evidence that the student was acquiring an education, the new system required the colleges to specify what they were aiming for and then to devise measures for adequate observations of achievement.

The result, however, was exhilarating for students and faculty alike. They were freed from the four-year plague of course credits. Since the federal government increasingly financed the education of needy students, colleges no longer had to keep bright young people on the campus for four years, just to collect the tuition.

The system which emerged was pioneered in California. Virtually all California students went from high school to a junior college. After an average of two years at such an institution, the top one-third of the students, plus some who entered advanced vocational programs, went on to college. From college, approximately the top 12 per cent advanced to the university—though even at this rate, university enrollments grew enormously.

The important point was that students progressed through this system with complete flexibility. The principles of early admission, and admission with advanced standing, which did so much to facilitate the transition from high school to college fifty years ago, were applied to the transition from college to graduate work. Standard measures of achievement in each basic subject were worked out. But students could meet these standards at their own rate of learning, and in a variety of ways. Thus it was the criteria of achievement, rather than the students, which were standardized.

Fifty years ago educators spent their time trying to determine how all students could be given basically the same course of instruction in the same amount of time. The results were disappointing: students emerged from the standard program with very different levels of competence and mastery. Now we have a more fruitful approach. We have concentrated on defining with some precision what we want students to know and to be able to do at the end of their liberal education. Then we have provided as many different paths to that goal as the diverse talents and interests of the students demand. The results have been extraordinary. Today it is unusual for any two students to take the same sequence of courses with the same balance of lecture, small-group discussion, and independent study. The "mix" is determined for each student on the basis of his needs and capacities. But at the end of the road, we can ascertain with some accuracy that each student has indeed achieved a comparable degree of true liberal learning.

As we look back over the progress of higher education in recent decades, we may wonder exactly when the major changes began to develop. Colleges and universities in the mid-twentieth century, we may recall, were run pretty much the way they had been run for the past hundred years. As Professor Jerrold R. Zacharias, of the Massachusetts Institute of Technology, expressed it in the 1950's, only about 2 per cent of the total educational expenditures in those days was used for books, films, laboratory equipment, and other means of communicating "substance that did not come directly through the teacher's larynx."

When did the great transformation begin? When did our colleges and universities begin catching up with the technological revolution which had transformed the world but left the campus untouched? When did the colleges begin to use the new techniques of communication and organization, to which they had contributed so much, to improve their own operations?

It is difficult to fix an exact date for the beginning of this movement. But I believe an unquestionable turning point occurred in the mid-1950's and 1960's. First, after 1957, we were spurred by Sputnik. Then—in the years 1964, 1965, and 1966—the colleges felt most sharply the upsurge in the demand for higher education. Educators had known quite well that the college population was likely to double, and perhaps treble, during the 1960's. In fact, due to demographic factors, the most acute increases came in the mid-1960's.

It was this event, I think, which galvanized the leading colleges into action. They could see that the conventional methods of collegiate instruction were inadequate to meet the enormous challenge. The students were ready, willing, and able to absorb the best education the colleges could offer. It would have been disgraceful for the institutions of higher education to refuse to find a way to meet their needs.

Of course, many institutions failed to rise at once to the challenge. Some of the most prominent universities simply announced that they could not handle more students than they already had enrolled, and refused to consider ways of increasing their student bodies. This attitude could not last, of course. It collapsed when other institutions, more sensitive to their own responsibilities and the nation's needs, pioneered in designing improved instructional methods which could provide a first-rate education for more students. Through such relatively simple reforms as year-round operation, control over proliferating courses, and better use of independent study, many colleges found they could enroll up to one-third more students without any significant increase in instructional costs.

But these reforms are merely the beginning. Changes will come more rapidly and more sweepingly—of necessity—in the early decades of the twenty-first century; changes so great, so fantastic, that the imagination can barely keep pace.

EPILOGUE

So we have come to the end of our fantasy. Whether we are now in the wagon wheel, the steam engine, or the automobile phase of higher education, I am not sure. But I am sure that we will need to progress through the airplane, jet, and satellite stages.

Some weeks ago I had the pleasant experience of driving back to New York from Connecticut on a Sunday afternoon with a bright eight-year-old boy. Through a combination of circumstances, which include his own impelling curiosity, he is fully absorbed in the space age. As we drove, the boy fell asleep—something he seldom does in an automobile. After an hour or so he woke up, opened his eyes, and said, "I've had a dream." "And what did you dream?" "I dreamt I was twenty years old, and was in college." "Fine," I said. "But," he said, "I died while I was in college." "That's a shame," I said. "And you didn't get a degree?" "Oh, yes I did," said the boy. "I got a scholarship to Venus. And you know," he added, "They're way ahead of us up there."

My story naturally represents one man's view. Each of us can make his own projections—they will differ widely, of course—but the point is, we must make them. The old ideas will no longer do. We will do well perhaps to begin with the thoughts of a boy, as free of the old world that imprisons us as we were of the world of our parents. If we start now to plan for the years to come, with the vision of a bright child of today, we are more likely to be ready for him when, ten years hence, he comes knocking at the door to demand his share of our cultural heritage.

Take-off to Revolution

JAMES D. FINN

Professor of Education, University of Southern California,
and Director, Technological Development Project
of the National Education Association

Historians of the future could mark this era as the beginning of a technological revolution destined to sweep through the entire educational system of America.

But the concept of a technology of instruction is not widely understood. When confronted with the proposition that a technological revolution in education is likely, a substantial segment of the profession—from basic educationists to old-time progressives, from professors of micropaleontology to nursery school teachers—becomes greatly disturbed.

A superficial concept of technology equates it with hardware. If educational technology is seen to consist of hardware, then the ancient bugaboo of machines replacing men (in this case, teachers) instantly arises. More important is the worrisome notion that education will become a completely automated, robot-directed process with all its humanity squeezed out.

At times a third, slightly more vague, worry is added: that an organization of machines, such as a television system, removes control of the educational system from local, professional or professorial levels and moves it somewhere else—to the state of federal government, to a foundation, or to a group of physics professors somewhat smarter than the local variety.

Now it may be that all these events will come to pass. If they do, however, it will be for social reasons—not because of the existence of a technology of instruction. For technology is by no means exclusively hardware. Technology obviously includes machines, but it also includes systems and organization patterns, plus both an attitude toward problems and a method of solving them.

No one familiar with the general history of technology would deny that technology directly affects the social order; on the other hand technology is, at bottom, the tool of a society on the move and is used for whatever purposes the society deems important. In this second sense, technology is neutral. A technology of instruction will not make education less humane, will not destroy the personalities of teachers or students, *unless a social decision is made to use it for that purpose.*

Admittedly, also, a highly organized technological system of instruction would easily permit the installation of new and different controls upon education. Again, however, the possibility is not the requirement. The issue remains the issue of control and who is going to do the controlling. This issue was present before instructional technology existed as a possibility and would remain if man were suddenly reduced once again to writing on the walls of a cave.

We have to evaluate the possibility of a technological revolution in education, then, in terms of the serious problems faced by American society in the remaining decades of this century. Since we must solve or alleviate many of these problems in the next few years, educators must think about instructional technology in the prospective of these problems; it is in this context that the crucial social decisions must be made.

Any American who has remained conscious most of the last twenty years, let alone the educator who must by his very business be sensitive to social problems, should know about these problems now. It seems unnecessary to list them here in any detail. There are problems of the cold war, of the population explosion, of the explosion in knowledge, of the race for space, of finances and natural resources, of urbanization, and the problems created by automation itself in terms of human beings and industrial production. And there are others. But these problems all have one element in common. They cannot be solved without more and better education than we now have.

To say that we can continue to use the old ways of Horace Mann or of any of his successors of whatever stamp or variety and meet these new educational demands is to say that we will use a cow as transportation to the moon. More and better education for all the American people demands new ways. We have little time and cannot afford to take the position of the educational ostrich with its head buried in the hand-tooled past.

TECHNOLOGICAL GROWTH

This brings us full circle back to the machines. For the new ways that are suggesting themselves are technological

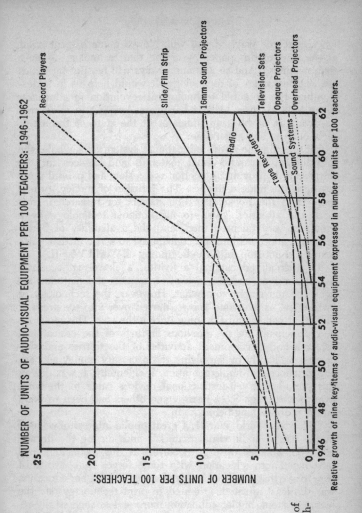

Fig. 1. Growth of instructional technology.

NUMBER OF UNITS OF AUDIO-VISUAL EQUIPMENT PER 100 TEACHERS: 1946-1962

NUMBER OF UNITS PER 100 TEACHERS:

Relative growth of nine key items of audio-visual equipment expressed in number of units per 100 teachers.

Record Players
Slide/Film Strip
16mm Sound Projectors
Radio
Tape Recorders
Television Sets
Sound Systems
Opaque Projectors
Overhead Projectors

ways—machine ways, if you will. Now I made a great point
at the start of this paper by crying that technology is more
than machines. And so it is and always will be. But machines
are the best index of technology. It would help us in understanding the potential technological revolution in education
if we took a closer look at hardware, keeping in mind that
hardware is, at best, an indicator of the state of the art of
technology at any given time.

Considering the entire educational system as a whole, the
introduction of audio-visual materials and devices for the
purpose of improving instruction was a slow and painful process until the middle thirties. The infusion of money, principally from the Rockefeller Foundation, for research in this
field, the attention given to instructional technology by a
group of very talented men, and the availability of better
materials and machines, all contributed to a rise at that point
which did not stop until the beginning of World War II.

As with all educational activities, a slowdown occurred
during the war, and the lack of equipment and materials set
back the movement somewhat. However, the technology of
instruction, as everyone knows, moved over into the areas of
industrial and military training during the war. This move relied principally on the previous findings of the educational
research and development activities of the thirties and succeeded brilliantly by supplying the necessary money and talent for successful implementation. Incidentally, it was during
this period that self-instructional devices came to the forefront even though S. L. Pressey and others had been working
on the problem long before.

Following World War II, a great public interest developed
in the use of audio-visual materials and, during the decade
1945–55, another upsurge occurred as this technology was
introduced into education with some force. Here, we must
stop to say that of all the levels of education, higher education
was the least affected. Oriented to print technology and the
lecture system, higher education more or less successfully re-
sisted this movement.

Since 1955, due to a variety of causes—the application of
television, the influence of Ford Foundation projects, the
attempts to find solutions to the problems of quality and quantity in education, the National Defense Education Act, and
similar efforts—our curve of instructional technology development has again started up sharply with no leveling-off point
in sight in the immediate future.

Walt W. Rostow, in his book *The Stages of Economic Growth,* postulates five stages which occur during the growth of a traditional culture into a high-order technological culture: (1) the traditional society, (2) the preconditions of take-off, (3) the take-off, (4) the drive to maturity, and (5) the age of mass consumption.

It is my thesis that American education, considered as a culture in tradition, is now beginning the take-off stage into a high-order, high-energy culture, and that it is the first educational system in the world to reach this stage.

If we take the period of the last curve and project it slightly into the future, say 1955–65, the dimensions of this potential technological revolution in education become clearer.

INSTRUCTIONAL TECHNOLOGY—PRESENT DEVELOPMENTS

1. *Equipment*
   a. Television
      (1) broadcast
      (2) low-power translators
      (3) closed-circuit
      (4) videotape
      (5) airborne (stratovision)
   b. Electronic Teaching Laboratory
      (1) language laboratories
      (2) language laboratories plus visuals
      (3) mobile laboratories
   c. Self-instructional Devices
      (1) reading pacers
      (2) individual listening and viewing devices
      (3) programed and scrambled books
      (4) teaching machines
   d. Newer Developments
      (1) 8mm sound film
      (2) thermoplastic recording
      (3) multiple projection systems
      (4) classroom communicators
      (5) computers
      (6) data and data-transmission systems
2. *Instructional Systems*
   a. Massed Film Systems
      (1) EBF series in physics, etc.
      (2) AIBS series in biology
      (3) etc.

   b. Instructional Packages
   c. Instructional System Prototypes
       (1) PSSC system-physics
       (2) Heath de Rochemont, *Parlons Français*
3. *Organization Proposals*
   a. Stoddard
   b. Trump
   c. Team Teaching
4. *Operating Organizations*
   a. Ford Foundation
   b. National Science Foundation
   c. Learning Resources Institute
   d. Educational Media Council
   e. Educational Facilities Laboratories
   f. Department of Audio-visual Instruction, NEA
5. *National Defense Education Act*
6. *Industrial Development*
   a. Publishing
   b. Electronics
   c. Non-educational Industries

The list of developments is interesting enough. However, a list is not a statement of trends. Due to the more rapid development of audio-visual devices such as the film, the first technological developments apparent to educators were those associated with mass instructional techniques such as the motion picture, radio, etc. in the thirties and later, of course, television. By 1960 we had the possibility of a fairly sophisticated technology for mass instruction.

In the meantime, a technology of individual instruction was also being developed, although much more slowly. As mentioned before, S. L. Pressey had been working at Ohio State University even before 1920 on what turned out to be a testing or teaching machine. However, it wasn't until the early fifties, with the work of B. F. Skinner at Harvard and related but independent work of military psychologists like Crowder and Chapman, that teaching machines and programed learning came to the forefront. The work of Pressey was also revived. Suddenly, it seemed, American education was presented with a technology of individual instruction.

Actually, there were other elements in the developing technology of individual instruction which are now being fitted into the teaching machine and programed-learning picture. These other elements, whose ancestor was probably the old Keystone stereograph, included listening units for individual or small groups of students, individual filmstrips and slide-viewing devices, etc. Teachers in the western part of the United States have been using such devices singly and in combination with some success since immediately after World War II.

Teaching machines, programed books, listening and viewing devices, reading pacers, etc., all make up the basis for a technology of individual instruction. It was inevitable that research workers would start inquiring into the possibility of combining these two technologies—individual and mass. About ten years ago C. R. Carpenter at Pennsylvania State University experimented with a program analyzer device in a classroom. This combined film with individual response, including knowledge of results.

More recently, Lumsdaine and Klaus at the American Institute for Research have studied the Harvey White physics films as used on television in combination with a programed book. Corrigan and Luxton have developed a response device designed to apply teaching machine principles to television viewing. This device is being initially tested in California by the California State Department of Education. Several other classroom communicators have appeared on the market lately, and Carpenter and his associates are now experimenting with group programed learning techniques.

This trend of combining the technology of individual instruction with that of mass instruction suggests another trend. If you would, for lack of a better category, call every other instructional technique used in the classroom "conventional instruction," the possibility of developing an instructional *system* presents itself with the combination of the two technologies with conventional instruction.

INSTRUCTIONAL SYSTEMS

There are several prototypes of instructional systems in existence. One is the Heath de Rochemont system for teaching French, *Parlons Français*. The earlier Zacharias program in physics developed under the sponsorship of the Physical Science Study Committee has some of the earmarks of such a system. In addition to a new textbook built around new content and concepts, there are paperback books for supplementary reading, films, a laboratory manual, and an apparatus manual. Some of the material is now being programed in both machine and book form. It has been suggested that the sponsors intend to make other materials such as filmstrips and tapes. Now this is a whole course and it is, to some degree, programed by the instructional materials and the teachers' manual into a *system* of teaching physics. Technically, it is not such a system because it has been built atomistically rather than in accordance with the still nonexistent principles of instructional system design. The suggestion of the possibility, however, is there.

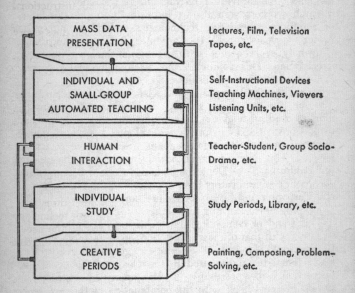

Fig. 2. Instructional systems—black-box concept.

This possibility leads us far out into the realm of prediction. Figure 2 introduces the "black-box" concept of instructional systems. *If* we had much greater knowledge of the instructional process than we now do, we might be able to set up such a black-box system. Consider, for purposes of speculation, that the instructional process can be broken down into the elements of (a) mass presentation techniques, (b) individual and small group automated teaching, (c) human interaction, (d) individual study, and (e) creative periods. (There may be more or less.) Assuming a clear understanding of objectives and content and further assuming that we had sufficient hard knowledge about the nature of these processes, such a system might be applied to an instructional problem.

Information concerning the nature of the students, the specific objectives, and content, etc., would be supplied the teacher-designer. Decisions would be made as to which black box to insert into the system at which point and which subsystem to trade off with another in the interests of the students, the facilities, the cost, etc. At this point an instructional system would have been designed.

It can be argued that this is what the teacher does every day at the present time. But such an argument, while containing an element of truth, actually does not cover the situation; for we are talking about two orders of magnitude.

Speculation about the possibilities of instructional systems by no means exhausts the discussion about the potential trends and growth of a technology of instruction. We have not touched, for example, on the conceivable role of computers, data processing in general, and the new possibilities of storage, retrieval, and display of complex information.

Enough, however, has been said to back up the thesis that we are at the take-off stage for a technological revolution that promises to engulf education. I use the word "promises" deliberately instead of the threadbare fear-word "threatens." For it is only by this promise of the application of technology to education that I feel we have a chance to make the necessary educational contribution to the solution of our difficult and exasperating national problems.

The New Technology and the Educational Decision

DONALD A. COOK

*Director of Programing,
Basic Systems Incorporated*

The general problem before us is how to integrate the two chief demands of education: that it disseminate increasing amounts of highly specific technical information to growing populations, while at the same time imparting the capacity for intellectual distance, discipline, and detachment, together with love of knowledge and fundamental criticism which is our educational heritage. The role of what is loosely called "the new media" or the "new technology of education" will be shaped by its capacity to help solve this problem. To make clear the issues at stake requires some clarity about what the "new" trends really are, and how they may affect the process of education.

The new media, which are often spoken of in a single term, actually consist of a number of devices and developments. What is happening, I believe, is not a single revolution of one sort, but several, with various currents and counter-currents going on at the same time.

These devices and developments have in common their newness, their dependence upon electronic technology, and the fact that the traditional educational devices of speech, books, and chalk board are being supplemented. But the process of supplementation may also change the manner in which decisions are made in the educational process. The term "supplements" may conceal the deeper issues of the nature of educational decisions.

I would like to suggest some categories into which various aspects of the new technology may be classified, and then to make some points about the implications of each one, for the kinds of decisions that go into the educational process.

DISPLAY

The first I shall mention are devices whose primary function is the display and distribution of information: filmstrips, tape recorders, flannel boards, overhead projectors, all kinds of flexible visual devices.

Such devices act primarily to display information in new ways, or to distribute it from more centralized sources of information. Some devices permit decentralized use. The overhead projector is an example. The control of its use lies at the point, in space and time, of imparting information to the student. It is directly in the teacher's hand. He can place a book into the projector, or make a sketch, and thereby multiply access on the part of a large group of students to stimuli. He may at the same time be violating an outmoded copyright law —an issue which is coming to attention under the impact of modern methods of cheap and rapid reproduction.

Other devices are more centralized, in the sense that films or tapes of great lectures, for example, must be chosen by the teacher from an available supply. Content is predetermined, and the teacher must gain access to a piece of already-stored information. The film or tape is not a device which simply amplifies or multiplies his own informational or stimulus material. Similarly, with closed-circuit television, he may choose whether or not to employ a given sequence, but the control of the sequence is not in his hands.

Use of some of these devices may require curriculum-adoption decisions, since they pertain to content. Others do not. In either case, the use of new materials which must be ordered, rented, requested, or scheduled requires advance planning on the part of the teacher. Such advance planning in turn requires knowledge that the materials and devices are available, an evaluation of their relevance and usefulness, and sometimes prior approval of the decision to use.

LIBRARY TECHNOLOGY

The second main group of new devices includes the cataloging and access devices, the traditional analogue for which is the card catalog of the library. Here modern technology is making its contribution to the system by which information is classified, stored, accessed, and retrieved. There is a great revolution going on in the library science area, and it is inevitable that changes will accelerate as electronic and computer devices, the micro-recording of information on cards, etc. become available, and as the storage, classification, and request problem continues to mount.

Library technology will affect the educational process by changing the ease of access to stimuli. The direction is potentially that of enrichment, but as always with enrichment, there is the problem of an "embarrassment of rules." Where so much is available, guidelines are required, and search skills also, or student and teacher alike may leave the riches untouched for want of a way to read the menu and digest the meal.

RESPONSIVE DEVICES

The examples mentioned so far have to do with the display of information, with the control of its organization, and with access to it. However, the *distribution* of stimuli or information can occur without any *response* to such information on the part of a learner. Furthermore, stimuli which can govern and control the attention of a person do not necessarily generate the behavior that the teacher wants generated. It may often be the case that we use stimuli to hold the attention which are irrelevant to the behavior changes which we really want to see in the learner. In this case the educator is following the false trail of the advertiser. So I would like to mention thirdly, then, devices which take into account the response of the student.

Of the many such types of devices, some allow the student's behavior to enter in some way into the decision making of the teacher. The classroom-communicator illustrates this provision. The classroom-communicator may let the teacher know the level and direction of class response, and he may modify any aspect of his presentation accordingly.

The technique of programed instruction also incorporates response on the part of the student: that is, he must reply or respond to each instructional frame. But programs go further than this and provide feedback to that student in some form. The most common form is the correct answer to each frame, which the student checks immediately after he has made his own response.

Programed instruction at its best goes further yet. Student response and feedback to the student are offered to material which incorporates a pedagogic design in the very sequence of the frames which are presented.

Consider the following example: A frame gives a picture of a quadrilateral and says, "A straight line connecting opposite corners of a quadrilateral is a diagonal line. Line A-B is a _____." The student would respond "diagonal" and turn the page of his program or advance the teaching machine and see the correct response, "diagonal."

The reason I named this example was to impress upon you the importance of curricular or pedagogical design. The frame I described will be responded to correctly; but it is a very bad frame because it can be answered correctly without any reference to the diagram whatsoever. The student guesses the answer correctly without having his perceptual behavior changed at all. And many programs available incorporate this kind of sloppy pedagogy.

If, on the other hand, the diagram were to present not only line A-B (as diagonal) but line C-D, connecting opposite sides of the same figure, the frame were to define "diagonal" and then say, "Which of the lines in the drawing is a diagonal, A-B or C-D?" it would still be very easy to get the correct answer, but the learner would be required by the design of the contingencies to examine the stimulus material and to respond to the relevant aspects. He begins to make a discrimination of diagonals from nondiagonals.

This single example could be amplified endlessly and applied to entire sequences of frames. The main point I wish to make here is that not anything which engages active behavior on the part of a learner in small steps and tells him then how he is doing is necessarily a well-designed program in terms of imparting the behavior changes it is supposed to.

In this sense, programed instruction is not a "medium" of instruction at all. In the first place, the stimuli involved, although now more often printed than in any other format, can be presented in any available media which may be relevant. For example, a program in listening skills may employ auditory inputs via tape, and require spoken responses. Programs can use any kind of stimulus input. The essential thing about programing is the design of the instructional cycle in which this input or increment of information calls for use on the part of the learner, response by the learner, followed by feedback in some form, such as the correct answer.

Teachers sometimes express concern about self-instructional programs as follows: "How can I make sure that the program is suited to the particular needs of my students? Can I adapt programs to local needs?" Such concern is not new. It properly exists in the case of textbooks. Its renewed statement may reflect the sensed power of a technology which not only "presents" information but actually *engages behavior*. An adequate solution to the problem depends upon effective methods of integrating programs into courses, and monitoring their effects so that local curriculum needs can be accommodated. The logistic requirements which would permit this—such as self-study rooms and methods of tabulating errors and other student variations—are now only in the stage of anticipation and design.

MACHINES

Fourth, I should mention computers and machines of several types. Once again there is a general feeling that since computers and machines are changing everything else in the world, they are changing education in some uniform and irreversible manner.

However, the functions which machines may perform are not generally distinguished. I would like to mention three.

1. The first is purely administrative. That is the role of computers as record-keeping devices, keeping cumulative records in order, grade point averages and so on. The information here never makes direct contact with the student, but is mediated through decisions on the part of faculty and staff.

The student feels the impact of the record-keeping function through more effective decisions on the part of educators.

2. Second, machines may be used in a more direct kind of contact with the student to accommodate individual differences. An example would be sampling the error rate of the student on a unit of programed instruction, and as a result of such data (generated by the students), giving more or less of a certain type of item, branching him ahead, allowing him to skip over material he already knows, branching him back, causing him to review material that he is learning weakly, speeding up the rate of presentation or slowing it down, switching to a more dense track or a less dense track of the same material, etc.

3. The third main function that machines can perform in the educational process is much more closely related to the moment-by-moment interaction with the student. This function rests upon the design of the contingencies of instruction. This is the teaching machine of the form envisaged and developed by Skinner and his associates.

Here the emphasis is not upon groups, individual differences, slow tracks and fast tracks, but rather matters such as the following. When a unit of programed instruction is put into an appropriate teaching machine, each frame is isolated from the frames before it and the frames that follow. Therefore, the student cannot look back to find help in getting the correct answer. He cannot turn the page and cheat. He must respond on the basis of this fixed piece of information in a given frame. This feature of machines puts a terrific burden upon the designer of the program to design that sequence of frames so that it will perform its function.

Secondly, the frame response and feedback may all be present together. In the programed text form, the learner either turns pages to reveal the right answer, with the result that he no longer sees the frame to which he had responded; or he moves a slider down the available page to expose the correct answer—a situation which may expose previous frames which cue the response to the frame at hand. The teaching machine allows for simultaneity of stimulus, response, and feedback, while at the same time permitting isolation of frames in a sequence.

There is no time lag in an ideal teaching machine; that is, the frame, your response to it, and the correct answer are all present simultaneously. There is no problem of short-run immediate memory storage on the part of the learner. This is likely to be critical in generating new behavior, such as a sense of rhythm; or sequences on induction, such as James Holland at Harvard has developed with children; or preverbal matching of stimulus patterns such as Wells Hiveley has developed, wherein children learn to match forms of alphabetical shapes before they learn reading and writing; or in programs in developing drawing skills.

These immediate "zero-second" feedback acts are of extreme importance in strengthening the behavior that is being developed. That is another function which machines might perform.

The fact is that few machines in existence today perform these functions adequately. For example, when programs are advanced to expose the correct answer, the frame to which it is the correct answer disappears from view. If the frame aperture is widened to prevent this, two frames at a time can be seen. These and other limitations will not be overcome until responsible developmental work is given adequate support.

SIMULATION

The fifth process I should like to mention is that of simulation. A simulation is simply a small-time copying device for some large-time process. The game *Monopoly* is a simulation of a certain kind of economic situation.

Simulation first appeared in business games—in an attempt to compress the process by which management decisions were made: how to price, how to inventory, how to distribute, how to market, how to mix products, and so on.

But in education, simulation is beginning to make an interesting appearance. Economists at Chicago and Michigan have developed an economy which second- and third-grade children play with, and as they play with each other in making the decisions of this economy, they gradually evolve such things as barter, the division of labor, the price structure, the competitive market, price-fixing, regulative legislation—in short, a social system. These institutions and practices need not be taught as out-of-the-book abstractions, because the processes, coalitions, and agreements actually develop in the classroom. Then they get named, discussed, and serve as the object lesson for discussions about the economic system in the social order.

James Coleman at Johns Hopkins has simulated political campaigns and the election process for students to participate in, to provide experience with coalitions, long-run versus short-run effects, ways of aligning different interest groups, and other phases of the political process.

Some simulations involve other people directly, and the response to your "move" is the decision of one or more players, whose identity you may or may not know. In other cases an individual simulates with a computer or other device into which the decision rules have been programed. In others, players are in touch with each other, but anonymously, through a computer which mediates their decisions so that nobody knows who is who. Many interesting variations are possible.

Coleman has also had adolescents of high school age simulate the "rating and dating" process, with apparently profound effects upon the social outlook of some of the participants.

All simulation has the feature that time is "collapsed"; that is, the long-run consequences of behavior appear quickly, with a heightened instructional effect upon the learner's behavior.

Some simulations have the property that roles may be explored. In a business game you may be asked to be the manager on a given day; another day the seller; another day the advertiser. Whatever the nature of the roles, performance in any one of them comes to be affected by exposure to the full set of roles in the network.

A student may be asked, in a biology course, to decide about the evolution of the species, whether to step up or slow down the rate of random mutations, and thus simulate over very rapid stretches the effects of small changes upon many, many generations of the species. Whether the mutation will contribute more toward the survival value of the species or to lethal effects will appear quickly in the simulation. Evolutionary models, in other words, can be simulated.

EDUCATIONAL DECISIONS

Now, all of these trends and techniques, as they move from the laboratory, out into the special school, and gradually become selectively implemented, will bring changes of many kinds to the roles of the teacher. Many questions about the "role of the teacher" under the impact of the new technology are really hidden questions about the *status* of the teacher. That is, will the status of the teacher move up or down? Is this not the hidden question? I think, however, the question points to an anxiety which has to be explored rather slowly and in some detail. It seems inevitable that roles will become more diffuse; that is, teachers who are used to participating in a given pattern of decisions will find that pattern shifting with respect to the kind and amount of control they have over the flow of material to students. Some will have to participate even more than they have in some decisions, and some will participate less in other areas. What is likely to result is a new pattern of stratification for the teaching process.

There would, for example, be greater demand for preparation, always a very difficult aspect of the educator's role. The time that gets lost first and early in the game, as the course load increases, is the time to prepare and keep up. I think it will be incumbent upon educational institutions to build buffers which will allow more and more preparation and keeping-up time.

We will probably see a distinction between clerical assistants and professional assistants, between people who handle details such as data collection and tabulation at a white-collar but nonprofessional level, and the professional assistants, who may also participate in such activities but who are in teaching training themselves, and who will gradually move up into the more advanced professional positions.

SOME DILEMMAS

As these aspects of the new technology get implemented, there are certain kinds of polarities, "either/or" issues, which I expect to see come to the surface in a rather sharp way. They already exist and they are characteristic of dilemmas of contemporary education already, but the new technology is likely to make them more acute.

One of them is that of specialization versus the broad fundamental liberal education. I think it would be a false hope to believe that the new devices which do teach effectively and faster are going to relieve us of the problem of making fundamental decisions, to lull us into the belief that since all this new gadgetry can teach anything, there's no need to decide what is essential; that we can just expose students to anything that anybody might claim is worth their learning, because our new methods will just pack it into their heads.

Well, it isn't so. It especially isn't so if the new technology is put to work at teaching students the intricacies and details of highly specialized performances which may be well out of date five years from now or a decade from now.

That decision will become more acute, I suggest, rather than less acute, as educational technology becomes more powerful.

I believe that one of the major impacts upon higher education of programed instruction specifically will be the delivery of freshmen who have greater skills of analytical thought. There is ample evidence to believe that programing in very basic subject matter can build up verbal repertoires which turn people into better readers and better thinkers. I am now talking about the impact of materials introduced from the second to the eighth grade, even.

But remember that our new skills in imparting "information" will not affect the very important role of *undoing* in education, and for this the wise teacher is of great importance.

By "undoing" I mean that by the time people arrive at school, they are already packed with a lot of mad ideas, and you know where they get them as well as I. The role of the educator is to allow the encapsulating shell of those ideas, whether they be from mass media, from the local community, from the family, to meet the test of liberal criticism.

To teach logic and history effectively is to generate canons of criticism, consistency and perspective, which will encounter enemies in the student himself. The teacher must help the student grapple with those enemies.

I have taught students who refused to believe me when I said that the Communist Party had once been legal in America. Not whether it *should* be, mind you, or not; simply that it once had been legal in this country. They refused to believe a matter of historical fact.

These same students could not understand magazines like *The Nation* and *The New Republic,* not even because of what they say, but because *there were no major advertisers in them!* When I told them that it was not the function of the magazines to make money, they were even more disbelieving. It was unacceptable to them. Some of these students believed that *Consumer Reports* was probably a Communist organization because it dared to look askance at the claims made in advertising.

This one example, drawn from experience at an overblown "community college," could be extended in subject and multiplied across the country.

What I am trying to say here is that the role of the wise, intelligent person will become even more acutely in demand because, in my opinion, such people are always in short supply. There is a scarcity not only of people who are "full of knowledge," but of people who know how to confront students with the interactions that they are now having with whatever it may be: computer-mediated teaching, programed instruction, new mathematics, new science, new social science, etc. These things have powerful effects upon the young learner, and he will always need an individual who can evince a deep and genuine care for the intellectual meaning of what is happening to the student. The effect of the new technology in extending the educational process, will be to increase the demand for this kind of teacher.

CLOSING THE LOOP

When I was at Princeton—fortunately it was my first college year—I had access to the library stacks, as any undergraduate did at Princeton.

When I moved to Columbia, I no longer had access to the stacks. Books were "located" in the card catalog and requested at a desk. (Fortunately, the graduate libraries maintain open collections.) If the effects of the new technology are that anybody can get anything as long as he knows how to ask for it, we must remember that part of what is learned is simply *what there is to ask for*. That year of mine "hanging around" in the stacks at Princeton taught me an enormous amount about man's attempts to organize his knowledge, and brought me to materials I might never have encountered otherwise. New automated libraries may become extremely efficient in getting in ten seconds any book asked for, but knowing what book to ask for may require its own equivalent—perhaps automated also—of the "random walk" in the library stacks. This is the requirement that we "close the loop," and encourage and permit the learner access back up the path to the sources of knowledge which are flowing towards him in even greater amounts.

Facts and Fallacies about New Media in Education

DONALD ELY

Director, The Audio-Visual Center,
Syracuse University

No one can speak authoritatively about *all* of the new developments in educational technology. The new frontiers are too vast, too complicated, and changing too rapidly.

There is probably no better statement concerning the tenor of our educational climate than the opening lines to the *Tale of Two Cities*.

It was the best of times, it was the worst of times, it was the age of wisdom, it was the age of foolishness.

As we survey the numerous technological innovations which have direct implications for solving some of our educational dilemmas, we certainly wonder whether it is truly a time of opportunity or merely a time of trouble. And as we survey the new developments today, I am afraid we are in the position of the clerk who was asked for a compass. The clerk replied that he had only the kind that you could make circles with but not the kind from which you got your directions.

There are many claims being made for new technological instruments which are reported to be *the* solution to our complex educational problems. There are many rumblings about replacement of teachers because of new machines which will handle certain instructional functions. At a time like this it is imperative that we analyze these claims before we are carried away by irrational thinking in an attempt to find panaceas.

I would like to make a series of statements about new media which are frequently heard today. We might call these statements the "Facts and Fables about New Media in Education." Answer "fact" or "fable" to the following statements. My answer given to each statement is based on personal experience and should not necessarily be considered as the "final word."

1. *New media are "audio-visual aids."* FABLE. The "new media" term has come into use primarily as a result of several titles of the NDEA (National Defense Education Act). The

term actually includes all the traditional audio-visual media (motion pictures, filmstrips, slides, recordings, pictures, overhead transparencies, exhibits, displays, community resources, etc.), but it also includes television, teaching machines and programed materials, the so-called language laboratories (I prefer electronic classrooms), computers, and other techno-

POTENTIAL DEVELOPMENT OF INSTRUCTIONAL SYSTEMS

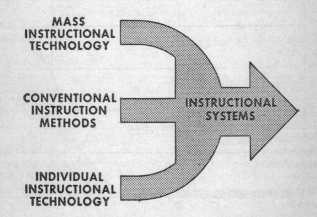

MASS INSTRUCTIONAL TECHNOLOGY

CONVENTIONAL INSTRUCTION METHODS

INDIVIDUAL INSTRUCTIONAL TECHNOLOGY

INSTRUCTIONAL SYSTEMS

logical devices. Technology is not just machines and men; it is a complex, integrated organization of men, machines, ideas, procedures, and management. New media by themselves are neutral; nothing but distribution systems, but as we relate machines, men, ideas, and procedures in an organized fashion we begin to see an instructional system.

2. *New media are being used to solve educational problems.* FACT. The problem comes first; technology follows as a possible solution to the problem. For example, the problem of increased enrollments has been solved, to some degree, by the use of television. The case studies involving the use of broadcast TV and CCTV seem to multiply weekly. One of the most dramatic programs utilizing TV is the Midwest Airborne Television Experiment. The two primary objectives in using instructional television seem to be *instructor multiplication* and *image magnification*. Another problem is centered around the

increased emphasis on spoken language, but how to teach more people a skill which requires individual practice and instruction? The phenomenal growth of language laboratories confirms the potential of technological solutions. But let's get away from the language laboratory term and call it the electronic classroom. There are many uses besides language in-

LANGUAGE LABORATORIES IN THE PUBLIC SCHOOLS: 1955 - 1962

(in thousands)

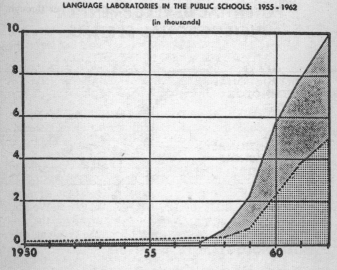

Total number of language laboratories in the public schools, 1950–1962. The dotted line indicates estimates as compared to actual survey figures of the Technological Development Project.[1]

struction. Various educational institutions are using this type of facility for speech, stenography, music, and other fields. The basic ingredients for the language laboratory or electronic classroom are a message source and a headset. In an elementary school it may be as simple as this. This situation may be multiplied by adding a microphone, and finally the whole classroom can pick up material from one or more sources with each student using an individual tape recorder. The instructor

[1] "Studies in the Growth of Instructional Technology, I: Audio-Visual Instrumentation for Instruction in the Public Schools, 1930–1960 A Basis for Take-Off," Occasional Paper No. 6, by James D. Finn, Donald G. Perrin, and Lee E. Campion, published by The Department of Audio-Visual Instruction, National Education Association.

uses a master control panel which permits individual communication with each student.

The advantages seem to center around the following:

a. Student actively participates for the full period.
b. Interest and motivation are increased because the student is given convenient facilities for immediately evaluating his work.
c. Student can get private assistance from the teacher through his inter-communication facility.
d. Systems provide facilities for student to progress at a rate equal to his ability. Talented students need no longer be retarded by slower students.
e. Both the administrative and teaching talents of the instructor are increased. He can control and instruct more students in less time.

The disadvantages are primarily financial, and also in the time required for the preparation and evaluation of materials by the teachers. Some schools are using portable electronic classrooms.

A third educational problem is the increased responsibility we want students to assume for their own learning. The teaching machines (or autoinstructional devices or programed materials) offer a partial answer to this problem. Dael Woelfle, Executive Director of the American Association for the Advancement of Science, has said this about the teaching machine: "There are several reasons for watching this development with continuing interest. It is the first major technological innovation in education since the development of printing." I don't agree entirely with this point of view, but I do believe that a major contribution will be made by this movement.

The unique advantages of the teaching machine are:

a. Every student is continuously involved with the task, a condition seldom obtained in the classroom.
b. Learning is completely self based: the learner can proceed as slowly or as rapidly as his ability requires.
c. Motivation to learn becomes very great as the result of continuous success built into the program.
d. The teacher is relieved of his responsibility for insuring routine learning, thus leaving time for the development of creative and critical thinking skills.

The only major disadvantages to the teaching machines seem to center around the time required for the development of programs and the general lack of availability of programs at the present time.

There are many developments in the area of self-instruction which are not programed in the manner of teaching machines or programed textbooks. Other new technological developments which offer less obvious applications to education are the devices which are enabling industry and the military to miniaturize all types of matter. Photographic images are effective. Transistors are "old hat" as one observes the new field of molelectronics which uses the molecule as the basic electronic element.

One danger I continually see is that technology is almost always ahead of education. If we try to adapt new technological developments to education *before* a problem has been defined, we are in danger of a misuse of these new tools.

3. *Teachers will be replaced by new media.* FABLE. Teachers will not be replaced but their roles will be changed. They will never replace the teacher, any more than the automatic washing machine or the coffee percolator will replace the housewife. They won't eliminate the teacher shortage, although they should help the teacher to do a better job with more students. These are teaching tools, and their greatest promise lies in their use by thoroughly competent teachers.

I also believe that no school should expect a teacher to perform any task that can be performed as well or better by modern technology: radio, television, films, etc. If a machine can replace a teacher, perhaps it should.

As one scans the history of technological innovations in education, he would observe pronounced fears on the part of educators. Most recently teaching machines have received this treatment. Ten years ago it was TV. Thirty years ago it was the sound film and radio. Then we have to jump back 500 years to the Gutenberg era. And finally two thousand years ago (280 B.C.) to the concern expressed by Plato in his *Phædrus:*

> This discovery of yours will create forgetfulnes in the learners' souls, because they will not use their memories; they will trust to the external written character and not remember of themselves. The specific which you have discovered is an aid not to memory, but to reminiscence and you give your disciples not truth but only the semblance of truth; they will be hearers of many things and have learned nothing . . . they will be tiresome company, having the show of wisdom without the reality.

Two thousand years of manuscript culture lay ahead of us when Plato made these notes. We can imagine what he would say about Gutenberg and Marconi. Technological innovations will change the role of the teacher—not replace him.

4. Innovations such as the introduction of new media are usually activated by administration. FACT. A recent report on educational change in New York State reports that

> New types of instructional programs are introduced by administrators. Contrary to general opinion, teachers are not change agents for instructional innovations of major scope. Implication: To disseminate new types of instructional programs, it will be necessary to convince administrators of their value.

This statement is made not about classroom practice, but about new types of instructional programs, which usually touch several teachers and which may require breaking up old work patterns.

Instructional changes which call for significant new ways of using professional talent, drawing upon instructional resources, allocating physical facilities, scheduling instructional time or altering physical space—rearrangements of the structural elements of the institution—depend almost exclusively upon administrative initiative.

Authority is a critical element in the shaping of institutional decisions. Schools depend heavily upon administrative authority in decision-making. Consequently, the control center of the institution, as schools are managed today, is the administrator. He may not be—and frequently is not—the original source of interest in a new type of program, but unless he gives it his attention and actively promotes its use, it will not come into being.

5. Technological innovations in education will save money. FABLE. Technological devices cost money. This money is usually a major capital outlay item. Any major innovation, such as a closed-circuit TV installation or an electronic classroom, is a major investment. This equipment will not replace teachers, as we indicated earlier. Why, then, do we expend these funds during a time when the expenditure of every educational dollar is carefully scrutinized? Primarily for the *improvement of instruction*. This is difficult to measure in a quantitative fashion, but I am convinced that it does occur when technology is used to solve specifically defined educational problems.

The most intensive study made regarding cost of technology, in this case television, was by Carpenter and Greenhill at Penn State University. ("An Investigation of Closed-Circuit Television for Teaching University Courses.") The graph below is a summary of their findings. The break-even point between conventional instruction (in groups of 45) and television instruction was estimated to be about 200 students. There are many facts in the report that clarify this statement.

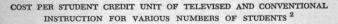

COST PER STUDENT CREDIT UNIT OF TELEVISED AND CONVENTIONAL
INSTRUCTION FOR VARIOUS NUMBERS OF STUDENTS [2]

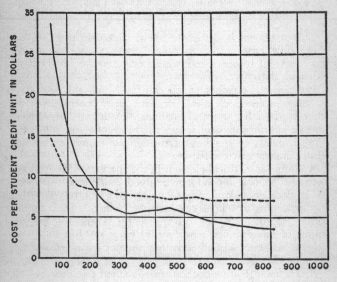

STUDENTS

Cost per credit unit: television instruction _____
Cost per credit unit: conventional instruction - - - - - -
1956–1957

6. *The option to use new media is decreasing.* FACT. We must face the fact that we are in the midst of a great revolution. Population, knowledge, and technology. We know that there are 83 babies born into this world every minute. This

[2] "An Investigation of Closed-Circuit Television for Teaching University Courses," Report No. 2, *Instructional Television Research*, C. R. Carpenter and L. P. Greenhill, The Pennsylvania State University, Spring 1958.

results ultimately in an increased school population. In 100 years mankind has doubled. In just three more decades, the world population will nearly double again. Are you beginning to feel this push in your institutions?

We know that over 40 million people are in school in our country and that nearly one-tenth of them are in higher education. How will we handle this flood?

There is an explosion of knowledge. Oppenheimer has said that over 90 per cent of the scientists who have ever lived are alive today. Literature in the field of chemistry doubles every eight and a half years.

As we look at technology we see the fruits of new knowledge. (New consumer goods continue to appear on the market. Think of the developments over the past five years: stereo sound, improved automobile maintenance schedules, products, etc.)

In the social sciences and humanities we see new nations, new literature, and implications of new knowledge facing us.

The fantastic growth of missiles and rockets compounded with the computer control systems force new demands on education to provide the trained personnel to handle information.

Add to these explosions the fact that we continue to report shortages of teachers and classrooms, and we end up with a simple statement of our total educational dilemma: There are so many, needing to learn so much, in so little time, and with so few teachers.

The development of kits of instructional materials compels teachers to use many media. Major revisions in the science and mathematics curricula incorporate new media. Kits of materials are appearing with increasing frequency on the educational market.

The option to use or not to use new media in teaching is rapidly disappearing. Thirty years ago the farmer had the option to use a team of horses or a tractor. Today the farmer's option is gone. Twenty-five years ago the secretary had the option to use longhand writing or a typewriter. Today the secretary's option is gone. Twenty years ago the carpenter had the option to use the hand saw or the power saw. Today the carpenter's option is gone. We had better accept the challenge that faces us today.

When we look at the new-media field we are looking at a field concerned with information: its movement, its reduction, its coding, its processing, its manipulation, its storage and retrieval, and its presentation. This is the library of the future —a computer-based system. New data-exchange systems are information-processing units.

SUMMARY

So what. What can you do about these new developments? If the use of new media is so inevitable, what can you do to handle the demands which will confront you?

1. Decide upon specific objectives when you plan. Define objectives in behavioral terms—then select the materials and equipment to help solve the problem. Try the Lasswell formula. (Who, says what, to whom, how, and with what effect?)

2. Experiment with new media. Use a tape recorder as a "second teacher" in the classroom. Try programed instructional materials with a group of students. Become informed about the new development and investigate the resources locally available for implementation of those ideas which are most feasible for your curriculum.

3. Once you know what you want to do with new media, be firm in your request for specific materials and equipment. Indicate that you are ready to show that increased productivity can result from intelligent application of technology.

4. Start where you are, with what you have, and do what you can. You can do no more, but as teacher-leaders you should do no less. A friend of mine told me about his high school principal, who said, "Edgar, if you and I don't do this, who will?" I ask you the same question about our part in improving the teaching-learning process: If you and I don't do it, who will? It has been said that "For the triumph of evil, it is only necessary that good men do nothing."

It was the best of times, it was the worst of times, it was the age of wisdom, it was the age of foolishness.

It is out of such times that brave men forge their victories.

Conflicting Values in the Secondary School

EDWARD J. GORDON

*Associate Professor of English
and Director of Teacher Training,
Yale University*

Anyone who has a concern for American secondary schools is bound to be both encouraged and discouraged by what has been happening to them in the past five years. On the one hand, the schools are more and more accepting the fact that one of their major purposes is to present a quality program in subject matter; on the other hand, the very emphasis on subject matter makes it too easy to neglect the emotional life of a student and in so doing neglect his system of values. Challenge and high standards are the seeds from which all good will grow, but challenge, in a heterogeneous school, can quickly become brutality.

Never before have the possibilities been greater. The liberal arts colleges, after neglecting the schools for fifty years, are doing penance. Not only are they moving into Master of Arts in Teaching programs to prepare teachers for the high schools, but also are they working with the best of those teachers to produce curricular materials in languages, in mathematics, and in science. We wait for a national push in the humanities.

More and more good minds are going into secondary school teaching. Now the schools are left with only the central question: Why do they exist? What are they expected to accomplish?

And I suggest that the answer ought to be what it has always been: to produce a free, reasoning person who can make up his own mind, who will understand his cultural tradition, and who can live compassionately with his fellow man. In judging a school, I would want to know first what its graduates care most about.

The world that I am asking for is a long way off, but it should be our next point of business. The most bitter attack in recent years on the secondary school philosophy was made, not by Admiral Rickover, nor Arthur Bestor, nor the Council for Basic Education, all calling for more subject matter, but by John Hersey in his book *The Child Buyer*. He argued there that the nation is more interested in using its children than in educating them. Defeating the enemy seems now a more pertinent objective than the true education of the young. We see this in various trends. Government money goes largely into retraining science teachers; state legislatures, in increasing numbers, are ordering courses in communism versus democracy; and censorship of materials in the humanities is the central fact in the choice of books for too many schools. I agree with Mr. Hersey's thesis that we are losing sight of why schools exist.

I said that the possibilities were never greater, but we may go wrong on the use to which we put these possibilities. Even children's games are being replaced by push-ups and chinning contests to see if we are stronger than the Russians. Society's pressures, reflected in the schools, may subvert the whole process of education.

The teacher and the student live in a world mad with dichotomies. The teacher is asked to teach the American experience and the values of the Founding Fathers. If he teaches them so well that students believe them, he is often castigated for being un-American. If he teaches kindness, generosity and good will, and tries to make his school a real house of learning, the teams may not win; they may not have that knock-'em-down spirit—or they may be too busy reading. If a man dedicates himself to becoming a fine public school teacher and works hard at his subject, he finds himself in the only profession where no matter how good he gets, he will too often be paid the same as a loafer working behind the next wall. He is soon made aware of the fact that quality of teaching is respected only by a small group of grateful parents who suddenly discover what can happen to a child in contact with a vigorous mind. But within his own profession of secondary school teaching he knows that *up* means *out*. Advancement is restricted to those who have not made teaching the center of their lives. The only way to become a "success" in too many schools is to give up teaching.

OPPOSING VALUES

The student operates in a world in which he is asked to accept two opposing sets of values; the one that is in theory taught in the books he reads and the one which is operative in the school and in the society which makes up his larger world. He is caught between what he is expected to believe and what the world rewards as beliefs. And this split is what according to Karen Horney causes the neurotic personality of our times and the high incidence of mental breakdowns.

The student is exposed to a world of movies which emphasize a world of sex; he knows which ones to attend because they are labeled "For adults only" and he finds them on a page headed "Get more out of life; go to the movies." On TV he finds a world of violence where it is commonplace to kick a man when he is down, or to shoot him in the back. It is a world of brass knuckles. He learns about the good life in the hands of the image makers and the status seekers. No longer can he believe the poetic corn, "Getting and spending, we lay waste our powers." He learns soon that a man is judged by the car he drives. And teachers might fight back against this attitude with a play like *Golden Boy* wherein Joe Bonaparte, and his name is significant, says, "When you drive a car, you're looking down at the world . . . how I love to stroke that gas." So far that is 100 per cent American, but when Joe dies in the very symbol of his success, the book teaches a different lesson, a lesson that English teachers learn early in life it is not healthy to talk about in class. *We* know that the most prevalent plot in the twentieth-century novel is the plot of the golden touch. Midas wishes for the golden touch, he gets it, and in using it destroys what he loves most. We see the modifications of the pattern in the twentieth century's concern with the Faust legend, that a man will sell his soul to get what he wants and what he wants is no longer knowledge but gold. But we prefer to teach the Sunday School lessons of *Silas Marner* and *A Tale of Two Cities*, emphasizing how a good woman can reform a miser or a drunk. And so we teach girls to marry sad people in the hope of reforming them. And so with these "happy books" we spread desperation in the world because we teach what is not true to life. We even transform the Faust legend. In *The Devil and Daniel Webster*, a safe book, we prefer to think that one can sell his soul if he has a fast-talking lawyer like Dan Webster who can outtalk the devil and so redeem a man before it is too late. The generality I want most to emphasize is that we cannot teach worthwhile values without grappling with reality—and reality is one of the last things we can teach.

And so we come to my central concern, the teaching of values; and I don't know how to define the word *value*. I find it the most elusive term in education—and the most oversimplified. Whenever I think about the idea, I am left with many questions. How do I know a person holds a particular value? Can I find out by asking him? I don't think so. We know the person who said, "I can't hear what you are saying because your actions speak louder than your words." In other words, what a person believes can be worked out only by observing him over a long period of time, in many places and situations. And students are always surprising us. When I have seen them need great moral courage, there are often reversals in the behavior one would expect. And to what degree will a person hold a value if he is put in a moment of extreme tension? I know this man is religious; he says all the right prayers, but would he die on a flaming pyre with St. Joan? What is his breaking point? *Are* there issues on which he would not break? And so it is with kids. Those who will take a stand have to be ready to walk a very lonely road. The lesson of the crucifixion is no idle legend. A society always kills, in one way or another, its best people; and is redeemed afterward by the knowledge of what it has done.

A WORLD OF CONTRADICTIONS

We see, then, the child of our schools growing up in a world of contradictions, a world that encourages him to pick the worst of its value system because that is what to the superficial glance seems most rewarding. We also have the second dilemma of attempting to fathom the ocean that is the human mind; we understand these problems only by bringing to them the simplest of simple minds, and by misunderstanding all the real issues.

We can now turn to a further problem: How do people take on a value system? In an essay written by an educational psychologist I find that students accomplish this through the process of identification. But try as I may in this book, I find no answer to the more central question: Why does the student identify with *this* person rather than with *this* person? We can be sure of one thing, however; most of the graduates of a particular school do take on most of the values of the people who make up the community of the school: the faculty, the parents, and the students. What I am trying to say, Peter Arno said more tersely in a *New Yorker* cartoon. A father is speaking to his wife, as they look out of a picture window at their son who is about to take off on a motorcycle. The son is appropriately arrayed for such activity with the hair-do, the boots and the jacket, in direct imitation of Marlon Brando. The father's words: "I can't help thinking that things would have been different if George had gotten into Groton."

What the school values, then, the students will tend to believe is important.

Let us probe further on the relation of a school to a value system. I don't know how good values are taken on, but because I don't know, I do have strong convictions on the subject. The first is that the school itself as an institution cannot contradict what it is trying to teach in the classroom. It cannot teach the value of freedom of inquiry and at the same time censor books and ideas. It cannot teach the value of individual dignity and disregard student opinion. It cannot call for responsible behavior without allowing students—and teachers—to have responsibility. It cannot be built around the governmental structure of a boss who dictates school policy and then expect to produce students who really believe in a majority rule, or even that a human being matters.

My second major conviction is that values are taken on only through concrete experiences. Let me modify this idea a bit. What we call the intelligent person is the one who can see connections between things and see them quickly. He can understand a death in a family without living the experience. He can develop empathy for other human beings by reading about them. To understand how another person will feel under an unkind word or act, he does not have to be severely hurt himself. The slow person will not make connections quickly; he understands unkindness only when one is unkind to him. Abstractions mean little to him because he cannot connect them with concrete instances. I have worked in one school that spent much time deliberately manipulating the environment to encourage a valid system of values in its students. I have worked in another in which to raise a question of value would have been as ridiculous as to suggest a course in the mating habits of the penguin. In the latter school we asked that the students study; we even gave them homework. We also offered an extensive program of night basketball so that the students would not have lonely evenings with a book. We were surprised when they went to the movies on other nights. We wondered about their parents and forgot about our own example.

COMMUNITY SERVICE

In the former school the students, many of them, spent weekends in workcamps, painting and plastering in the slums. They spent their summers working among Indians, for example, building recreation centers for young people, or digging irrigation ditches. In the city they cleared vacant lots for playgrounds and staffed them on weekends when they could have been hanging around the drug store. Many of them worked for an hour or so, a couple of days a week in a hospital, carrying trays or rolling bandages. They worked with adults on committees dealing with housing problems in newly integrated neighborhoods, on racial tensions growing in the community. In a word, the philosophy of this school was that we should be of service to the community. The outside world was a place for testing and shaping what we believe. The other school thought of itself as an entertainment center for the community. The community came only to admire, to build the egos of those few who could shine. What we *do,* then, matters far more than what we *say.*

My third conviction is that we need to be more clear in schools about the values we want people to have. Because one doesn't just have values; he values something. We should be clearer on what that something is. Everyone has values; the difficulty in life comes from those who value themselves more than others. The major purpose of education is the overcoming of selfishness.

My fourth conviction, and these convictions are mounting in intensity, is that no one can value anything until he values himself. And the only way to get a student to value himself is to give him a sense of accomplishment, an idea that something he has said or done is worth while. We then build his sense of self-respect. But schools are too full of defeat for all but the best students, the best athletes, and the best-looking girls. The very structure of the typical class is based on finding out what the student does not know. We too often ask: When was Jackson elected, instead of what did you learn in your reading about Jackson? The former question eliminates all those who didn't notice, or didn't think it important. The latter question gives everyone a chance to participate, to feel important. Winston Churchill said of his days at Harrow: "The teacher was always trying to find out what I didn't know, instead of what I did know. I knew a lot of history but never got a chance to say so."

In the Yale–North Haven Summer School, a part of our teacher training program, to take a further example, we gave no marks; we had none of the usual holds on students. We had many for whom school had represented one defeat after another. We tried to give some successful experience every day to each person in the class. We set general problems that each could solve in his own way. We tried to make each person value himself. We made special efforts to search out those overly quiet people, of whom there are so many, who have learned that keeping their mouths shut is the best way to face the challenge of a hostile environment. Our Yale students tried to be friendly with them, to find out and to encourage their interests. The last idea would seem platitudinous to those who have had much success in the world of schools, but it is central to the process of living and learning. The ability to get along with our neighbors depends largely on our ability to get along with ourselves. And getting along with ourselves depends on our own sense of self-respect, the image that we have built of who we are. Happy people are content with themselves; they have no other role to play. They need no victims. Respect for themselves will be mirrored in the respect they allow to others.

ENCOURAGEMENT AND BOOKS

Students are especially anxious about two main things; they want to belong and they want to be noticed. The psychologists talk of determination and how character is formed in the first six months of life. They tell us that from then on, in moments of tension we regress to childhood patterns of behavior. All well and good. As an intelligent reader and observer of life I agree with them; the evidence is on their side. As a teacher, though, I know that we can change a student's image of who he thinks he is. With encouragement and with books we can change the role he is playing in life. But this is a conscious process of getting the right books in the right hands, of providing the right experience at the right time. It means knowing the book and knowing the student. Needless to say, it means better educated teachers, who read books. And it means staffing the school with people who care about *all* the students.

And if we set ourselves the task of changing people, we have to set up many experiences in which a student can have success. How many students in a particular school during this year will have a chance to take part in a play, do dramatic readings before an audience, paint pictures, play or sing good music, produce a bit of sculpture, play on teams? How many in other words will get a sense of accomplishment and develop a sense of the proportions of beauty?

A good school must offer a student a sense of fulfillment which comes to those who use their talents and so develop

respect for themselves. We cannot ask support for public
education on the grounds that "frills" have been eliminated;
and we cannot assume, as so many recent public statements
have, that anything beyond Latin, mathematics, and physics
is a "frill." This type of thinking has been too prevalent since
the first Sputnik took off with a dog as cargo.

A humanistic education does not have a *use*. It frees individuals for a search after an elusive truth, and the search is
full of danger. But a greater danger, in our dealing with
totalitarian states, is that we may get to imitate them. We may
offer official answers for the problems before us.

If we fail to set our own standards and fail to center our
efforts on producing reasoning and kind people, we may find
ourselves in the position described, in a letter to *The New
York Times,* by Harry Rudin of the Yale history department.
He said more tersely in this letter what John Hersey said in
the novel I referred to earlier. Mr. Rudin's words, written
shortly after that Russian dog took off in Sputnik, were:
"What is the meaning of education in a world devoting most
of its talent and treasure for a war whose chief targets must
inevitably be the symbols of their culture—the great cities
with their industries, universities, libraries, art collections,
and so on? Is self-destruction, then, the high goal of education? Have men of religion and of learning no higher purpose?
Is the significance of our learning that of those endless zeroes
traced by a dead dog in the heavens above us? There can't
be much time left for men to find out what their learning is
really for."

The Challenge of Automation to Education

LUTHER H. EVANS

*Columbia University, formerly Librarian of Congress
and Director General of UNESCO*

Thomas Jefferson wrote, almost 150 years ago, "If a nation
expects to be ignorant and free, in a state of civilization, it
expects what never was and never will be." The United States
has pursued the Jeffersonian course. The one-room schools of
Jefferson's day have grown to a gigantic system of public education that takes most American children through at least
twelve years of public schooling. With the growth of our

public school system, we have given our schools an ever-increasing role in promoting citizenship as well as personal development. American schools have played a crucial role in furthering both political democracy and social mobility, while a high general level of education has aided economic and technological progress. On the other hand, man's store of knowledge has multiplied many times over in the intervening years. It is estimated that in this century our total knowledge doubles every ten years. The "state of civilization" for which we must be educated has grown ever more complex, and rapid technological progress has made the problem of "ignorance" far more important than even Jefferson could have imagined.

HOW AUTOMATION IN SOCIETY AFFECTS EDUCATION

Automation is part of this rapid sweep of technological progress. Its effects are already being felt in such widely separated places as the library and the factory, the office and the hospital. Automation affects workers and executives; it affects our concepts of work and leisure. The social and economic results of automation are far-reaching, and are increasing in importance. Because of this, automation is likely to have a significant effect on education in any country where it is widely introduced. It is particularly appropriate to discuss the relation of automation to education in the United States because our educational system is a major instrument of social policy, yet it is not centralized on a national basis: it can adjust to changing conditions only by a constant process of public discussion, by local communities who control the public schools, by their elected representatives, by the teaching community, and by other professional groups.

At this time, we can only guess at many of the long-range effects of automation. However, certain effects clearly visible today, relate directly to education at all levels.

The accelerated rate of technological change produces some of the most widespread effects. Industry and government now spend an ever-increasing amount on research and development. In 1941, the total spent throughout the economy was less than a billion dollars annually; today the annual rate is close to $15 billion, with much of this supplied by the government. When discoveries are made, they are put to use very quickly. More than 3,200 different products have already been developed as an outgrowth of our space research programs. Miniature computers and other electronic equipment, developed to fit into missiles, are quickly being adapted by private industry, where a smaller computer is less costly and becomes economically feasible for a greater number of firms. Research continues to promote miniaturization of electronic devices. Other products are far removed from the world of electronics and space. Materials first developed for the nose-cone of guided missiles, for example, have been used for several years to manufacture cooking utensils.

These examples illustrate the speed and ingenuity with which scientific discoveries are now converted into practice. The steam engine was not put into widespread use for twenty or thirty years after its discovery. Two or three years would be a much better estimate of the time gap in the 1960's between the drawing board or laboratory and the market. For example, a government occupational handbook, published in 1961, states that the rate of demand for computer operators cannot be accurately forecast for the next decade, because it depends on certain computer improvements still being developed.

This rapid change presents, first of all, the very practical problem, for both layman and professional, of keeping their own knowledge reasonably up to date. It also means that industrial and economic organization will change continually and rapidly, in response to the economic potential of new discoveries. It is unlikely, in such a situation, that any man or woman will be able to go through life with his original potential of new discoveries. Retraining, which we now consider a remedy for the few, will become a matter of course for all. As economic changes come more quickly, the social and political changes accompanying them will also come more quickly. This last is very important for a democracy, where public opinion tends to move slowly in adapting to new concepts and new problems.

What will the new jobs be? What skills will they require? The fact that we do not know with any degree of accuracy is in itself significant. Companies that have automated in whole or in part are being studied for some clue to the answer. What the worker in an automated operation actually does may not be more complicated than his previous job. There is an increasing emphasis on mental rather than physical skills and on the ability to correlate a great many facts. It is not surprising that the unskilled worker and the less educated worker have already suffered most from automation, and will probably continue to be the most seriously affected.

While the demand for unskilled workers continues to shrink, there is an increasing demand for scientists, engineers, computer programmers and qualified supervisory personnel. In the firms where it is introduced, automation integrates all the operations in the interest of efficiency and creates centralized control of these operations. By means of electronic data processing, it also provides management with a greater variety of information, in more detailed form, and much sooner, than in the past. Thus, managers can exercise much greater control, and make decisions about many things that were not within their power before. In view of this, the outlook and education of these new engineers and scientists become a matter of public interest.

The premium which automation, and the systems approach, put upon efficiency and uniformity of production can have consequences for industrial relations and human relations that should concern the educator. An industrial or clerical operation preplanned down to the smallest detail does not allow room for individual variations. This can create problems of employee morale in an automated plant, just as it created similar problems on the assembly line that preceded automation. Because automation eliminates many routine assembly-line operations, there may be fewer workers in any given plant who face the problem of routine, rigidly timed tasks. Many new positions are created which require creative intelligence. On the other hand, automation is entering whole new areas, such as the office, where the problems of the assembly line have not been experienced before. To the extent that automation emphasizes uniformity, efficiency and detailed central planning, it tends to stifle individualism. However, many by-products of automation, such as increased leisure and increased schooling, can help to strengthen our humane values, if we take advantage of the opportunities they present.

Increased leisure will be among the more significant long-run social effects of automation. As productivity has increased in the past, the average work week in this country has declined from 84 hours in 1800, to 60 hours in 1900, to less than 40 hours today. Automation, which increases productivity sharply, will encourage the continuing shrinkage of the work week, as well as the trend toward early retirement. Retirement at 65 or earlier is becoming quite customary for all segments of our population, and there are more than 16 million people over 65 in our country today. The leisure time thus created represents a great educational potential.

To speak of the growing complexity of our civilization is trite, yet necessary. Our increasing reliance on advanced technological methods in both government and business creates serious problems for the citizen. Part of current U.S. military strategy, for instance, relies on the calculations of computers. As our economic measurements become more sophisticated, they become more difficult for even the reasonably well-educated citizen to evaluate. How, then, can he make his own decisions on basic national issues, and not merely accept spoon-fed interpretations? The educational community alone cannot solve this problem, but any attempt to solve it must begin with a concerted effort in our schools.

RESPONSE OF THE SCHOOLS

These, then, are some of the challenges to education suggested by our present knowledge of automation. We have simply noted so far points at which automation impinges on some aspect of education. Considering these points separately, and in combination, how can our schools respond to this challenge?

The most urgent consideration is this: No part of our population will be able to function in our economy without an adequate grasp of basic language and mathematical skills. Because of the rapid rate of technological change, almost every worker will have to be retrained at some time, and such retraining usually is not successful with a worker who cannot follow written instructions and communicate his own knowledge and ideas capably. In addition to this, we can expect a generally rising level of education and skill requirements on all jobs. Despite all our efforts, there are today eleven million illiterate people in this country. In the past these people could not advance very far or live very well, but there were jobs they could fill. These jobs will become ever fewer. Accordingly, intensified effort must continue to be made to teach the basic skills well, and to keep all children in school long enough to learn them. At present, about 70 per cent of our children complete at least twelve years of public schooling. Another 20 per cent complete eight years or more. Measured by our own past performance, and that in other parts of the world, this is a very good record. But in an age of automation, it is not good enough.

Students who do not go beyond high school will generally need, in addition to basic skills, technical training to secure their first jobs. Our technological progress has created a growing demand for technicians to back up the scientist and the engineer. The first task is to keep these youngsters in school so that they can be trained. The second step, equally important, is to provide them with useful, up-to-date training. This is the traditional role of high school vocational courses, but such courses must be kept under constant review in order to meet the constantly changing needs of the economy. A major review of this program is, in fact, under way in the United States Office of Education. There is also a trend toward providing this technical training in one or two years of training after high school graduation. Such courses in electronics, laboratory assistance, business machines—are now offered in a variety of technical schools, and both public and private junior colleges. If our high schools, colleges, and universities are not to be overwhelmed by the specific needs of industry, the system of two-year community colleges and technical schools will surely have to be expanded.

The student who does not go on to professional training or a liberal arts college also needs to be imbued with a positive attitude toward learning. To lead a meaningful and productive life in an age of automation requires a new kind of morale. He must realize, when he leaves school, that the traditional words of commencement speakers have become more than clichés: the education he has received really is just a beginning. No one can safely predict the kind of work he will be performing thirty years hence, but it can be predicted with certainty that he will have to update his skills and his general knowledge if he is to remain a productive member of society.

The cause of adult education, which has already made great strides, attains new urgency in an age of automation. This may well be the most far-reaching educational implication of automation. As job requirements change at a rapid pace, along with every other aspect of our economic and scientific life, adults will have to go back to school, whether the school is formal or informal, within industry or outside, to keep from being left behind. Many of today's older workers, who have had no significant learning experience since childhood, present a very serious problem when they face the need for retraining. Some have lost confidence in their ability to learn; others actually show a serious loss in their ability to learn. Psychological studies of older people suggest that their learning experience, far more than their chronological age, determines their mental agility.

The solution appears to be a process of continuing education for all adults. Here, automation itself can help to solve the problem it creates. Increased leisure, a by-product of automation, makes such a program of continuing education feasible. The increase in leisure time also provides added incentive for adult education, which can help people to enjoy their leisure in a meaningful way.

Automation presents its greatest educational challenge in relation to the poorly and marginally educated. But automation will also have an effect, and should have an effect, on curriculum in general, and what our best schools offer our best students. The rate at which our store of knowledge changes, the requirements of new professional fields such as computer programing, and the analysis and design of systems —all must lead to a greater emphasis on the use of logic and on the analysis and integration of information and data, rather than mere memorization of facts or even of generalizations. The growing impact of science and technology on our daily lives highlights the need for intensive science instruction in our schools. As mentioned earlier, the rate of technological change will also speed the rate of economic, social, and political change and will reduce the time available to citizens and government for deciding how to cope with new problems. This makes it all the more important that our students receive a good education in the social sciences. Integrated social studies courses have provided high school students with a broad understanding of historical and political issues, but certain important areas such as geography and, especially, economics, have been seriously neglected.

If education in the social sciences is important for the average student, it is all the more important for the engineers and scientists who have roles of growing influence in modern industry. Automated industry will have fewer managers, but it is likely that more of them will come from engineering and related sciences. Thus, it is extremely important that they be sufficiently educated in the social sciences and humanities so that all decisions will not appear to them to be purely technical, and they will take cognizance of less measurable human and cultural factors.

Most of this discussion has emphasized the role of education in helping us adapt to change, for that is the first requirement of automation. The more rapid and basic the change, however, the more important is education's parallel role of preserving and passing on the basic human and cultural values of a society. Automation and other technological developments place a sometimes unfortunate emphasis on material achievements, efficiency and uniformity. The tradition of individualism and human dignity is strong in this country; it has benefited in the past from the support of our schools, and it will certainly need their continued support in the future.

The goals I have outlined for our educational system are vast. Most of them will require much more effort to achieve than is now being expended. In many areas, however, significant spadework has already been done, and progress is visible.

TRAINING OUTSIDE THE "SCHOOLS"

Adult education of all kinds has mushroomed in recent years. It is estimated that there are now about ten million Americans taking part in formal institutional adult education. Many universities offer extension courses for adults, not only on their own campuses, but often in widely scattered locations within a radius of several hundred miles. Over three million people are enrolled in adult education courses sponsored by local public school systems. Public schools offer these courses in almost all large cities, but fewer are available in small communities. An added difficulty in small communities is that the programs offered are not as comprehensive. Most do not offer, for instance, the opportunity to earn a high school diploma. An analysis of subject matter in public school adult education reveals that courses in trade, industrial and technical education are the most popular, followed by homemaking, high school academic courses, business education, and practical arts and crafts.

Often, it is true, the people who benefit from adult education are not those who need it most. People who had unsatisfactory school experiences usually will not take the initiative to enroll in adult education courses. To overcome this sort of resistance, efforts have been made in several communities to reach one group, adult illiterates, through television programs.

American industry and labor unions also make a significant contribution to continuing adult education. One expert, Professor Harold F. Clark of Columbia University, estimates that more people are being educated in industry than are enrolled in all our public and private institutions of higher education. There is no doubt that a great deal of training takes place within private industry. The largest companies not only train new employees and retrain their own workers for new methods, but they encourage all employees to enroll in courses for personal development and send their executives to intensive courses conducted for them at a variety of colleges and universities. Many labor unions also conduct both technical and general courses for their members. On two points there probably is general agreement: That the educational program in industry is very extensive and that it is not sufficient by itself to solve the problems caused by automation.

The federal government has recently entered this field on a broader scale than heretofore, under the Manpower Development and Training Act passed early in 1962. A new office of automation in the U.S. Department of Labor will help states and local agencies finance training programs for unemployed workers, workers who face future technological unemployment and young people just entering the labor market. It will also undertake a comprehensive research program to identify current and future manpower requirements and resources. This should make possible a co-ordinated response to some of the employment problems created by automation, and help workers to gain the new skills that are in demand.

Legislation has also been introduced in Congress to encourage technical education at the junior college level, and the U.S. Office of Education is conducting a study of our nation's technical training needs and resources.

A great variety of private and governmental organizations have been attacking the problem of the drop-out, the student who does not complete at least a high school education. Communities have sought to reach these students while they are still in school with films, counseling and other means; to work with their parents—and, in at least one project, Mobilization for Youth, with the entire community—in order to improve the motivation they receive from their home environment; to reach them after they leave school and encourage them to return for training; and to learn how to identify potential drop-outs early enough to help them with revised courses, counseling, and other means.

There has also been progress, in recent years, toward improving the course content in public schools. Science and mathematics courses have been reorganized to help prepare students for an age of automation and science. New study materials are being prepared in economics to help high school teachers present the difficult and controversial issues that many have avoided in the past. Frequently, curriculum revision that was precipitated by a need for updating in the physical sciences has, in the end, led to changes in almost every area of education. Automation has also begun to enter the classroom as a teaching aid, in the form of teaching machines and other technical devices which help to free the teacher's time for more creative tasks and allow students to learn at a more individual pace.

Thus American education is already in a state of flux. To meet the challenge of automation and other technological changes, it will have to make an even greater effort and move even more quickly than at present. If this is done, however, automation can help achieve a new and higher level of education, culture, and freedom for the entire people.

Education on the Nonverbal Level

ALDOUS HUXLEY
Distinguished author and philosopher

Early in the mid-Victorian period the Reverend Thomas Binney, a Congregationalist divine, published a book with the alluring title, *Is It Possible to Make the Best of Both Worlds?* His conclusion was that perhaps it might be possible. In spite of its unorthodox message, or perhaps because of it, the book was a best seller, which only showed, said the more evangelical of Mr. Binney's Nonconformist colleagues and Anglican opponents, how inexpressibly wicked Victorian England really was.

What Mr. Binney's critics had done (and their mistake is repeated by all those who use the old phrase disapprovingly) was to equate "making the best of both worlds" with "serving two masters." It is most certainly very difficult, perhaps quite impossible, to serve Mammon and God simultaneously—to pursue the most sordid interests while aspiring to realize the highest ideals. This is obvious. Only a little less obvious, however, is the fact that it is very hard, perhaps quite impossible, to serve God while failing to make the best of both worlds— of *all* the worlds of which, as human beings, we are the inhabitants.

Man is a multiple amphibian and exists at one and the same time in a number of universes, dissimilar to the point, very nearly, of complete incompatibility. He is at once an animal and a rational intellect; a product of evolution closely related to the apes and a spirit capable of self-transcendence; a sentient being in contact with the brute data of his own nervous system and the physical environment and at the same time the creator of a home-made universe of words and other symbols, in which he lives and moves and has anything from 30 to 80 per cent of his being. He is a self-conscious and self-centered ego who is also a member of a moderately gregarious species, an individualist compelled by the population explosion to live at ever closer quarters, and in ever tighter organizations, with millions of other egos as self-centered and as poorly socialized as himself. Neurologically, he is a lately evolved Jekyll-cortex associated with an immensely ancient brain-stem-Hyde. Physiologically, he is a creature whose endocrine system is perfectly adapted to the conditions prevailing in the lower Paleolithic, but living in a metropolis and spending eight hours a day sitting at a desk in an air-conditioned office. Psychologically, he is a highly educated product of twentieth-century civilization, chained, in a state of uneasy and hostile symbiosis, to a disturbingly dynamic unconscious, a wild phantasy and an unpredictable id—and yet capable of falling in love, writing string quartets, and having mystical experiences.

Living amphibiously in all these incommensurable worlds at once, human beings (it is hardly surprising) find themselves painfully confused, uncertain where they stand or who they really are. To provide themselves with a recognizable identity, a niche in the scheme of things that they can call "home," they will give assent to the unlikeliest dogmas, conform to the most absurd and even harmful rules of thought, feeling, and conduct, put on the most extravagant fancy dress and identify themselves with masks that bear almost no resemblance to the faces they cover. "Bovarism" (as Jules de Gaultier calls it) is the urge to pretend that one is something that in fact one is not. It is an urge that manifests itself, sometimes weakly, sometimes with overpowering strength, in all human beings, and one of the conditions of its manifestation is precisely our uncertainty about where we stand or who we are. To explore our multiple amphibiousness with a view to doing something constructive about it is a most laborious process. Our minds are congenitally lazy, and the original sin of the intellect is oversimplification. Dogmatism and bovaristic identification with a stereotype are closely related manifestations of the same kind of intellectual delinquency. "Know thyself." From time immemorial this has been the advice of all the seers and philosophers. The self that they urge us to know is not, of course, the stylized persona with which, bovaristically, we try to become identified; it is the multiple amphibian, the inhabitant of all those incompatible worlds that we must somehow learn to make the best of.

A good education may be defined as one which helps the boys and girls subjected to it to make the best of all the worlds in which, as human beings, they are compelled, willy-nilly, to live. An education that prepares them to make the best of only one of their worlds, or of only a few of them, is inadequate. This is a point on which, in principle, all educators have always agreed. *Mens sana in corpore sano* is an ancient educational ideal and a very good one. Unfortunately, good ideals are never enough. Unless they are accompanied by full instructions regarding the methods by which they may be realized, they are almost useless. Hell is paved with good intentions, and whole periods of history have been made hideous or grotesque by enthusiastic idealists who failed to elaborate the means whereby their lofty aspirations might be effectively, and above all harmlessly, implemented.

Just how good is modern education? How successful is it in helping young people to make the best of all the worlds which, as multiple amphibians, they have to live in? In a center of advanced scientific and technical study this question gets asked inevitably in terms of what may be called the paradox of specialization. In science and technology specialization is unavoidable and indeed absolutely necessary. But training for this unavoidable and necessary specialization does nothing to help young amphibians to make the best of their many worlds. Indeed, it pretty obviously prevents them from doing anything of the kind. What then is to be done? At the Massachusetts Institute of Technology and in other schools where similar problems have arisen, the answer to this question has found expression in a renewed interest in the humanities. Excessive scientific specialization is tempered by courses in philosophy, history, literature, and social studies. All this is excellent so far as it goes. But does it go far enough. Do courses in the humanities provide a sufficient antidote for excessive scientific and technical specialization? Do they, in the terminology we have been using, help young multiple amphibians to make the best of a substantially greater number of their worlds?

Science is the reduction of the bewildering diversity of unique events to manageable uniformity within one of a number of symbol systems, and technology is the art of using these symbol systems so as to control and organize unique events. Scientific observation is always a viewing of things through the refracting medium of a symbol system, and technological praxis is always the handling of things in ways that some symbol system has dictated. Education in science and technology is essentially education on the symbolic level.

Turning to the humanities, what do we find? Courses in philosophy, literature, history, and social studies are exclusively verbal. Observation and experimentation with nonverbal events have no place in these fields. Training in the sciences is largely on the symbolic level; training in the liberal arts is wholly and all the time on that level. When courses in the humanities are used as the only antidote to too much science and technology, excessive specialization in one kind of symbolic education is being tempered by excessive specialization in another kind of symbolic education. The young amphibians are taught to make the best, not of all their worlds, but only of two varieties of the same world—the world of symbols. But this world of symbols is only one of the worlds in which human beings do their living and their learning. They also inhabit the nonsymbolic world of unconceptualized or only slightly conceptualized experience. However effective it may be on the conceptual level, an education that fails to help young amphibians to make the best of the inner and outer universes on the hither side of symbols is an inadequate education. And however much we may delight in Homer or Gibbon, however illuminating in their different ways Pareto and William Law, Hui-neng and Bertrand Russell may strike us as being, the fact remains that the reading of their works will not be of much help to us in our efforts to make the best of our worlds of unconceptualized, nonverbal experience.

And here, before I embark on a discussion of these nonverbal worlds, let me add parenthetically that even on the verbal level, where they are most at home, educators have done a good deal less than they might reasonably have been expected to do in explaining to young people the nature, the limitations, the huge potentialities for evil as well as for good, of that greatest of all human inventions, language. Children should be taught that words are indispensable but also can be fatal—the only begetters of all civilization, all science, all consistency of high purpose, all angelic goodness, and the only begetters at the same time of all superstition, all collective madness and stupidity, all worse-than-bestial diabolism, all the dismal historical succession of crimes in the name of

God, King, Nation, Party, Dogma. Never before, thanks to the techniques of mass communication, have so many listeners been so completely at the mercy of so few speakers. Never have misused words—those hideously efficient tools of all the tyrants, war-mongers, persecutors, and heresy-hunters—been so widely and so disastrously influential as they are today. Generals, clergymen, advertisers, and the rulers of totalitarian states—all have good reasons for disliking the idea of universal education in the rational use of language. To the military, clerical, propagandist, and authoritarian mind such training seems (and rightly seems) profoundly subversive. To those who think that liberty is a good thing, and who hope that it may some day become possible for more people to realize more of their desirable potentialities in a society fit for free, fully human individuals to live in, a thorough education in the nature of language, in its uses and abuses, seems indispensable. Whether in fact the mounting pressures of overpopulation and overorganization in a world still enthusiastically dedicated to nationalistic idolatry will permit this kind of subversive linguistic education to be adopted by even the more democratic nations remains to be seen.

And now, after this brief digression, let us return to our main theme, the education of multiple amphibians on levels other than the verbal and the symbolic. "Make the body capable of doing many things," wrote Spinoza. "This will help you to perfect the mind and come to the intellectual love of God." Substitute "psychophysical organism" for "body," and you have here the summary of a program for universal education on the nonsymbolic level, supplemented by a statement of the reasons why such an education is desirable and indeed, if the child is to grow into a fully human being, absolutely necessary. The detailed curriculum for an education in what may be called the nonverbal humanities has still to be worked out. All I can do at this time is to drop a few fragmentary hints.

Two points, to begin with, must be emphatically stressed. First, education in the nonverbal humanities is not just a matter of gymnastics and football, of lessons in singing and folk dancing. All these, of course, are good, but by themselves not good enough. Such traditional methods of training young people in nonverbal skills need to be supplemented, if they are to yield their best results, by other kinds of training, beginning with a thorough training in elementary awareness. And the second point to be remembered is that education in the nonverbal humanities is a process that should be started in the kindergarten and continued through all the years of school and college—and thereafter, as self-education, throughout the rest of life.

At the end of a delightful anthology entitled *Zen Flesh, Zen Bones*, its editor, Mr. Paul Reps, has printed an English version of an ancient Tantrik text in which Shiva, in response to Parvati's questions about the nature of enlightened consciousness, gives a list of one hundred and twelve exercises in the art of being aware of inner and outer reality on its nonsymbolic levels. *Gnosce Teipsum*. But how? From the vast majority of our pastors and masters no answer is forthcoming. Here, for a blessed change, is a philosophical treatise that speaks of means as well as of ends, of concrete experience as well as of high abstractions. The intelligent and systematic practice of any half-dozen of these hundred and twelve exercises will take one further towards the realization of the ancient ideal of self-knowledge than all the roaring or pathetic eloquence of generations of philosophers, theologians, and moralists. (Let me add, in passing, that whereas Western philosophy tends to be concerned with the manipulation of abstract symbols for the benefit of the speculative and moralizing intellect, oriental philosophy is almost always essentially operational. "Perform such and such psychophysical operations," the exponents of this philosophy say, "and you will probably find yourself in a state of mind which, like all those who have achieved it in the past, you will regard as self-evidently and supremely valuable. In the context of this state of mind, speculation about man and the universe leads us, as it led earlier thinkers, to the metaphysical doctrine of *Tat tvam asi* [thou art That], and to its ethical corollary—universal compassion. In this philosophy it is the experiential element that is important. Its speculative superstructure is a thing of words, and words, though useful and necessary, should never be taken too seriously.")

Education in elementary awareness will have to include techniques for improving awareness of internal events and techniques for improving awareness of external events as these are revealed by our organs of sense. In his introductions to several of F. M. Alexander's books, John Dewey insisted upon the importance of a properly directed training in the awareness of internal events. It was Dewey's opinion that the training methods developed by Alexander were to education what education is to life in general—an indispensable condition for any kind of improvement. Dewey had himself undergone this training and so knew what he was talking about. And yet in spite of this high praise bestowed by one of the most influential of modern philosophers and educational reformers, Alexander's methods have been ignored, and school children still receive no training in the kind of internal awareness that can lead to what Alexander described as "creative conscious control."

The educational and therapeutic values of training aimed at heightening awareness of internal events was empirically demonstrated during the first quarter of the present century by the eminently successful Swiss psychiatrist, Dr. Roger Vittoz. And in recent years methods similar to those of Vittoz and to the Tantrik exercises attributed many centuries ago to Shiva have been developed and successfully used both in the treatment of neurotics and for the enrichment of the lives of the normal by the authors of *Gestalt Therapy*, Drs. Frederick F. Perls, Ralph F. Hefferline, and Paul Goodman.

All our mental processes depend upon perception. Inadequate perceiving results in poor thinking, inappropriate feeling, diminished interest in and enjoyment of life. Systematic training of perception should be an essential element in all education.

Our amphibiousness is clearly illustrated in the two modes of our awareness of external events. There is a receptive, more or less unconceptualized, aesthetic and "spiritual" mode of perceiving; and there is also a highly conceptualized, stereotyped, utilitarian, and even scientific mode. In his *Expostulation and Reply* and *The Tables Turned*, Wordsworth has perfectly described these two modes of awareness and has assigned to each its special significance and value for the human being who aspires to make the best of both worlds and so, by teaching his psychophysical organism to "do many things," to "perfect the mind and come to the intellectual love of God."

> "Why, William, on that old grey stone,
>   Thus for the length of half a day,
>   Why, William, sit you thus alone,
>   And dream your time away?
>
> Where are your books?—that light bequeathed
>   To beings else forlorn and blind?
>   Up! Up! and drink the spirit breathed
>   From dead men to their kind.

You look round on your Mother Earth,
As if she for no purpose bore you;
As if you were her first-born birth,
And none had lived before you."

One morning thus, by Esthwaite lake,
When life was sweet, I knew not why,
To me my good friend Matthew spake,
And thus I made reply.

"The eye it cannot choose but see;
We cannot bid the ear be still;
Our bodies feel, where'er they be,
Against or with our will.

Nor less I deem that there are Powers
Which of themselves our minds impress;
That we can feed this mind of ours
In a wise passiveness.

Think you, 'mid all this mighty sum
Of things for ever speaking,
That nothing of itself will come,
But we must still be seeking?

Then ask not wherefore, here, alone,
Conversing as I may,
I sit upon this old grey stone
And dream my time away."

In *The Tables Turned* it is the poet who takes the offensive
against his studious friend. "Up! up! my Friend," he calls,
"and quit your books." And then, "Books!" he continues im-
patiently.

Books! 'tis a dull and endless strife;
Come, hear the woodland linnet;
How sweet his music! on my life,
There's more of wisdom in it.

And hark how blithe the throstle sings!
He too is no mean preacher.
Come forth into the light of things,
Let Nature be your teacher.

One impulse from a vernal wood
May teach you more of man,
Of moral evil and of good
Than all the sages can.

Sweet is the lore which Nature brings;
Our meddling intellect
Mis-shapes the beauteous forms of things—
We murder to dissect.

Enough of Science and of Art;
Close up those barren leaves;
Come forth and bring with you a heart
That watches and receives.

Matthew and William—two aspects of the multiple amphibian that was Wordsworth, that is each one of us. To be fully human, we must learn to make the best of William's world as well as of Matthew's. Matthew's is the world of books, of the social heredity of steadily accumulating knowledge, of science and technics and business, of words and the stock of second-hand notions which we project upon external reality as a frame of reference, in terms of which we may explain, to our own satisfaction, the enigma, moment by moment, of ongoing existence. Over against it stands William's world—the world of sheer mystery, the world as an endless succession of unique events, the world as we perceive it in a state of alert receptiveness with no thought of explaining it, using it, exploiting it for our biological or cultural purposes. As things now stand, we teach young people to make the best only of Matthew's world of familiar words, accepted notions, and useful techniques. We temper a too exclusive concentration on scientific symbols, not with a training in the art of what William calls "wise passiveness," not with lessons in watching and receiving, but with the injunction to concentrate on philosophical and sociological symbols, to read the books that are reputed to contain a high concentration of "the spirit breathed from dead men to their kind." (Alas, dead men do not always breathe a spirit; quite often they merely emit a bad smell.)

It is related in one of the Sutras that on a certain occasion the Buddha preached a wordless sermon to his disciples. Instead of saying anything, he picked a flower and held it up for them to look at. The disciples gaped uncomprehendingly. Only Mahakasyapa understood what the Tathagata was driving at, and all that he did was to smile. Gautama smiled back at him, and when the wordless sermon was over, he made a little speech for the benefit of those who had failed to comprehend his silence. "This treasure of the unquestionable teaching, this Mind of Nirvana, this true form that is without forms, this most subtle Dharma beyond words, this instruction

that is to be given and received outside the pale of all doc-
trines—this I have now handed on to Mahakasyapa." Perceived
not as a botanical specimen, not as the analyzed and labeled
illustration of a pre-existent symbol system, but as a nameless,
unique event, in which all the beauty and the mystery of
existence are manifest, a flower can become the means to enlightenment. And what is true of a flower is true, needless to
say, of any other event in the inner or outer world—from a
toothache to Mount Everest, from a tapeworm to The Well-
Tempered Clavichord—to which we choose to pay attention
in a state of wise passiveness. And wise passiveness is the
condition not only of spiritual insight. ("In prayer," wrote
St. Jeanne Chantal, "I always want to *do* something, wherein
I do very wrong. . . . By wishing to accomplish something
myself, I spoil it all.") In another context, wise passiveness,
followed in due course by wise hard work, is the condition of
creativity. We do not fabricate our best ideas; they "occur to
us," they "come into our heads." Colloquial speech reminds
us that, unless we give our subliminal mind a chance, we shall
get nowhere. And it is by allowing ourselves at frequent intervals to be wisely passive that we can most effectively help
the subliminal mind to do its work. The *cogito* of Descartes
should be emended, said Von Baader, to *cogitor*. In order to
actualize our potentialities, in order to become fully human
and completely ourselves, we must not merely think; we must
also permit ourselves to be thought. In Gardner Murphy's
words, "Both the historical record of creative thought and the
laboratory report of its appearance today, indicate clearly
that creative intelligence can spring from the mind that is not
strained to its highest pitch, but is utterly at ease." Watching
and receiving in a state of perfect ease or wise passiveness is
an art which can be cultivated and should be taught on every
educational level from the most elementary to the most advanced.

Creativity and spiritual insight—these are the highest rewards of wise passiveness. But those who know how to watch
and receive are rewarded in other and hardly less important
ways. Receptivity can be a source of innocent and completely
harmless happiness. A man or woman who knows how to make
the best of both worlds—the world revealed by wise passiveness and the world created by wise activity—tends to find life
enjoyable and interesting. Ours is a civilization in which vast
numbers of children and adults are so chronically bored that
they have to resort during their leisure hours to a regimen of

non-stop distractions. Any method which promises to make life seem enjoyable and the commonplaces of everyday experience more interesting should be welcomed as a major contribution to culture and morality.

In *Modern Painters* there is a remarkable chapter on "the Open Sky"—a chapter which even by those who find Ruskin's theology absurd and his aesthetics frequently perverse may still be read with profit and admiring pleasure. "It is a strange thing," Ruskin writes, "how little in general people know about the sky. It is the part of creation in which nature has done more for the sake of pleasing man, more for the sake and evident purpose of talking to him and teaching him, than in any of her works, and it is just the part in which we least attend to her. . . . There is not a moment in any day of our lives in which nature is not producing (in the sky) scene after scene, picture after picture, glory after glory, and working always upon such exquisite and constant principles of the most perfect beauty, that it is quite certain it is all done for us and intended for our perpetual pleasure." But, in point of fact, does the sky produce in most people the perpetual pleasure which its beauty is so eminently capable of giving? The answer, of course, is No. "We never attend to it, we never make it a subject of thought. . . . We look upon it . . . only as a succession of monotonous and meaningless accidents, too common or too vain to be worthy of a moment of watchfulness or a glance of admiration. . . . Who, among the chattering crowd, can tell me of the forms and the precipices of the chain of tall white mountains that girded the horizon at noon yesterday? Who saw the narrow sunbeam that came out of the south and smote their summits until they melted and mouldered away in a dust of blue rain? . . . All has passed unregretted as unseen; or if the apathy be ever shaken off, if even for an instant, it is only by what is gross or what is extraordinary." A habit of wise passiveness in relation to the everyday drama of the clouds and mist and sunshine can become a source, as Ruskin insists, of endless pleasure. But most of the products of our educational system prefer Westerns and alcohol.

In the art of watching and receiving Ruskin was self-educated. But there seems to be no reason why children should not be taught that wise passiveness which gave this victim of a traumatic childhood so much pleasure and kept him, in spite of everything, reasonably sane for the greater part of a long and productive life. A training in watching and receiving will not turn every child into a great stylist but, within the

limits imposed by constitution, temperament, and the circum-
ambient culture, it will make him more sensitive, more intelligent, more capable of innocent enjoyment and, in consequence,
more virtuous and more useful to society.

In the United States life, liberty, and the pursuit of happiness are constitutionally guaranteed. But if life hardly seems
worth living, if liberty is used for subhuman purposes, if the
pursuers of happiness know nothing about the nature of their
quarry or the elementary techniques of hunting, these constitutional rights will not be very meaningful. An education in
that wise passiveness recommended by the saints and the
poets, by all who have lived fully and worked creatively,
might help us to transform the paper promises of a democratic constitution into concrete contemporary fact.

Let us now consider very briefly two other areas in which
an education in the art of making the best of all our seem-
ingly incommensurable worlds would certainly be helpful and
might also turn out to be practicable within the system now
prevailing in our schools and colleges. It is a matter of observable fact that all of us inhabit a world of phantasy as well as
a world of first-order experience and a world of words and
concepts. In most children and in some adults this world of
phantasy is astonishingly vivid. These people are the visual-
izers of Galton's classical dichotomy. For them the world
presented to their consciousness by their story-telling, image-
making phantasy is as real as, sometimes more real than, the
given world of sense impressions and the projected world of
words and explanatory concepts. Even in nonvisualizers the
world of phantasy, though somewhat shadowy, is still real
enough to be retreated into or shrunk from, tormented by or
voluptuously enjoyed. The mentally ill are the victims of their
phantasy, and even more or less normal people find themselves
tempted into folly, or inhibited from behaving as they know
they ought to behave, by what goes on in the superreal but
unrealistic world of their imagination. How can we make the
best of this odd, alien, almost autonomous universe that we
carry about with us inside our skulls?

The question has been partially answered by the apostles of
those numerous religious movements stemming from "New
Thought." Using a vaguely theological language and interpreting the Bible to suit themselves, they have given a religious form to a number of useful and practical methods for
harnessing imagination and its suggestive power in the service
of individual well-being and social stability. For about a

quarter or perhaps a third of the population their methods work remarkably well. This is an important fact, of which professional educators should take notice and from whose implications they should not be ashamed to learn. Unfortunately, men and women in high academic positions tend to be intellectually snobbish. They turn up their noses at the non-scientific, distressingly "inspirational" but still astute and experienced psychologists of the modern heretical churches. This is deplorable. Truth lives, proverbially, at the bottom of a well, and wells are often muddy. No genuinely scientific investigator has any right to be squeamish about anything.

And here is another truth-containing well abhorred by academic scientists of the stricter sort. Excellent techniques for teaching children and adults to make the best of the chaotic world of their phantasy have been worked out by the Dianeticists and their successors, the Scientologists. Their Imagination Games deserve to be incorporated into every curriculum. Boys and girls, and even grown men and women, find these games amusing and, what is more important, helpful. Made the worst of, our imagination will destroy us; made the best of, it can be used to break up long-established habits of undesirable feeling, to dissipate obsessive fears, to provide symbolic outlets for anger and fictional amends for real frustrations.

In the course of the last three thousand years how many sermons have been preached, how many homilies delivered and commands roared out, how many promises of heaven and threats of hell-fire solemnly pronounced, how many good-conduct prizes awarded and how many childish buttocks lacerated with whips and canes? And what has been the result of all this incalculable sum of moralistic words, and of the rewards and savage punishments by which the verbiage has been accompanied? The result has been history—the successive generations of human beings comporting themselves virtuously and rationally enough for the race to survive, but badly enough and madly enough for it to be unceasingly in trouble. Can we do better in the future than we are doing today, or than our fathers did in the past? Can we develop methods more effective than pious talk and Pavlovian conditioning?

For an answer to these questions—or at least for some hints as to the nature of a possible answer—we must turn to history and anthropology. Like many primitive societies today, many highly civilized societies of the past provided their members with realistically amphibious methods for dealing with negative emotions and the instinctive drives that are incompatible with communal living. In these societies morality and rational behavior were not merely preached and rewarded; they were made easier by the provision of religiously sanctioned safety valves, through which the angry, the frustrated, and the anxiously neurotic could release their aggressive or self-destructive tendencies in a satisfyingly violent and yet harmless and socially acceptable way. In Ancient Greece, for example, the orgies of Dionysus and, at a somewhat later date, the Corybantic dances, sacred to the Great Mother, were safety valves through which rage and resentment found an innocuous outlet, while the paralyzing inhibitions of anxiety were swept away in a wild rush of nervous, muscular, and hormonal activity. In this ethical and therapeutic context Dionysus was known as Lusios, the Liberator. His orgies delivered the participants from the dismal necessity of running amok, or of retreating into catatonia, or stoically bottling up their feelings and so giving themselves a psychosomatic illness. Corybantic dancing was regarded as a form of medical treatment and at the same time as a religious rite, cathartic to the soul no less than to the adrenalin-charged body. Which did most for morality and rational behavior—the dialogues of Plato or the orgies of Dionysus, Aristotle's *Ethics* or the Corybantic dances? My guess is that, in this competition, Lusios and the Great Mother would be found to have won hands down.

In a society like ours it would doubtless be impracticable to revive Maenadism or the congregational antics of the Dionysian orgies. But the problem of what multiple amphibians should do about their frustrations and their tendencies to aggression remains acute and still unsolved. Sixty years ago William James wrote an essay entitled *The Moral Equivalent of War*. It is an excellent essay as far as it goes; but it does not, unfortunately, go far enough. Moral equivalents must be found not only for war but also for delinquency, family squabbles, bullying, puritanical censoriousness, and all the assorted beastliness of daily life. Preaching and conditioning will never of themselves solve these problems. It is obvious that we must take a hint from the Greeks and provide ourselves with physical safety valves for reducing the pressure of our negative emotions. No ethical system which fails to provide such physical safety valves, and which fails to teach children and their elders how to use them, is likely to be effective. It will be the business of psychologists, physiologists, and sociologists to devise acceptable safety valves, of moralists and clergymen to provide rationalizations in terms of the local value systems and theologies, and for educators to find a place in the curriculum for courses in the indispensable art of letting off steam.

And there is another art that merits the educator's closest attention—the art of controlling physical pain. Pain, as recent studies have made abundantly clear, is not simply a mechanical affair of peripheral receptors and special centers in the brain, and its intensity is not directly proportional to the extent of the injury which is its cause. Pain may be aggravated or inhibited by numerous psychological and even cultural factors. Which means, of course, that to some extent at least pain is controllable. This fact, needless to say, has been known from time immemorial, and for the last century and a half (from the days of Elliotson and Esdaile) has been systematically exploited in hypnotic anesthesia. Neurological research is now discovering the organic and functional reasons for these old observations and empirical practices; a somewhat disreputable "wild" phenomenon is in process of being turned into a domesticated scientific fact, consonant with other well-known facts and safely caged within a familiar symbol-system. Taking advantage of the new-found respectability of hypnosis and suggestion, educators should now include elementary pain control in the curriculum of physical training. Control of pain through suggestion and autosuggestion is an art which, as every good dentist knows, can be learned by most children with the greatest of ease. Along with singing and calisthenics, it should be taught to every little boy and little girl who can learn it.

Training in a closely similar art may prove to be very useful as a part of ethical education. In his book *Auto-Conditioning* Professor Hornell Hart has outlined simple and thoroughly practical methods for changing moods, intensifying motivations, and implementing good intentions. There are no educational panaceas, no techniques that work perfectly in every case. But if autoconditioning produces good results in only 20 or 30 per cent of those who have been instructed in the art, it deserves to take its place in every educator's armamentarium.

That we are multiple amphibians is self-evident, and the corollary of this self-evident truth is that we must attack our problems on every front where they arise—on the mental front and on the physiological front, on the front of concepts and symbols and on the front of wordless experience, on the

rational front and on the irrational front, the individual front
and the social front. But what should be our strategy? How
are we to learn and successfully practice the art of attacking
on all the fronts simultaneously? Many valuable discoveries
were made by the amphibians of earlier times and alien cultures, and many discoveries are being made within our own
culture today. These empirical findings of the past and the
present should be studied, tested, related to the best scientific
knowledge now available, and finally adapted for practical
use within our educational systems. Ten million dollars from
the coffers of one of the great foundations would pay for the
necessary research and large-scale experimentation. Out of
such research and experimentation might come, within a few
years, a radical improvement in the methods currently used to
prepare young people to meet the challenges of their mani-
fold amphibiousness and to make the best of all the strangely
assorted worlds in which, as human beings, they are predes-
tined to live.

What Do We Know about Learning?

GOODWIN WATSON

*Professor of Social Psychology and Education
(on leave) Teachers College, Columbia University*

What do we really know today about learning? Although
no scientific "truths" are established beyond the possibility
of revision, knowledgeable psychologists generally agree on a
number of propositions about learning which are important
for education. The educator who bases his program on the
propositions presented below is entitled, therefore, to feel
that he is on solid psychological ground and not on shifting
sands.

Behaviors which are rewarded (reinforced) are more likely
to recur.

This most fundamental law of learning has been demonstrated in literally thousands of experiments. It seems to
hold for every sort of animal from earthworms to highly intelligent adults. The behavior most likely to emerge in any
situation is that which the subject found successful or satisfying previously in a similar situation. No other variable affects learning so powerfully. The best-planned learning

provides for a steady, cumulative sequence of successful behaviors.

Reward (reinforcement), to be most effective in learning, must follow almost immediately after the desired behavior and be clearly connected with that behavior in the mind of the learner.

The simple word "right," coming directly after a given response, will have more influence on learning than any big reward which comes much later or which is dimly connected with many responses so that it can't really reinforce any of them. Much of the effectiveness of programed self-instruction lies in the fact that information about success is fed back immediately for each learner response. A total mark on a test the day after it is administered has little or no reinforcement value for the specific answers.

Sheer repetition without indications of improvement or any kind of reinforcement (reward) is a poor way to attempt to learn.

Practice is not enough. The learner cannot improve by repeated efforts unless he is informed whether or not each effort has been successful.

Threat and punishment have variable and uncertain effects upon learning: They may make the punished response more likely or less likely to recur; they may set up avoidance tendencies which prevent further learning.

Punishment is not, psychologically, the reverse of reward. It disturbs the relationship of the learner to the situation and the teacher. It does not assist the learner in finding and fixing the correct response.

Readiness for any new learning is a complex product of interaction among such factors as (a) sufficient physiological and psychological maturity, (b) sense of the importance of the new learning for the learner in his world, (c) mastery of prerequisites providing a fair chance of success, and (d) freedom from discouragement (expectation of failure) or threat (sense of danger).

Conversely, the learner will not be ready to try new responses which are beyond his powers or are seen as valueless or too dangerous.

Opportunity for fresh, novel, stimulating experience is a kind of reward which is quite effective in conditioning and learning.

Experiments indicate that lower animals (rats, dogs, monkeys) will learn as effectively when they receive rewards of new experience or satisfied curiosity as they will when the rewards gratify physical desires. Similarly, stimulating new insights have been found to be effective as rewards for the learning efforts of human beings.

The sense of satisfaction which results from achievement is the type of reward (reinforcement) which has the greatest transfer value to other life situations.

Any extrinsic reward—candy, or stars on a chart, or commendation—depends on its dispenser. There is no need to strive if the reward-giver is out of the picture. Also, cheating can sometimes win the extrinsic reward. The internal reward system is always present for the learner, and he sees little gain in fooling himself.

Learners progress in an area of learning only as far as they need to in order to achieve their purposes. Often they do only well enough to "get by"; with increased motivation, they improve.

Studies of reading speed show that practice alone will not bring improvement; a person may have read books for years at his customary rate, but with new demands and opportunities he may be able to double that rate.

The most effective effort is put forth by children when they attempt tasks which are not too easy and not too hard—where success seems quite possible but not certain. It is not reasonable to expect a teacher to set an appropriate level of challenge for each pupil in a class; pupils can, however, be helped to set their own goals to bring maximum satisfaction and learning.

Children are more likely to throw themselves wholeheartedly into any learning project if they themselves have participated in the selection and planning of the project.

Genuine participation (not pretended sharing) increases motivation, adaptability, and speed of learning.

Excessive direction by the teacher is likely to result in apathetic conformity, defiance, scapegoating, or escape from the whole affair.

Autocratic leadership has been found to increase dependence of members on the leader and to generate resentment (conscious or unconscious) which finds expression in attacks on weaker figures or even in sabotage of the work.

Overstrict discipline is associated with more conformity, anxiety, shyness, and acquiescence in children; greater permissiveness is associated with more initiative and creativity.

In comparisons of children whose parents were most permissive in home discipline with those whose parents were most strict (both groups of parents loving and concerned), the youngsters from permissive homes showed more enterprise, self-confidence, curiosity, and originality.

Many pupils experience so much criticism, failure, and discouragement in school that their self-confidence, level of aspiration, and sense of worth are damaged.

The pupil who sees himself at his worst in school is likely to place little value on study and to seek his role of importance outside the classroom. He may carry through life a sense of being not good for much. He is likely also to feel resentment at schools, teachers, and books.

When children or adults experience too much frustration, their behavior ceases to be integrated, purposeful, and rational. The threshold of what is "too much" varies; it is lowered by previous failures.

Pupils who have had little success and almost continuous failure at school tasks are in no condition to think, to learn, or even to pay attention. They may turn their anger outward against respectable society or inward against themselves.

Pupils think whenever they encounter an obstacle, difficulty, puzzle, or intellectual challenge which interests them. The process of thinking involves designing and testing plausible solutions for the problem as understood by the thinker.

It is useless to command people to think; they must feel concerned to get somewhere and eager to remove an obstruction on the way.

The best way to help pupils form a general concept is to present the concept in numerous and varied specific situations —contrasting experiences with and without the desired concept—and then to encourage precise formulations of the general idea and its application in situations different from those in which the concept was learned.

For example, the concept of democracy might be illustrated not only in national government but also in familiar situations of home, school, church, jobs, clubs, and local affairs. It is best understood when it is contrasted with other power structures such as autocracy, oligarchy, or *laissez faire*.

The experience of learning by sudden insight into a previously confused or puzzling situation arises when (a) there has been a sufficient background and preparation, (b) attention is given to the relationships operative in the whole situation, (c) the perceptual structure "frees" the key elements to be shifted into new patterns, (d) the task is meaningful and within the range of ability of the subject.

The term "cognitive reorganization" is sometimes applied to this experience. Suddenly the scene changes into one that seems familiar and can be coped with.

Learning from reading is facilitated more by time spent recalling what has been read than by rereading.

In one experiment (typical of many), students who spent 80 per cent of their learning periods trying to remember what they had read surpassed those who spent only 60 per cent of the time on recollection. The students who spent all the time reading and rereading the assignment made the poorest record.

Forgetting proceeds rapidly at first—then more and more slowly. Recall shortly after learning reduces the amount forgotten.

Within twenty-four hours after learning something, a large part is forgotten unless efforts are made to prevent forgetting. A thing can be relearned more quickly than it was learned originally, however, and if it is reviewed several times at gradually increasing intervals, it can be retained for some time.

People remember new information which confirms their previous attitudes better than they remember new information which runs counter to their previous attitudes.

Studies consistently show that individuals who feel strongly on a controversial issue, and who are asked to read presentations of both sides, remember the facts and arguments which support their feelings better than they recall those on the opposite side.

What is learned is most likely to be available for use if it is learned in a situation much like that in which it is to be used and immediately preceding the time when it is needed. Learning in childhood, then forgetting, and later relearning when need arises is not an efficient procedure.

The best time to learn is when the learning can be useful. Motivation is then strongest and forgetting less of a problem. Much that is now taught children might be more effective if taught to responsible adults.

If there is a discrepancy between the real objectives and the tests used to measure achievement, the latter become the main influence upon choice of subject matter and method. Curriculum and teaching geared to standardized tests and programed learning are likely to concentrate only on learnings which can be easily checked and scored.

The most rapid mental growth comes during infancy and early childhood; the average child achieves about half of his total mental growth by age five.

In the first two years a normal child transforms the "big, buzzing, blooming confusion" of his first conscious experience to organized perception of familiar faces, spoken words, surroundings, toys, bed, clothing, and foods. He differentiates himself from others, high from low, many from few, approval from disapproval. He lays a foundation for lifelong tendencies toward trust or mistrust, self-acceptance or shame, initiative or passivity; and these vitally condition further growth.

Not until adolescence do most children develop the sense of time which is required for historical perspective. The so-called facts of history—1492, 1776, and all that—can be learned by children but without any real grasp of what life was like in another period or in a different country. Most instruction in ancient, medieval, and even modern history is no more real to children than are fairy tales.

Ability to learn increases with age up to adult years. The apparent decline is largely the result of lack of motivation. We can coerce children into school activities; adult education is mostly voluntary. Men and women *can,* if they wish, master new languages, new ideas, and new ways of acting or problem-solving even at sixty and seventy years of age.

PART TWO
THE NEW TECHNOLOGY

The Educational Promise of Television

SAMUEL GOULD

President, The State University of New York

The acceptance of television by educators nationally has in most cases been something less than enthusiastic. This tepid reaction has come about, I suppose, for at least three reasons, all quite understandable. The first is that some educators have confused the value of the technical tool of television itself with the value of what they see being broadcast daily. They have equated television with unrelenting commercialism, with repetitive and inane comedy, with an inordinate amount of violence, and with hours and hours of superficiality. Recognizing that these programs also educate, even if in a decidedly negative fashion, many in the academic profession have drawn back in horror. Their critical attitude has blinded them to the fact that television occasionally provides magnificent programs of high cultural content as well as superb documentaries and special-events coverage. Some have even taken the extreme view that so far as they are concerned this medium of communication does not exist, feeling for some unexplainable or at least illogical reason that if they ignore it long enough, television will somehow disappear from American life.

Of course, I must admit that in comparison with normal standards of educational speed, the progress of educational television has bordered on the sensational. Television itself became a part of American life less than twenty years ago. During the first ten years it was virtually ignored by education authorities, but the second decade has seen remarkable advances. Yet when one considers the important possibilities of this tool of communication in relation to the needs of our time, my criticism of the pace at which television is being utilized educationally has validity.

The second reason, therefore, for the slowness of acceptance of educational television is the innate conservatism of the teaching profession and its unwillingness to adapt to a changing world. I have often said that if one is to live happily in educational circles, he must adjust himself to a geological approach to change. We progress in educational methods and techniques, but we do it so reluctantly and in the face of such resistance that only the brave among us dare to be innovators. With knowledge increasing yearly by almost geometric proportions, we are still a long way from cleaning out the Augean stables filled with obsolescent materials and reclassifying or regrouping what is pertinent and contemporary. This time lag was once tolerable and even amusing; now it is dangerous and tragic.

The third reason the educational world has looked coldly upon television is one based upon fear, fear which, as in so many other instances, is grounded in ignorance. Many teachers and professors consider television a potential threat to their livelihood and an inevitable dilution of academic quality. The fact of the matter is that neither of these fears is valid when television is used intelligently. It is true that there has been much loose talk about the economies that can be effected by substituting television instruction for the regular classroom. And indeed, in some geographical areas television can and does provide higher quality and greater quantity of instruction where there may have been insufficient and poor instruction previously. Schools and colleges too small and too poverty-stricken to maintain a full curriculum of studies may well be helped academically and economically by the use of this new electronic means, since they can experience the beneficial effects of superb teaching they would otherwise not be able to bring to their classrooms.

It is well within the realm of present fact and future possibility, also, that a properly organized curriculum of television courses can help to ease the pressure of campus or school population increase without sacrifice of instructional quality and with certain economic advantages. The experiment carried on in Chicago recently along this line has been so successful that it is now a regular part of the Chicago educational plan. Here was an instance, as you may recall, in which more than 500 students completed a full two-year junior college curriculum and received their associate degrees, taking all their courses through television. There was no difference in course content between their courses and those given on the campus. In fact the courses were actually interchangeable, as were many of the instructors. Interestingly enough, the television students performed as well as those in conventional courses. Another noteworthy fact is that after three years of operation the plan reached the point where its costs were 24 per cent below those of the conventional junior college in Chicago. It can readily be seen that there are important implications here for institutions or localities facing temporary or even long-term shortages in building space and other facilities.

Such approaches, however, will not lessen our need for as many able and qualified teachers as we can possibly find. Television is no threat to the good teacher. On the contrary, it can provide supplementary and enriching elements to the less able teacher, and for the one who is truly gifted, it can expand his influence. He can be a participant himself, or he can free himself from certain routine teaching duties through the use of television for more factual aspects of his subject, giving himself more time for creative and stimulating classroom time with his students.

It is true that television has occasionally been employed as a high-grade boondoggle by some classroom teachers just as films and other audio-visual aids have been similarly used. There are never enough ways to be protected against the lazy or even unscrupulous instructor who chooses to waste his own and his students' time. No new device or technique can sufficiently overcome this obstacle at any educational level.

But when used properly and in normal circumstances, television is an enriching tool for the teacher to use, augmenting and enhancing his normal classroom procedures and making his own presence more, rather than less, necessary. It can add a dimension to learning which he can create in no other way, and thus it can broaden and deepen the thrust of the learning process by supplying him with new methods and new materials hitherto inaccessible. It should not be measured in terms of financial economy; it should rather be measured in terms of what it provides educationally that augments what was available hitherto.

II

It was almost inevitable in America that television, the brain child of scientific and technical workers, should have had its major force devoted to promoting ideals that stem from technology and materialism. The pattern of radio had previously been spread along the way as a guide, and television followed willingly and even eagerly. It will be recalled that originally a large number of AM radio frequencies were assigned to educational purposes by the FCC. One by one, however, they either failed to be taken up or after educational stations were established, they found themselves financially unable to develop. Gradually these AM radio frequencies were taken over by commercial interests, and a great opportunity was lost to give education its place in the sun.

When television came into being, it was soon apparent that once more education was neither ready nor willing to take on the expense and responsibility of operating VHF channels. Thus the term "commercial television" came into being and a tremendous and powerful industry emerged to give life to the term, pointing its energies toward reaching and holding a great mass audience of all age levels and of all social, economic, and educational conditions.

We have now had a goodly number of years in which to observe this new medium and to come to some conclusions as to the impacts it has had. In commenting upon these, let me make clear that I am being analytical rather than critical. It is not my purpose to castigate or praise, but instead to hold the light of reality squarely upon what television has done by way of influencing the American people.

The very fact that the first television activity of consequence in this country was geared to commercial purposes is in and of itself significant. Its artistic possibilities were sublimated from the very beginning to those essential for advertising and sales. If programs of quality and variety develop out of a policy based upon commercialism, it may be no more than happy coincidence. For if it were shown conclusively that only the very worst kinds of programs in terms of quality entertainment or good taste invariably stimulate the greatest sales, there is serious question as to whether station owners would feel obliged to do more than the minimum of public service programing insisted upon by FCC edict. What would be the nature of commercial television in America today if there were no restrictions brought about by the grant or renewal of licenses? In other words, what would station owners do if they were completely free to do as they wish?

Whatever our conjectures may be on such a hypothetical set of circumstances (and I am sure, incidentally, that many broadcasters would act at least as responsibly as they do today), the realities are that television through its commercial pressures has had tremendous influence upon consumer habits. This is so self-evident as to make discussion of the matter superfluous, except to note it as one of television's achievements.

Today's concentration upon advertising products and development of programs that are sure to please and are rarely designed to tax the mind—such concentration has led to an emphasis upon those values in life which are compatible with a technological and materialistic society. The possession of *things* in larger quantity and better quality than ever before, already a dominant part of American life before the existence of television, has become even more important. Adventure has been so completely equated with violence and bloodshed that a callousness toward the dignity of individual human life has been allowed to develop, with a minimum of countervailing portrayals of gentleness and graciousness. Conformity of many sorts has been encouraged, whether in dress, habits of eating, drinking, smoking, and the like, recreational pleasures, transportation, and even in family relationships; correspondingly a strong sense of the importance of security and the almost pathological avoidance of controversy have made their mark upon the values of the viewer. Statements have been heard that he watches without ill results, or indeed without results at all. The whole experience is purported to be passive, peripheral, and innocuous. But if this is true, how does one adjust this argument to the admittedly great effects upon the viewer of commercial messages, effects borne out by tangible actions of purchasing on his part? Can we say that television has force and power only in its commercial aspects and is harmless otherwise? Of course we cannot.

Just as this medium affects and alters consumer habits and values, so does it also affect and alter the standards of taste. If ratings are to be believed, the mass taste of our citizenry tends very largely toward western drama, family situation comedy, detective fiction, popular ballad singers, and comedians. It reflects a willingness to view the same stock plots and stereotype characters offered week after week in series after series together with an equal willingness to forego any subtleties of dramatization or characterization. It reflects wholesale acceptance of the slick, the smooth, the competent program in preference to the provocative. It reflects a kind of hypnosis or suspension of critical judgment that overcomes the viewer as he sits before his set hour after hour.

One unmistakable influence that television has exerted relates to the gradual disappearance of regional differences in our country's population. Through network broadcasting and syndicated programs the same drama, music, comedy, special events, and even commercial messages are seen in every part of our land. The urban and rural citizens are subject to the same stimuli, sometimes simultaneously, and eventually register identical responses. The same catchwords can be heard all over the country, parroted from the television screen, and the same star performers are idolized. All this is only a continuation of what radio started as a trend many years before and testifies to the power and importance of the word "mass" inherent in the term "mass communications."

Still another impact of television has been its ability to keep the citizen aware and up to the minute on world, national, and local events. In addition to the news reports which have become so important a part of each day's schedule, the special reports on major issues and crises, on-the-spot coverage of presidential news conferences and other meaningful occurrences, documentaries that summarize and crystallize the problems of our time—all these constitute a very bright spot in an otherwise lackluster landscape and are among television's finest and truly superb achievements. This has taken us a step forward toward the American ideal of a thoroughly informed public and offers new emphasis to the argument that television has great and yet untapped potential as a communicator.

We must not forget, as we look upon these phenomena of mass taste, that a minority of respectable size has also emerged, a minority that searches for the occasional program of high purpose and merit with which the over-all television schedule is dotted. Given time and encouragement, this minority could someday become a major audience, responding to depth and complexity of content in programing as well as to sophistication of style. What makes this audience so important is that in spite of the comparative smallness of their numbers thus far, they represent the thinking public and the leadership citizenry. They exert a power and an influence which is disproportionate to their numbers. They are thus most worthy of attention and cultivation. It is with this audience that educational television starts.

III

Educational television is only now beginning to come into its own in this country. Its history, covering the past decade or so, is one of laborious progress, always with inadequate financial support and often with unimaginative and unskillful programing and production. Yet there *has* been progress on all fronts, and it appears as though educational television is now making a breakthrough to the consciousness of the American people. For this we can largely thank the ten-year effort of the Ford Foundation. Through its Fund for Adult Education, as well as on its own, it has encouraged the establishment of stations and has created the National Educational Television and Radio Center, a major distribution and production agency. It has spent about $75,000,000 in its attempts to strengthen educational television and no doubt will spend more. These expenditures, augmented by local support, have made the first breakthrough possible so that now millions of people can be reached with a new kind of television broadcasting.

At present there are 71 educational television stations, with more to come. Many of these are broadcasting on ultra-high-frequency channels, which means that they have rather limited potential audiences. Several, however, are in the very-high-frequency band, and these represent the most influential stations. Boston, Chicago, Pittsburgh, and, more recently, New York are examples. New York's channel 13/WNDT has a potential audience for its community programing of 15,000,000 people in three states. Besides, it broadcasts regularly to 1,500,000 school children in elementary and secondary schools. The establishment of this channel has given tremendous new impetus to educational television. Annual operational budgets for the 71 stations vary from about $250,000 to over $3,000,000, as is the case with New York's Channel 13. A few of the very small stations that originate few or no programs of their own operate on annual budgets of less than $100,000.

At the risk of dealing in what may seem fundamental and obvious, it may be wise to review the purposes for which educational television is intended. It has three such purposes, the first two instructional. It can offer instruction at all levels by means of open-circuit transmission, which means that the broadcasts are available to anyone who wishes to tune in, whether in school or at home; it can also offer instruction by closed-circuit transmission, which means that the broadcasts are confined to a single building or to the school system and cannot be seen by the general public. Finally, it can provide programs of a more generally cultural nature to the community, programs encompassing discussion of literature, art, or current events, performances of music, dance, drama, and so on. There are definite educational reasons for all its activities, even though there is no reason why many of the programs should not have entertaining elements.

Probably the most important characteristic of educational television comes out of the tradition of education itself, when properly interpreted and developed. This tradition holds the individual human being in great respect, recognizing his potentiality for growth and endeavoring to help him toward fulfillment of that potentiality. A sound process of education, as you well know, does not assume all students to be of the same capacity, nor does it place that capacity at a single level. On the contrary, it tries constantly to raise the level of understanding, to encourage students to higher expectations of their own possibilities, and to protect them from being frozen into a conformist mass. If educational television is to perform its mission well, it must operate according to this selfsame tradition, for if it questions the intellectual capacity of its viewers, it ceases to be creative and merely perpetuates mediocrity. Even in the comparatively short life of American commercial television, it has been proved again and again that splendidly creative programing is not beyond its skill. Sadly enough, however, it has also been proved that such programing is too often beyond its aspirations. In its own modest way, and particularly because of its educational concern for the individual, educational television can and should do something toward reawakening such aspirations.

The great attention focused upon program broadcasting has unfortunately tended to cause educators to forget the very real possibilities inherent in television as an audio-visual instrument in the classroom. There are examples to be cited from many parts of the country indicating the uses of cameras, television monitors, and other equipment in ways that add effectiveness to the teaching process, particularly with large classroom or auditorium groups. In most of these instances the classroom teacher himself is the demonstrator. As an illustration, I have seen a biology course in which students are taught with the help of a special camera and monitors in such a way that wherever the student sits he has a close-up view of what the instructor is demonstrating. You are undoubtedly familiar with similar illustrations in your own experience. Much more experimentation needs to be done in this area of television use, including the wider utilization of closed-circuit equipment. On the other hand, a good deal of experimentation that has proved successful in one or two institutions has not been adopted as educational practice elsewhere. A considerable body of literature exists describing such experimentation, but it is not often enough consulted. The tendency seems to be for each university or school system to insist upon its own experimentation regardless of the fact that this particular experiment has already been carried out to its conclusion.

I wish there were space to explore the specifics of the many ways in which educational television can be used both in open- and closed-circuit opportunities. Thus far I have given only a hint of what is possible.

But I must not trespass upon your patience, and thus I shall not enumerate examples nor shall I get into the consideration of equally important subjects—namely, how an institution should prepare itself for the use of television, how it should orient its faculty, how it should estimate its financial needs in such use, what it should expect as results, where it can look for guidance, and so on and on. Since I could not possibly cover all this adequately in a single paper, I am merely trying to sketch the total picture.

One aspect, previously unmentioned, I must take a moment or two to touch upon, however. This is the necessity for some attention to be paid in our schools to the problem of developing more discriminating and selective viewing habits among our students. You will forgive me if I sound somewhat bitter about this, but twenty-five years ago in New England I made the same plea in regard to radio before educational organizations by the score, both administrative and academic. I urged teachers and teacher-training institutions to find a place for instruction in the art of listening with some measure of critical judgment. In my own classes I developed units of instruction to cope with the problem and demonstrated them to be successful. But it all fell on deaf ears, and today we shall probably repeat our earlier folly.

Twenty-five years ago school children were listening to the radio over five hours a day; now they are watching television at least the same amount of time. We did nothing to refine their tastes or discipline their habits a quarter-century ago; we are doing nothing now. A glance at the list of the ten most popular programs currently being shown is sufficient to point up the results of our unconcern. In the face of this, I fail to see what right we as educators have to criticize modern television for being what it is when most of us have never lifted a finger to educate children to be as discriminating in its use as we do in regard to books, music, and the other arts. Most of us have found it too much of an effort to learn anything about this mass medium ourselves, even though we could plainly see the power it has in influencing the mind and spirit. We ourselves, by our apathy or our antagonisms, have allowed a great mass generation to mature who sit apathetically in front of their sets hour after hour, completely content with whatever is offered so long as it provides escape from reality.

And so, eternally optimistic, I make the same plea once more. This is an area of television education that requires no great outlays of money, no complicated equipment, no governmental subsidies, no bond issues. Yet it could be the most vital and crucial area of all in shaping the next twenty years of television programing, whether commercial or educational.

Finally, and by way of summary, may I say a word about the place of television in education whether we think of it philosophically or practically. In its commercial framework, this comparatively new medium of communication has shown a degree of effectiveness already that is in some ways almost frightening. At the same time this effectiveness holds great promise for education. Even though television's major strength has been devoted to fulfilling the profit motive by sales of time and products, the medium has demonstrated an equally strong possibility for the dissemination of information, the exploration of ideas, and the presentation of the performing arts. In this second possibility rests an almost limitless potential for our schools and colleges and universities.

Educational television, furthermore, has the ability to offset as well as augment commercial television in that it can counter the current emphasis on materialistic values with continuous and increasing attention to the humanistic side of life and the importance of the individual as a thinking being. It can make of the viewer an active rather than a passive participant and can show him the pleasure and satisfaction that come from stretching and exercising his mind.

The conditions under which higher education must function during the next twenty years throw an additional spotlight upon television. The tremendous numbers of students to be served and the inevitable struggle to acquire enough faculty and enough facilities call for real innovations in our present methods and almost radical departures from what we have hitherto considered normal. Thousands upon thousands of young men and women will soon be denied the opportunity for higher education if we persist in holding fast to our present procedures and limit ourselves to these alone. A time lag is already beginning to set in, for with the crisis already upon us, many institutions are still doing nothing to change their current situations, whether to include television or anything else. A few more years, and we shall be in extremely serious trouble. Television is one and only one of several innovations and departures that should be carefully considered. There has now been enough experience with the medium educationally to show many of the patterns it ought to follow as well as those it should avoid. We should swiftly capitalize on that experience and add new experiments to refine and augment what has already been done.

Five hundred years ago, the invention of the printing press revolutionized man's possibilities for learning; later, the motion picture film and the recording created other revolutions for him; still later, the radio pushed even further back the frontiers of his communicative resources. Now, through television, another revolutionary advance has caught up with him, expanding still more the potential range and breadth of his intellectual and cultural life. Education—all education, but particularly higher education—must make of this new revolution a deeper and more penetrating attribute of human growth than it has been up to now. It must do this realistically, steadily, imaginatively. I hope it will also do it enthusiastically.

Educational Television and Films

STEPHEN WHITE

Assistant to the President,
Educational Services, Inc.
Watertown, Massachusetts

The motion picture film and the television transmitter, as media of communication, are likely to be immediately attractive to the educator. It is clear that the possibilities are enormous, both for extending the range of his influence and the depth of his presentation. It appears particularly obvious that in an era when the number of trained teachers must inevitably steadily decrease in relation to the number of students, television and film offer an extraordinary opportunity to redress the balance without a sacrifice in the quality of teaching.

All of this is quite true, but it is equally true that in seeking to make effective use of television and motion pictures, the educator enters a world for which little in his training has prepared him. He must begin to deal with two extremely elaborate communications media, in each of which techniques have been developed to which the educator is a total stranger, and which to some degree may be inimical to his purposes.

The central fact is that both these media have an existence quite separate from any use that may be made of them within the educational system, and that their development has been dominated, and will continue to be dominated, by the necessities of these other uses. They are mass media, and as such have been designed primarily to entertain and, in the case of television, to propagandize, neither of which should be a primary purpose of education. As a consequence, the motion picture establishment and the television establishment are thoroughly alien to the educational establishment in outlook, criteria and purposes. When these differing establishments meet, they do so—in the first instance at least—not as partners but as adversaries.

To get the kind of film or television program he wishes to have, the educator must be prepared to struggle, and if he is to do so confidently, he must have some knowledge of the medium with which he plans to deal. He will be waging his struggle against men who call themselves experts, and who are within their own field experts indeed. The educator must learn to recognize when their expertness is relevant to his own problems, and when it is not. He must also have some notion of how to distinguish the true expert from the man who pretends to a competence he does not have. And he must exercise these judgments in relation to an extremely complex field of activity.

In each of these two media, there are obligations which must be met if the process of communication is to be carried on properly. This state of affairs is not peculiar to television and films; to state it is no different than to say that books must be printed in readable type, on appropriate paper, and proofread before they are issued. And as in publishing, so in television and films: these requirements are for the most part common to all production, whether for the classroom or for the living room.

Thus, on film or on television, the picture must be well defined, the sound intelligible and the lighting such that what should be seen will be seen. But these are the trivia of production, just as type face and paper are the trivia of book design. The real production problems are a great deal more complicated than any of these.

Consider, for example, a fairly characteristic classroom

situation in which an instructor elucidates a point before his class, and then proceeds to read briefly from relevant literature. This is not difficult to photograph, and the outcome will be a series of pictures on film. But they will not constitute a motion picture.

To begin with, the students who witness such a sequence on film rather than in the classroom will have their eyes fixed on a small screen and what they see will be shadows, in two dimensions. In the classroom there may be a blackboard, with words scribbled over it; in the real situation this is of no moment, for the student will concentrate on the instructor and effectively will not see the blackboard. On the screen, blackboard and instructor are on the same plane, and the mixture will be a constant irritation and distraction. They are likely, in fact, to be utterly incompatible, and the viewer will not usefully see either one or the other. In short, the classroom and the classroom "set" are two entirely different things; the set must be carefully designed to frame the communicator, to give assurance that he is in a real and a familiar educational setting, and yet to reinforce the act of communication rather than to subtract from it.

On film or in class, the instructor must expect the student to watch him and to listen attentively to what he has to say. Even in the real classroom, this requires considerable effort. It is difficult for the best of us to fix our attention and to keep it fixed over an extended period of time. But in the real classroom, the warmth and reality of the person who is addressing the student comes into play. There is a presence in the room which in some degree commands attention. Much of this is inevitably lost on film, and the film-maker has been forced to learn how he may help compensate for this loss. One of his tactics is to change the picture on the screen, so that the eye is confronted from moment to moment with a new image, and the brain is seduced with an illusion of motion and activity. The protagonist is seen in a long-shot, a close-up, from this angle and from that, and usually on each occasion for only seconds at a time. This may sound absurd—to the educator making his first film it appears ludicrous as well as exhausting —but the fact is that it works. (And the fact that nothing comparable was possible on radio precluded the use of radio as a significant instructional medium.)

These are merely two minor elements in film-making. The process is far more subtle than this. Lighting a set, for example, is an art in itself, and must be done skillfully if the scene on film is to make any impression upon the viewer. The picture, frame by frame, must be carefully composed. There must be continuity of action on the screen to match the continuity which the real world provides in the classroom. These are not mere pretensions of the film-maker; they are vital to the act of communication.

These are a few of the exigencies which are inherent to the medium. But there are others which relate not to the medium itself but to the use that has been made of it. Short as the time span may be with which we are dealing, there are traditions of motion picture and television production which are quite as real as any of their aspects and which can not be ignored. The student, whether he realizes it or not, is immersed in these traditions, and he will react against any film or television program which breaches them. What is more, as long as most of his film and television viewing takes place in an extra-educational context, he will remain bound by those traditions.

We spoke above of the instructor who reads from the relevant literature. On screen, the page from which he is reading must be shown. There is nothing reasonable about this—it adds little to the act of communication and may even be a distraction. But the technique of film production over the years has created in the viewer the firm expectation that he will see the printed page, and if it is omitted he will be oppressed by a sense of incompletion. The viewer has learned to expect that anything which can be shown will be shown. This expectation is so real that it is frequently used in dramatic films to increase tension, and when it is so used there is an obligation upon the director to release the tension at some appropriate moment.

The traditions of motion pictures and television are by no means the same. The motion picture, for example, has engendered a tradition of perfection in detail. Because a scene can be photographed indefinitely until the detail is perfect, and because Hollywood has recognized that this perfection of detail heightens the illusion of reality and hence has insisted that it be achieved, it has come to be part of the basic requirements of film-making. As a consequence, the viewer, whether he is consciously aware of the fact or not, rejects a film in which this perfection is lacking. If a microphone boom slides into the top of the picture, that film will no longer be received seriously.

Yet the same mishap, occurring on television, will be ignored by the viewing audience. Television, whatever the reasons, has never sought to establish the tradition of totally clean production, and the viewer neither expects it nor is disturbed by its absence. Peculiarly enough, this tolerance even extends to television that has been stored on magnetic tape, where corrections might have been made. It is because of this tolerance that the television producer can denominate his production, "live on tape"—tape production, so long as it explicitly mimics live production and it is accepted upon the same terms. Film production is different; even when it is transmitted over television it is always recognized as film by the viewer, although he may not be aware that he has recognized it and in any case would be helpless if he attempted to say how the identification was made.

THE EDUCATOR AND THE TECHNICIANS

This brief discussion of the demands of the two media and their traditions has not attempted to describe either in any depth or detail. It is intended only to point out that they exist, that they are real, and that the educator who plans to deal in films or in television must take them into account. They confront him with two distinct sets of problems.

Motion picture and television production are intensely collaborative activities. To film a scene, or to transmit it over television, may require the services of 30 or 40 technicians, and is never likely to require less than a dozen. If the production is to be worth while, they must all be in some degree creative men and women who bring something more than a journeyman's attitude to their tasks.

It is most difficult for the educator to deal effectively with these men and women. He is likely to be aware that they possess a body of knowledge and experience which he himself lacks and which he finds somewhat arcane; this knowledge and experience, moreover, are intimately related to the activity in which he is participating. It is extremely easy to defer to them when they insist that a scene must be produced in such and such a way, or even that it should not be produced at all. It is difficult to resist when a director says confidently that a certain pedagogic point must be distorted in order that a cinematic point may be made. The director, presumably, knows what makes a motion picture and what does not, while the modest educator is likely to be acutely aware that he himself possesses no such knowledge.

The better the producer, director or film editor, the more

likely he will be to seek to create the film or television production in his own image. To be first-rate at his job, he must have a great deal of assurance in his makeup; he himself will certainly not defer without resisting.

This would be only beneficial if there were any assurance that his decisions would be predominantly the proper ones. The hard truth is that they will not be. For one thing, his criteria will be the criteria of the entertainment business, because he and his fellow technicians have been trained in production for entertainment and not for education, and the nature of their training will have been fixed by the demands of the major portion of the motion picture and television effort. His decisions, therefore, although they are likely to be right for show business, will frequently be wrong for education.

Somehow the educator must learn to distinguish between those pronouncements which relate to the actual demands of the medium in which he is trying to work, and those which merely reflect the technician's bias toward the entertainment industry. It is not easy to learn, but if an educational production is to accomplish any part of the job the educator wishes it to accomplish, he must learn to discriminate, and he must be prepared to be stubborn about it.

There is no reason why the educator should be diffident about making his views known and insisting that they be acted upon. There is no one, in show business or out of it, who knows better how to communicate what he wishes to communicate than the good educator. He, too, has his show-business side, and reflects it every minute he is before a class. The skilled teacher is quite as much a professional communicator as the skilled film or television producer, and has every right to have his skill respected.

Yet in actual practice it is not, and as a consequence not one educational motion picture film or educational television program in a thousand is worth the effort that is required to watch it. This is not hyperbole. A colleague has recently screened 200 hours of educational films in his specialty and has yet to find a film he would be willing to show in a classroom. The Physical Science Study Committee, six years ago, did much the same and found one-half of one film that was worth considering—and that film was produced not as an educational film but as an industrial public relations film.

Yet educators continue to permit film producers and television producers to turn out worthless material, and even lend their names to the product. I have in mind an extremely distinguished scientist who was asked to take primary responsibility for an elaborate educational film. When he was taxed with the result, he protested: "It really was a first-rate film, but it ran fifteen minutes too long and they cut the wrong fifteen minutes." *They* cut the film because *they* had convinced him that *they* alone knew the intimate secrets of film editing. He was irresponsible in not insisting that the film be edited according to his own specifications, and submitted to him in edited form until he gave his approval.

But to see that a film or television production turns out as he intended is only one problem. The second problem is paying for it.

It is clear that production is not cheap. It requires first-rate people, drawn from industries where the rates of pay are extremely high. It requires long periods of time: in motion pictures, for shooting, revising and editing; in television for rehearsal and other preparation. I do not believe that any extended series of motion picture films or television programs can be produced for anything less than $1,000 a minute of screen time, and I suspect that for first-rate production the correct figure is nearer $2,000. (Both these figures presuppose that the time of the educator himself is provided free, or very nearly so.)

At either of these prices, it is well worth while. A teaching film made at a cost of $20,000 or $30,000 can reach hundreds of thousands of students every year for half a dozen years, and the cost quickly reduces to pennies per student. A television program can reach a million students at one time, or on tape can do precisely what the film does. In relation to the return, the investment is small. But the investment must be found, and except for science films, where the National Science Foundation does some part of the job, there is no source for funds of this magnitude to be used for motion picture or television production.

It is a reflection of our native gadget-mindedness that unlimited funds appear to be available for the means of transmission, and little or nothing for the matter to be transmitted. This has been most noticeable recently in the case of television. We have not only managed to build several dozen educational television stations and to equip an extremely large proportion of our schools with receivers, but we have even found a good many millions of dollars to fly airplanes over the Midwest, capable, in principle at least, of putting signals into schools in several states at once. The machinery is there, but the message is simply ignored. I know of at least one case where a producer of educational films was asked to supply some of his produce free to Midwest Airborne Television because there were "no funds for programing."

I am not sure that this is a problem for the educator, but it is certainly a problem for education. Until it is solved, no amount of discussion of the use of television and motion pictures in education will make any difference. I am convinced that these two media contain possibilities for education that are comparable only to the possibilities that lie in the printed word—not the same possibilities, but possibilities certainly as great. I am convinced also that no attempt has yet been made to exploit these possibilities, and at the moment I see no signs that this situation is likely to change.

Programed Instruction: Miracle or Menace?

RICHARD MARGOLIS

"Human history," wrote H. G. Wells half a century ago, "becomes more and more a race between education and catastrophe." The race today is being run at breakneck speed. Stung by the Russians' orbiting of Sputnik in 1957, Americans have come to assess their schools as they assess their rocketry: as a weapon in the Cold War arsenal.

"Only a dramatic upgrading of our scholastic standards," wrote Vice-Admiral Hyman Rickover in his crotchety but influential book, *Education and Freedom*, "can guarantee the continued safety and prosperity of the Republic."

In their somewhat frantic search for a better method of teaching, our schools have hit upon a new and still controversial technique called "programed instruction." Nearly everyone by now has heard something about this remarkable innovation, and probably more about the hardware that often accompanies it—the teaching machine. In less than five years the technique has spread from a handful of experimental classrooms to more than 3,000 schools across the nation—and the number might easily triple by next year.

For many, programed instruction has become a glittering symbol of America's supremacy in the so-called "education race" with Russia. One educator has termed it "the most important breakthrough in the field of education since the printed textbook." Another has prophesied that it will ultimately replace teachers. A famous psychologist has asserted flatly that "teaching machines can teach twice as much in half the time."

Yet not all the experts are in agreement. Many educators who had at first enthusiastically embraced the new technique are now backing away and taking a second look. Some feel it has been grossly overestimated; others, that it is downright dangerous. In at least two states indignant individuals have demanded legislation barring programed instruction from schools.

What is the truth about programed instruction? Will it really give us the edge in the ongoing race with catastrophe? Or is it just another classroom gimmick, comparable to overhead film projectors, closed-circuit television and green blackboards? Perhaps the most urgent question to be asked is: What effect will the new teaching method have on your child's education?

Chances are your child, at some point in his school career, will be taught by a "program." While it may look like an ordinary workbook, it will "behave" in ways similar to a private tutor. It will present the subject in very small steps, beginning with simple, easy-to-understand information and gradually building to more difficult and complex material.

Like a tutor, the printed program will try to make sure the child understands his lesson, by asking him a question at each step and immediately correcting a wrong answer. The child must answer the question before he is allowed to tackle the next step.

Here, for example, is a small portion of a widely used program that explains the solar system to sixth and seventh graders. This program comes equipped with a "mask" or "slider" to cover up the answers. The student unveils them one at a time, checking his own answers against the master list.

The nine planets in our solar system revolve around the _____.	sun
The diameter of the sun is about 864,000 miles. The sun is the largest body in our _____ system.	solar
If the sun were hollow, it would be large enough to hold more than 1 million planets the size of our _____	earth
The sun is a huge ball of flaming gases which emits its own heat and _____.	light

In this example, as you see, the student is required to fill in a word at every step. Other programs may require him to solve problems, or to select one of a series of multiple-choice answers; all demand *some* kind of response to each item.

In conventional textbooks or in classroom lectures, the student who loses his way in the explanation is all too likely to *stay* lost. With a program, he can check his comprehension at every point, and correct his errors instantly. As a delighted fifth-grade girl commented about her grammar program, "It's just as if somebody is talking to you. And it doesn't yell or scream, either!"

Sometimes the program is housed in a teaching machine. If so, the machine is of no special importance. Despite a good deal of publicity to the contrary, the new technique has nothing to do with "robot" learning or automated wizardry. Even the most elaborate machines—those electronic wonders which cost as much as $4,000—are little more than boxes to hold programs. "No matter how well the machine is built," explains Laurence M. Stolurow, a psychologist and programmer at the University of Illinois, "the results produced are determined, in the final analysis, by the program."

Most educators concede that the results produced thus far have been uncommonly good. "Research leaves us in no doubt that programs do teach," writes Wilbur Schramm, director of Communications Research at Stanford University. In his special study on programed instruction, sponsored by the Fund for the Advancement of Education, Schramm observes, "A great deal of learning seems to take place, regardless of the kind of program or the kind of student. Even a bad program is a pretty good teacher."

From the classroom has come considerable support for Schramm's contention. In Roanoke, Virginia, eighth graders learned about as much algebra in one semester by means of programed instruction as ninth graders are ordinarily expected to learn in a full year.

At Manhasset Junior High School, New York, students using a programed text learned a year's worth of grammar in just twelve hours.

In an experiment sponsored by the United States Office of Education, sixth graders learned spelling with a program in one-third the normal time—and scored much higher on achievement tests.

At Hamilton College the average grade in a freshman logic

course jumped 30 per cent after programed instruction was introduced.

In an experiment at Yale, programs are being used successfully to teach two- and three-year-olds how to read and type.

The findings would seem, at first glance, to point to a major breakthrough in education. If so, we can thank the psychologists. For programed instruction originated not in the classroom but in the psychologist's laboratory—and that is where any realistic assessment of the new technique must begin.

Programed instruction owes its existence mainly to Harvard's brilliant behavioral psychologist, B. F. Skinner. His life work has been an investigation of the learning process and an attempt to pin-point the "laws" that govern it. About ten years ago, while experimenting with pigeons, Skinner discovered his birds could be taught to accomplish many astonishing feats—such as whirling in a circle or pecking out a tune on a toy piano—providing each step of their behavior was rewarded with a grain of corn. Psychologists call this process of rewarding "reinforcement," and reinforcement is central to Skinner's theories about programed instruction.

In 1954 Skinner published an article in which he argued that people could be taught the same way he had taught his pigeons—that is, they could be "reinforced" each time they took a correct step toward mastering a subject. The article signaled the birth of programed instruction.

In a program for people, the reinforcement factor is not corn but an oblique kind of encouragement. The student is "rewarded" at each step by being told instantly that his answer is correct. That is why a programmer arranges his material so as always to invite a correct response.

For example, a spelling program for second-grade students begins by spelling the word "fish." In the next step the child must complete the word "fis_"; the third step asks him to fill in the rest of "fi__"—and so on, until he has learned to fill in all four letters. Chances are he will get each of these simple tasks right—and getting things right, says Skinner, is a pleasant experience which will encourage him to learn more.

If a student commits errors on a program, it is considered the fault of the program, not of the student. "There are no wrong answers," runs the programmer's slogan—"only wrong questions."

Most programs being produced today still follow the rules formulated in Skinner's laboratory a decade ago. Indeed, it is precisely this fact—the rigid application of laboratory theory to classroom practice—which disturbs many educators. As at least one irate teacher has remarked, "People aren't pigeons." Critics of the new technique are alarmed by the programmer's attempt to transform teaching from a subtle art into a precise science. They warn that the new technique contains a number of serious defects. These can be briefly summarized:

(1) Programed instruction discourages critical thinking.

(2) Programed instruction fosters *only* rote learning and memorizing of facts, but prevents the student from exploring a discipline on his own and from discovering basic principles.

(3) Programed instruction is both mechanical and monotonous; it is a joyless and uninspiring way to learn.

There is a patness to programed instruction, the critics point out, an either-or quality which interferes with genuine learning. By their nature, programs often produce the erroneous impression that for every question there is one, and only one, correct answer.

"Programs to date," writes Lee J. Cronbach, professor of education at the University of Illinois, "reward the student only for agreeing with what the programmers believe. If composition, literature, languages, social studies and science are reduced to responses that can be evaluated by a clerk, education will have settled for considerably less than half a loaf."

Another professor of education, George Kneller of U.C.L.A., sees in the new technique an even greater hazard. "If we seek exact responses and reward only those who conform to the demands of the machine," he warns, "we are likely to snuff out the precious spark of revolt that is necessary to healthy growth and activity."

In their zeal to reshape the learning process into a workable science, programmers are often accused of overlooking the only elements in the process that really matter. There is a French proverb: "Everything a child learns in school he forgets—but the education remains." By stressing rote learning and ignoring critical thinking, many programs seem to have turned this proverb upside down.

"Dr. Skinner," writes Benjamin Fine in his book on *Teaching Machines*, "has developed a program to help a student memorize a long poem, but he has not yet found one which will teach a student to enjoy poetry!"

Noting that the new teaching technique is "one-dimensional," Fine goes on to ask, "How can it teach a course in

American history which must deal three-dimensionally with events, people, ideas, and the subtle relationships among them?"

Good teaching, everyone agrees, requires an exciting give-and-take between student and teacher. "You have to fling challenges at a student," a teacher explains. "The idea is to get the student excited . . . pique him . . . *argue* with him. A teacher who has never lost an argument to a student is not a good teacher."

It is well known among school children who have been exposed to the new technique that programs never lose an argument. As Cronbach has remarked, "It is difficult to see how a program can contribute to divergent thinking and creative imagination. . . ."

The programmer's notion that children should not be allowed to make errors appears to be open to serious question. "Trying to prevent students from making errors," a Harvard mathematics professor acidly commented, "is like trying to arrange for a track team not to get out of breath. It can't be done. Furthermore it shouldn't be tried. Making mistakes is essential to learning."

It is possible, say some critics, to go through an entire program without making a single error—and not learn a thing. This is because programmers, in their anxiety to prevent students from making errors, give absurdly broad hints to the answers. Here is a typical instance:

Beethoven wrote m _ _ e symphonies than Brahms.

Most students will answer this correctly by filling in "more," but their answer will not show that they know anything about Beethoven. It will merely show that they took the hint. "If things continue the way they are now going," warns one authority, "programing is going to become more and more a 'word game,' a kind of didactic anagram or 'find the cue' affair."

Insistence on "errorless" programs can lead to what David Sohn, a programmer and English teacher in Darien, Connecticut, calls "simple-minded exercises." And that, in turn, leads to boredom. "Many programs are painfully monotonous," Sohn says. "They have no style and no sense of humor. A student may learn from them, but he won't *like* it; and since there's no joy in it, he won't pursue the subject, he won't use it and, in all probability, he won't remember it."

"It's so tedious!" or "It's so cut-and-dry!" are frequently heard comments from students using programs. A sixth grader wrote a terse note to his English teacher: "These little spoonfuls of information do not agree with me." In Westport, Connecticut, I visited a class of eighth graders who were using a programed text in first-year algebra. I asked them what they thought of the new teaching method. From the back row a boy named Jay had an answer. "It's all right," he said. "I mean you can learn quite a lot from it. Trouble is—you're not going to go through life always getting multiple choices."

There is a curious irony here: a technique based on the use of rewards may turn out to be a kind of punishment. By reducing a subject to tedious simplicity, programed instruction can discourage a process which, even under the best conditions, is difficult: the process of education.

Many of our schools today are reshaping their curricula. They are emphasizing basic principles and throwing out the traditional mixed bag of disjointed facts and rules. The New Math, for example, attempts to demonstrate *why* two plus two equals four. The thinking behind this trend is that children will "learn how to learn." As Schramm describes it, "They are not to be taught laws and theorems and relationships; they are to be taught how to *generate* and *discover* laws, theorems and meaningful relationships." In a word, they are to be taught how to *think*.

Yet this new approach to the various disciplines appears to be at loggerheads with the new teaching technique. It is generally conceded that most of the programs being used today are restricted to the teaching of facts. They have fallen into a trap which Henry Adams once described as "the accumulation of ignorance . . . in the form of inert facts."

In fairness, it should be noted that many programmers—a group which includes both psychologists and teachers—are aware of this trap, and are working manfully to revise the technique along more sophisticated lines. It is the contention of the faithful that programed instruction can teach anything, providing the programmers are smart enough. "Anything that can be verbalized can be taught in a teaching machine," Skinner has stated.

Thus far the evidence in support of this claim is sketchy, but what there is of it suggests that programs are gradually being improved to meet at least some of the criticisms. Some programmers, for example, are forsaking the rigid Skinnerian style and moving toward an approach developed independently by Norman A. Crowder, a former Air Force psychologist. Crowder's programs tend to be chattier and more informal. His steps contain large chunks of information—a good deal larger than Skinner's—and end with a series of multiple-choice answers.

It is sometimes just as rewarding in a Crowder-type program to answer a question incorrectly as to answer it correctly. The wrong answer leads you to still another block of information and possibly a pep talk. "Now, now," the student may be told, "you're getting excited."

This system of directing the wrong-answer students along one route and the right-answer students along another is called "branching." Here is how branching works in Crowder's Trigonometry program:

Angles, as you know, are measured in degrees. A circle contains 360 degrees (360°). You should remember the answer to this question:
How many degrees are there in a right angle?
45 *page 29*   90 *page 38*   100 *page 42*

Students who choose either the first or last answer are obviously in need of additional information, which they will get when they turn to the pages specified. Once they've mastered the right-angles problem, they will be directed back to the "main trunk" on page 38. Meanwhile, the students who have shown they already know there are 90 degrees in a right angle are forging ahead at their own crisp pace.

In this way the slower students get the help they need, when they need it, while the faster ones are allowed to proceed at a more challenging pace.

The Crowder vs. Skinner debate has caused a good deal of commotion in the field, but the upshot seems to be a gradual blurring of the two schools. Programmers are selecting devices from both and are writing programs that are identical to neither.

A considerable sum of money, most of it from foundations and the federal government, is being spent for research in the new technique. Last year's research bill has been estimated at $25 million. Five years ago only eight known research projects were underway; last year there were more than 200. At Harvard a Committee on Programed Instruction, operating on a $300,000 grant from the Carnegie Foundation, is conducting 18 different research projects, all of them aimed at creating programs to challenge the student's intellect and excite his imagination. The wide range of subjects being programed there includes geography, music, crystallography, and "English for Foreigners."

The kind of research going on at Harvard is fairly typical of undertakings at dozens of other universities across the country. Unfortunately, though, not much of the experimental work as yet has influenced the commercial programmers—the big publishing houses which produce and sell most of the programs being used by school children today. With a few notable exceptions, the quality of programs being written today remains depressingly low.

One reason for this, as Wilbur Schramm has pointed out, is "the great commercial pressure to produce programs. In a new field of publishing," Schramm says, "the race is to the quick. Traditional programs can be made more quickly, and sold more readily, than experimental ones."

Schramm reports that "the commercial agencies have supported almost no research on programing." I asked a vice-president of one large publishing company, which produces both teaching machines and programs, why his firm had rushed into the market so early, when relatively little was known about the new technique.

"We honestly wanted to do more research to perfect the technique," he replied. "But research is a costly business. Somebody has to finance it."

A good program may require two years to produce. To make certain that it will be clearly understood, a program should be tested—sometimes again and again—on students comparable to the students who will eventually use it. This takes time. Yet some publishers, in their haste to beat the competition to the cash register, have been producing programs in as little as five weeks. James G. Holland, a colleague of Skinner's at Harvard, has noted sadly that "some programmers today seem to have taken seriously the axiom in one of James Thurber's *Fables*: 'Don't get it right, just get it written.' "

Again, there are exceptions. One textbook firm has recently published a book called *Poetry: A Closer Look*, which includes an imaginative programed analysis of a poem by Robert Frost. To avoid the charge that "programs never lose an argument," this one is sprinkled with such phrases as, "If we accept this interpretation . . ." "*Some* readers of this poem go even further . . ." and "a third *possible* symbol . . ." The program goes a step beyond rote memorization toward critical thinking.

In 1957, when publishers began to appreciate the profit potential in the new technique, there was a great flurry of commercial activity. Most firms in those days concentrated on selling teaching machines. "Even the publishers were deluded," says Schramm. "One respected firm sank $50,000 in an abortive attempt to create a machine." It never produced one, finally giving up on machines and turning its attention to the production of programed books.

Other firms were more fortunate. They began to peddle gadgets with such alluring names as Learn Ease, Teachall, Edumator, and Redi-Tutor—and they sold them, in many cases, not only to schools but directly to parents. Teaching machines and programs are still being sold today on a door-to-door basis (frequently by encyclopedia salesmen), via direct mail and even in supermarkets and drugstores.

One thing educators seem agreed on: salesmen are not competent to prescribe for a child's educational needs. The Center for Programed Instruction, a non-profit organization in Manhattan, devoted to research and to spreading the word about the new technique, is particularly outspoken about consumer sales. Its president, P. Kenneth Komoski, has berated "companies that use programed instruction as a gimmick to sell encyclopedias door-to-door or to relieve the housewife of a few dollars as she leaves the supermarket."

A CPI booklet warns parents that "there are programs in existence which have not been able to teach anybody anything. It is also unfortunate that several producers of teaching machines and programs have resorted to deceptive, sensational advertising. . . ."

Obviously, if programed instruction is ever to become an effective arm of learning, it will be through its use in the classroom, not in the home. And in the classroom there will be, as always, the one indispensable element in education: a teacher.

The teacher's place in programed instruction is still a matter of spirited debate. Some teachers fear that the traditional little red schoolhouse, in which the teacher has always held stage center, will be exchanged for "rows of little red school booths," where each student sits in splendid solitude and works with his program, while the teacher goes out for a cup of coffee—or to look for another job.

An official of the American Federation of Teachers gave

voice to this fear when he called teaching machines "just one
more method the school boards will use to cut the sacred tax
rate."

When a community in upstate New York bought twenty
teaching machines for the classroom, one citizen was heard to
comment: "Wonderful! Those twenty machines are a good
omen. This fall we can get rid of twenty teachers!"

And in Salt Lake City the local newspaper ran this provocative news item:

> The first Utah teacher already has been shouldered aside by a
> machine. He is a mathematics teacher at Weber County High
> School, and Superintendent T. H. Bell assigned him to a junior
> high school next fall.
>
> His place at Weber will be taken by an automated teaching
> machine and the materials it uses.

This sort of publicity is hardly calculated to soothe teacher
fears. "The idea of being replaced by a machine just infuriates
me," one teacher has remarked—and no doubt she reflects the
feelings of many of her colleagues. Yet most educators are
convinced that the teacher's place of pre-eminence in the classroom is secure.

Francis Keppel, the United States Commissioner of Education, has given this conviction a folksy twist. "I'll accept the
machine as a replacement for a teacher," he has said, "when
it can run a birthday party for my young daughter, when it
can comfort a sick child or encourage a child who needs
assistance. Then I'll go along with the idea that a machine is
as good as a teacher."

Teachers who have used programed instruction frequently
discover that, far from replacing them, the new technique
saddles them with greater responsibilities—or, as school
administrators would describe it, "affords them greater opportunities." For one thing, the technique frees them from the
tedious necessity of drilling and redrilling the class in basic
information, a process which Skinner has described as "white
collar ditch-digging." With the extra time, the teacher can
concentrate on individual problems; she can hold lively group
discussions, prepare more inspiring lessons—in short, be a
better teacher.

"I like this new way of teaching," an elementary school
teacher has remarked. "It gives me more time to spend with
students who are having trouble. Before, the children who

knew the work would often sit back and wait with almost patronizing looks on their faces while I drummed information into the heads of the duller students."

"Among us English teachers," observes William E. Hoth of Wayne State University, "are many who suspect the machine because it is not a book. They should not fear. For the machine presents an exciting challenge. At last good teachers can demonstrate their unique skills."

A good deal of teacher hostility to the new method must be blamed on school administrators who sometimes force programs on teachers without bothering to explain to them how they work or why she should use them. "There has been no widespread movement of school systems," Schramm points out regretfully, "to train their teachers in the expert use of programs, nor any general movement of teachers colleges to make use of programed instruction."

The consequences of this omission can be dismal. Teachers resent the new technique and, perhaps unconsciously, undermine it. In Roanoke it was found that when teachers were hostile to machines, the students performed badly. "I would never use a teacher in programed instruction unless she was sympathetic to this method of teaching," declares Clifford Rall, superintendent of schools in Port Chester, New York.

In Newton, Massachusetts, the school administration successfully introduced the technique by first setting up workshops and seminars, and sending nineteen teachers to a short course on programed instruction at Harvard.

One healthy side effect of the new technique, according to its advocates, is the good example it sets for teachers. According to this view, a program presents information with such striking clarity that the observant teacher can't fail to follow suit. "The programing not only helps the kids learn," a fourth-grade teacher from Niskayuna, New York, has commented, "but it helps me to learn *how* the kids learn."

Certainly the basic elements in programing—the idea of breaking up the material into small steps, asking the student to respond to each item, and rewarding him for correct answers—have been practiced by good teachers for centuries. Horace, who lived 2,000 years ago, referred in his writings to the practice of giving sweets to children who learned their letters. Another Roman, Quintilian, wrote that education "should be a matter of play. The pupil must be questioned and praised, and must never be made to wish he had not

spoken." Quintilian stressed the importance of having the
student make a series of correct responses, in order to achieve
"speed without error."

What programmers have done, in effect, is to refurbish these
old concepts and make them available to students on a mass
basis. By this means they have compelled at least some teachers to focus their attention on a question long ignored: what
do we mean when we speak of "the learning process"?

"Those who are most actively concerned with improving
education," Skinner has written with a touch of scorn, "seldom
discuss what is happening when a student reads a book,
writes a paper, listens to a lecture or solves a problem. . . .
In short, there is general neglect of educational method." If
the new technique does nothing more than to alert teachers
to their weaknesses, it will have done an inestimable service.

As a "teacher" in its own right, programed instruction
remains a crude instrument, though at some future date it
may become everything its enthusiasts claim it to be now.
But first psychologists will have to revise their theories to
conform more closely to classroom practice. They will have to
get clear the distinction between people and pigeons, and
accept the fact that good teaching, with its many fine shadings
and subtleties, is an art.

If we mean by education something more than rote learning, then we will have to rely on something more than programed instruction. As the Center for Programed Instruction
has pointed out, "Programs can help . . . but education of
a child is a complicated process involving hundreds of problems, and programed instruction like anything else cannot
solve all of these in one moment."

Each year some four million children enter our schools. No
previous generation of beginners has had so much to learn;
no previous generation of adults has been quite so anxious to
teach them. "We do not know what education could do for
us," declared Robert Hutchins seventeen years ago, "because
we have never tried it." It is conceivable now that we are beginning to try it—tentatively, awkwardly, and one step at a
time.

Team Teaching in the Elementary and Secondary Schools

ROBERT H. ANDERSON

Associate Professor of Education,
Harvard University

The form of school organization to be examined here did not even exist, except in incipient or primitive form, in America (or anywhere else) until forty-nine months ago. The phrase "team teaching" cannot be found in the *Education Index* prior to the 1957–59 volume, and there are only a few dozens of people in the United States who have ever taken a course in team teaching or team leadership.

Yet I dare say that at this moment there are several thousands of American schools in which teachers and administrators will state that they are seriously studying, and perhaps a thousand schools engaging in, one or another form of team teaching. Even the most casual examination of state and national convention programs shows that team teaching is among the most prominent topics for discussion and debate. Almost every national magazine in education has already given the topic signal attention, and the research agencies of the NEA, the U. S. Office of Education, and affiliated groups have in some cases been swamped with appeals for information and help. The pioneer school system whose team-teaching enterprises have been described in the burgeoning literature are, similarly, flooded with requests for information and for permission to visit. It may well be wondered whether any other arrangement has created so much excitement in so short a space of time.

My first obligation to you is to put team teaching into some sort of reasonable perspective. Most of the aforementioned excitement is, in my judgment, premature and unwarranted. Team teaching, in essence, is a major stage in an evolutionary process that has been going on for some time. Before turning to its history, however, I will define team teaching and urge you to the realization that the fundamental ideas underlying team teaching are on the whole misunderstood or misapplied by the bandwagon jumpers who constitute perhaps the majority of the thousands to whom reference has already been made. To prevent misunderstanding as to my own role in the team-teaching movement and in this immediate situation, let me also state (1) that team teaching has no mysterious or magical powers, (2) that I strongly advise against its widespread adoption at this time, (3) that my purpose, rather, is to stimulate thoughtful, objective, and open-minded examination of the ideas and practices represented in the team-teaching mechanism.

Having disclaimed an evangelistic purpose here, let me swing around to the admission that I have great faith in the ultimate potential usefulness of team teaching to the progress of American schools. Though I worry that this promising arrangement may fail of acceptance because of impatience, or the absence of theoretical understanding, or misapplication, or (at the other extreme) the stubborn and close-minded resistance of the Old Guard among us, I see reason for optimism about its survival. The research data and the fast-changing attitudes apparent within the profession seem to suggest that a solid movement may be underway.

DEFINITIONS

First, moving counterclockwise, let me tell you what team teaching is *not*.

(1) It is *not departmentalization*. Though team teaching encourages the idea of complementary specializations existing within teams, team teaching is in no sense an imitation, a distortion, or a perversion of the conventional pattern of departmental organization.

(2) It is *not large-group instruction*. Although it is true that most teams do a good deal of teaching in large groups (*i.e.*, assemblages of up to 100, 150, 180 pupils), it is theoretically legitimate and possible to have scarcely any large-group lessons in team teaching. Certain projects, where the customary sequence calls for large-group teaching followed by small "sections" or subgroups for follow through, probably should not be labeled as "team teaching."

(3) It is *not merit rating in disguise*. Merit rating implies the payment of higher salaries to those teachers whose effectiveness and usefulness is judged to be (relatively) superior to other teachers of equivalent background who are performing in the same role. Team teaching is indeed an arrangement which attempts to pay higher salaries to the more effective and useful teachers, but it does so by assigning such persons to different (and presumably more difficult) roles.

There are other things that team teaching is not, but these three cover the questions most frequently raised. Now then, what *is* it?

Taking note of the great diversity of team-teaching projects and pointing out that there is danger in too many exclusive definitions, my colleague Shaplin has prepared this definition: *"Team teaching is an effort to improve instruction by the reorganization of personnel in teaching. Two or more teachers are given responsibility, working together, for all, or a significant part of the instruction of the same group of students."* [1] My own preference is for a definition which requires *three* or more teachers to be involved, on grounds that role differentiation, effective subdivision of functions, and the profitable exchange of ideas and criticism are necessarily limited when only two adults are involved. By the way, at this moment I see six or seven as the likeliest maximum number of team members, though experience may lead to a different view.

Team members work together in all three teaching functions: planning, actual work with children, and evaluation. The obvious limitations of time, space, and other resources make it impossible for all these functions to be co-operative all the time, but the general idea is that (1) all team members (including children where possible) should participate in the formulation of broad over-all objectives for the total program; (2) all team members should participate at least weekly in the formulation of the more immediate objectives of the total program; (3) all team members should be given at least periodic opportunity to contribute to the specific daily planning of colleagues and vice versa; (4) all team members should at all times be at least minimally conversant with the specific daily plans of the other team members; (5) all team members should at least occasionally (*i.e.*, several times weekly) carry on teaching functions in the presence of colleagues whose own roles might alternately be to assist, to observe pupil reaction, or some other factor, and to offer constructive criticism in subsequent discussion; (6) all team members should participate in periodic (weekly?) evaluation of the total program and in as much specific evaluation discussion as time and energy allow. (See 5, above.)

It becomes obvious that such a pattern of operations would require a quality and quantity of professional conversation to

[1] Judson T. Shaplin, "Team Teaching," *Saturday Review*, XLIV (May 20, 1961), 54.

stagger the imagination! Each team's success in arranging for such extensive communication will obviously be limited. The quality of leadership, the over-all efficiency of the team's members, and the quality of the school curriculum itself can have great bearing on a team's ability to maintain good communication at a reasonable expenditure of energy.

This raises several additional questions about teams. Is leadership necessary? If so, need it be formalized? Do teachers find hierarchical organization objectionable? Cannot the leader function be rotated? On these matters we have only scant experience, and several different theories have been offered. My own view, which has if anything been intensified and confirmed in our experience to date, is that leadership is indeed necessary; it *does* need to be formalized; teachers do live comfortably within a hierarchy (if the leader is at least minimally qualified for the role); and rotation of leaders is appropriate only in situations where persons are "in training," or its equivalent.

ADVANTAGES AND LIMITATIONS

One presumed advantage of team teaching is that it allows the more competent, the more committed, and the more influential teachers to play a more significant role in the life of the school. Until team teaching came along this kind of person tended to remain in his own classroom, with relatively little direct effect upon the decisions and professional performance of colleagues. Also, such teachers would work directly with only thirty-or-so children each year. The road to "advancement" was to the principal's office, where of course there was no longer the same opportunity to practice the aforementioned teaching skills.

Team teaching now offers to the "born teacher" an intermediate leadership role which is still a teaching role. Further, the team leader works, ultimately, with many times the usual number of children. His skills and insights become directly available to colleagues. He is, at once, a teacher, an influencer of teachers, and a master craftsman in the eyes of his colleagues and the community.

Yes, this is the idea at its best. It does not always work out this happily. If the basis of his reputation as a "born teacher" proves upon inspection to be shallow or superficial, there is of course trouble ahead. If over time he does not keep his substantive knowledge up-to-date, with commensurate retooling of his technical-professional skills, again there can be embarrassment. If, as appears rather often to be the case, he does not have those intuitions and attitudes that allow some persons to feel comfortable in a role of leadership and responsibility, again there is potential unhappiness.

Despite heroic efforts over many decades to provide teachers with supervision and in-service growth opportunities, the typical teacher is insufficiently well-informed in content areas and insufficiently proficient in technical-professional performance. Under the false label of academic freedom, individuality —call it what you will—we tolerate all sorts of idiosyncrasy and unsuitable or indefensible teaching behavior. By encasing each teacher in a private classroom not generally visible to his peers and vice versa, we allow such idiosyncrasy to flourish and crystallize until remedy or modification becomes almost impossible. Team teaching, if it has one supreme virtue, causes teachers to look at themselves and one another and provides the opportunity for seeing alternatives, recognizing correctable faults, and in various ways developing over time a technology that may be confidently defended.

I would in no sense argue that the result can or should be a uniform or standard approach to teaching. Though I strongly believe that "best" ways do exist or can be found for many situations (hence, teaching becomes in large part a "science"), I am equally convinced that many alternatives are possible in most situations and that there will always be room for individuality and artistry within each teacher's classroom. But the artist must possess a defensible art!

Team composition, in fact, should take differences into account and capitalize upon them. The most productive teams, I have found, are those peopled by individuals somewhat unlike each other in a professional personality. These people are more likely to engage in healthy argument and create a stimulating salt-and-pepper atmosphere than are teams of look-alikes.

There remains at least one aspect of team organization which must be explained. Some teams make extensive use of nonprofessional assistants, while others do not. Which of these is bona fide team teaching? The answer is, both. Actually it is largely coincidental that the pilot projects have tended to use noncertified personnel extensively: the original intent in at least some cases was to free the teachers from routine tasks in order that they might have additional time available for curriculum revision and other research-and-development activities. However, it soon became apparent that nonprofessional assistants are invaluable and that teaching teams can make more efficient use of such helpers than can teachers in conventionally organized schools.

Though nonprofessional workers are not inevitably assigned to teams, it is clear that: (1) perhaps 25–30 per cent of what typical classroom teachers do, can and should be delegated to less expensive nonprofessionals; (2) until teachers are at last relieved of direct and continuous involvement in such duties there can be no real dignity or prestige to the teaching role.

Next, a few words about grouping and class sizes. In teams, it is possible to arrange groups of many different sizes at will, the only limitations being the number of available instructors and the physical spaces available. Thus far, most pilot teams have tended to use the conventional 25–30 as the modal group size, probably due to habit and the familiar architectural setting. Large groups are probably used too often in some projects (the defense is that some teachers are thus released for necessary planning), and in most cases there is as yet too little development of arrangements for small-group instruction. However, there seems now to be a growing awareness of the advantages and disadvantages, for each specific content or purpose, of the various-sized groupings, and it seems probable that useful guidelines will slowly emerge. Even more important, teaching techniques specifically appropriate for large-group instruction and small-group instruction will gradually develop. Experience to date suggests that, upon first going into team teaching, most teachers will use essentially the same teaching procedures whenever they confront children, regardless of their number. Lest this point be misunderstood, it seems to mean that despite a century of practice with groups of thirty or less, teachers have not developed enough different strategies or techniques for dealing with small-group opportunities.

Perhaps by now you will appreciate some of the reasons for my caution against willy-nilly enthusiasm for team teaching. The definition emphasizes that an enormous amount of staff planning and intrateam communication is necessary. Membership in teams makes very different intellectual and emotional demands upon teachers, and it calls for the acquisition of new skills and attitudes. Hasty venturing into so complicated an arrangement could well prove disastrous for a sizeable number of the present teaching force. Many of these more fragile or vulnerable persons ought not to be teaching even in conventional classrooms.

Editorial comment on the presumed advantages and strengths of team teaching has also crept into my remarks thus far. Team teaching offers hope of greater flexibility in utilizing instructional resources including personnel and in responding to the whole range of each child's educational needs. It offers to teachers a remarkable opportunity for professional growth through the constant exchange of professional information and criticism. And it serves as an almost certain stimulant to fundamental curriculum reconstruction, which in the long run may be its most practical advantage.

HISTORICAL BACKGROUND

Now that you have a broad definition in mind and have been alerted to one man's view of its promise and its dangers, let us stop for a moment to inquire further, "How on earth did team teaching come about?" Perhaps you will agree that the answer is a fascinating and reassuring one.

It is difficult to decide where to begin the historical narrative. The first known effort to train teachers for the "new" plan of team teaching took place at Harvard in the summer of 1957, and the first full-scale project in team teaching was launched in an elementary school in Lexington, Massachusetts, by those teachers in the 1957–58 school year. At approximately the same time, numbers of related projects were launched by several other universities and in certain secondary schools associated with the NASSP's Commission on the Experimental Study of the Utilization of the Staff in the Secondary School.

Every profession can point to certain significant events, or series of events, which stand out over the long course of the profession's development. To cite only a few such instances in our own history, we might point to the appearance of the Quincy Grammar School in 1848, or the half-century dominated after 1836 by the McGuffey Readers, or the opening in 1873 (in St. Louis) of the first permanent public kindergarten, or the early work of John Dewey in the University of Chicago Laboratory School. At this moment it is my prediction that the decade which began in 1955, and through which we are still churning, may ultimately come to be regarded as one of the major turning points in American public education. That we may reach this verdict is by no means due solely to the emergence of team teaching, however. The year of 1955 seems to have been a year when a number of conventional arguments and practices were discovered to have lost their validity, when certain long-building forces for change seemed all at once to combine their strength, and when certain unusual or unfamiliar arrangements seemed rather suddenly to come to mind.

Allowing for the fact that historical threads run through each of them so that the identification of specific dates is essentially improper, we may nevertheless point to several major developments which either began or "took hold" about 1955: (1) the nongraded elementary school, after a dozen or so years of trial development, emerged as a definite alternative to conventional graded structure, and national magazines and conferences reflected a lively interest in the movement. (2) Educational television emerged from the crude experimental stage, accompanied by a surge of interest in other audio-visual aids to instruction. (3) Pioneer efforts to make use of nonprofessional assistants to teachers, as in Bay City, Michigan, and in the Yale-Fairfield Study, became almost overnight a *cause célèbre* and touched off (sometimes violent) discussion of what is and what is not teaching. At the same time, energetic discussion of merit rating was enlivening the literature and pumping smoke into meeting rooms. (4) The teaching machine and programed instruction, as exemplified in the work of Skinner and his colleagues, appeared as a dramatic alternative to conventional procedures of program organization, instruction, and evaluation. (5) Criticisms of public education by various writers and scholars outside the public school establishment, as well as attacks by Rudolf Flesch and others, reached a kind of crescendo and led, sometimes profitably and sometimes not, to local and national re-examination of the school enterprise. (6) More important, university professors and scholarly societies in the various disciplines, especially the sciences and mathematics, began at this time to engage in fundamental curriculum revision. Such projects as the School Mathematics Study Group, the University of Illinois mathematics and arithmetic projects, the Biological Sciences Curriculum Study, and the Physical Science Study Committee were either under way or about to be, with the result that public school teachers would shortly have not only new resources at their disposal but new needs and opportunities for personal study and training. (7) "Gifted" children became the object of special concern and attention, and this along with other forces led to a sharp increase in the literature on a long-familiar problem, pupil-grouping practices. (8) New approaches to teacher education, such as the internship plan launched by Harvard in the summer of 1955, brought the school systems and the college staffs into a more intimate working relationship. The Harvard–Newton Summer Program, which called for four or five apprentices to work simultaneously with a gifted master teacher, revealed both the capacity of children for multiple relationships with adults and the advantages of co-operative and collaborative teaching arrangements.

Prior to 1955, when the foregoing developments were stirring up the national scene, there had been many decades of slow but steady erosion of certain conventions in curriculum and staff organization. There were, of course, certain dramatic episodes and "giant steps" along the way, each being primarily an effort to arrange more appropriate and individualized instruction, or to utilize personnel and instructional resources more effectively, or to translate more recent knowledge about child development into operational terms. Let none of us underestimate the relevance and importance of the Batavia Plan, the Lancastrian Plan, the Dalton Laboratory Plan, the Winnetka Plan, Wirt's work-study-play Platoon School, Hosic's Co-operative Group Plan, or the earliest nongraded programs launched by Preston W. Search, Leonard Wheat, and Lowell Goodrich, to mention only a few.

Any serious effort to trace the history of team teaching and related organization plans (especially nongrading, which is by all odds the most important of the arrangements now being developed), would inevitably uncover hundreds if not thousands of little-known advances, in Europe as well as America, in the direction of truly individualized instruction. The historian would probably be startled to discover a remarkable little book by Search, published in 1901,[2] and daring to propose an ideal school which astonishingly resembles certain "new ideas" on the horizon. Apropos of our current interest in team teaching, for example, Search proposes to free teachers from routine functions, to join teachers in a federation for planning purposes, to build teacher-training functions into the very fabric of the school itself, to pay adequate salaries which "should be discriminative" [sic], to afford opportunity to observe in the best schools, "or better still, by association

[2] Preston W. Search, *An Ideal School: or, Looking Forward* (New York: D. Appleton & Co., 1901). International Education Series.

in the same school with co-workers who represent, in their selection, the best personnel and the best methods," [3] among other recommendations.

The historian might also note that various efforts at informal co-operation or collaboration among teachers have been made at an increasing rate for the past quarter-century or more. Teachers for many years have been exchanging function, combining classes, pooling their classes prior to temporary regrouping for (*e.g.*) reading instruction, and subdividing the total workload. Informal hierarchical organization, even though voluntary, has existed in many schools. Especially in larger high schools and in those with core programs, teachers in the same department or division have functioned much like teams. At the college level, even the phrase "team teaching" was used as early as 1941 to describe the efforts of the teachers to work together.[4] The very existence of these arrangements would tend to support the argument that team teaching was an inevitable development on the American scene, probably not as an ultimate form but as one of the major events in the centuries-old search for an adequate system of school organization.

Before concluding this historical review I would reiterate that the nongrading of schools [5] is by far the most fundamental and important of the current trends in school reorganization. And in this connection I would point out that multiage groupings appear to have notable advantages for children both socially and academically.[6] Nongraded secondary schools are already on the scene (*e.g.* in Melbourne, Florida), and many of the pilot team-teaching projects have built nongradedness into them, for example, by including pupils of two or more age levels in the teams.

RESEARCH FINDINGS

Research in team teaching is a frustrating activity, since appropriate research models and instruments are not available

3 *Ibid.*, p. 305.

4 Reference is here made to a project at Troy State Teachers College, Alabama. See G. F. Stover, "The Freshman Program in General Education for 1940–41," the College's *Bulletin*, XXVIII (October, 1941), p. 8.

5 See John I. Goodlad and Robert H. Anderson, *The Nongraded Elementary School* (Tarrytown: Harcourt Brace and World, 1959).

6 See W. Hamilton and W. Rehwoldt, "By Their Differences They Learn," *The National Elementary Principal*, XXXVII (December, 1957), 27–29.

or at least are untried.[7] Our conservative habits prompt us to ask the wrong questions about pupil growth and welfare, and on the whole the research has thus far ignored the no less important questions about impact on teachers. Nevertheless, certain useful studies are under way and findings of a sort can be reported.

In general, it may be stated that team teaching appears to have essentially the same academic and personal-social advantages for children as the conventional school, plus certain advantages not obtainable in the conventional school. Equivalent outcomes of pupil achievement and personality development have been measured in the pilot and control settings, and in view of the newness of team teaching these results are regarded as encouraging. Evidence is rapidly building to the effect that team pupils have more initiative, self-sufficiency, and enthusiasm for schooling than pupils in regular classrooms. The brighter children and the slow learners appear to benefit particularly from team teaching.

Reports indicate, further, that teachers on the whole respond favorably to hierarchically organized teams. However, there is much frustration because adequate guide lines to daily operations do not yet exist, personnel are generally untrained for their new roles, necessary resources are frequently missing, and team planning makes heavy demands upon time. Even more serious is the fact that enormous curriculum deficiencies come to light as a result of team activities, and team members tend to become caught in the quicksand of long-overdue curriculum reforms.

Much of the research to date has been chiefly exploratory and precautionary: exploratory in the sense of "Let's see what the problems are"; precautionary in the sense that "We'd better make sure the children will not suffer while we try to develop this idea." Now that the research problems are better understood and now that there is reason to believe that the children are in no sense endangered, a new and more solid attack on the research front will be possible. Furthermore, the recent construction of exciting new school buildings [8] appropriate for team teaching and the initiation of university training programs for team personnel, such as the Harvard-

---

[7] See Esin Kaya, "Problems in Evaluating Educational Plans in the School Setting," *Journal of Educational Sociology*, XXXIV (April, 1961), 355–59.

[8] See Evans Clinchy, *Schools for Team Teaching: A Profile* (New York: Educational Facilities Laboratories, Inc., 1961).

Lexington Summer Program, will eliminate some of the obstacles to full-blown development of team teaching.

A SANE APPROACH

The last question to be asked is, "What position should the typical educator take with respect to team teaching?" I would say, as the Boy Scouts do, "Be prepared." Acquaint yourself with the literature and exploit every opportunity to become better informed. Take stock of your own staff and situation— adequacy of curriculum guides, adequacy of instructional and physical resources, quality and amount of supervisory and specialist personnel available, and so on—and estimate the amount of erosion already taking place on the cinderblock walls that separate your teachers. Try to predict which of your teachers have the aptitude for team leadership and devise means for testing your hunch. Inventory the external resources that could be brought in, *e.g.*, a nearby college staff. Make sure you already have the minimum requisites of a good school program, especially a strong kindergarten, and the right relationship between elementary-junior high and junior high-senior high! Above all else, look for evidences that your staff is disenchanted with graded organization and is hungry for an alternative arrangement. When these preparations have been made, perhaps modest steps toward team teaching will be warranted.

Libraries and Information Retrieval

HENRY J. DUBESTER
*Chief of the General Reference and Bibliography Division
of the Library of Congress*

Although no generalization can ever be immune from challenge, a generalized characterization of libraries may serve as a useful point of departure for a discussion about libraries and information retrieval. All libraries have certain common and continuing functions. They must exert effort to acquire materials. The materials must be processed and organized before they are merged into the files or collections of the library. Efforts must be developed to ensure that desired items can be identified and called from the collections in response to a determined need. The proportion of endeavor distributed among the three functions of *acquisition*, *organization*, and *retrieval* varies with the size of the library and with its policy or service goals. The parameters of size and policy are not necessarily independent of each other.

THE EVOLVED FUNCTIONS OF LIBRARIES

In the evolution of libraries from simple accumulations of rather homogeneous bodies of materials to their present varied collections representative of the many different types of records resulting from man's attempts to communicate, there has been a gradual transition in the concentration or focus of effort. In their earlier state, for reasons which need not be elaborated and can be assumed to be obvious, the emphasis was placed on acquiring materials. With the influence of democratization on libraries, together with their incessant and possibly exponential growth rates, this shift was forced into concentration on identification and organization of collections, and their individual constituents. There is presently manifest a newer tendency to focus attention and consequent effort upon identifying for the purpose of retrieval not the physical items in the collections but rather the information for which these items are vehicles.

The reasons for the latter change and the nature of the resulting problems require elaboration. The development of a systematic organization of large collections of books embracing the so-called universe of knowledge can be traced to seminal events less than two centuries old. The efforts to introduce order into the collections of the Bibliothèque Nationale and the library of the British Museum led to the search for reasonable rules for the treatment or cataloging of books. Panizzi's notions still represent the basic expression of the functions of library catalogs—to identify the books in a collection so that the catalog can inform whether a given book is present, to bring the works of an author together, and to bring editions of a work together. These requirements are basic to the complicated structure of the rules which describe the largest single expense of librarianship today, that of cataloging.

The professional librarian distinguishes between descriptive cataloging, the aforementioned function, and subject cataloging, designed to lead to a work when no identifying information is available, when the need is expressed in terms of desire for information on a subject. Here the continuity of tradition introduces recognition of a significant constraint. Traditionally, a book has been devoted to the treatment of a given subject or problem. The book is assumed to possess a unity in relation to its subject. The task of the subject cataloger is to recognize this unity and to express it as economically as possible, in a single term or phrase, as a subject heading. The subject heading is thus required to be specific to the subjects or concept of the book. If the cataloger's knowledge of the subject is inadequate or faulty, he will exhibit a tendency to use more than one subject heading to express the subject, or he will utilize a more general rather than a more specific term to ensure that he embraces the various choices among which he is reluctant to make definitive discrimination. Because of the anticipated life expectancy of the collection and subject catalog, terms are chosen to reflect both current and expected usage; new terms are deferred until usage is known. The basic function, whether realized in ideal or imperfect manner, leads to a catalog which informs the user what materials are contained in the library on a given subject or on a related subject. Because of internal requirements, this type of subject catalog contains an inner communication network, a syndetic structure, which refers the user from more general to more specific subject headings, rarely to the reverse.

To complete the perspective another tradition requires recognition. Our contemporary large research libraries are the continuations of the private scholar's library of an older period. The arrangement of books admits of many possible patterns. The most prevalent pattern in American libraries is one that places books on the same and related subjects in relative juxtaposition by means of such familiar classification schemes as the Dewey Decimal Classification, the Library of Congress Classification, and a few others. Libraries have recognized that classification of books designed to recover a book on a desired subject does not require that the books themselves be ordered according to the classification on the libraries' shelves. A classified catalog, together with an index to the classification nomenclature, would better serve the purpose of subject retrieval, as opposed to the classified arrangement of books which serves the individual's need or purported need for browsing among the physical containers of information. The classification of books cannot be divorced from classification of knowledge. The latter effort is always a delayed recognition of the state or order of knowledge as it has progressed to the moment; it has very limited predictive virtue.

Thus, and in partial summary, libraries have concentrated on efforts to organize their collections, strongly centered on the book as the unit of information, developing methods and rules which organize books for effective recall from the shelves when their identity is known, or suggest desirable books by virtue of specific subjects assigned to them or through browsing among their classed arrangement. This general situation is not to be deprecated. It is generally coherent, prevents chaos, and serves quite adequately the educational purposes for which most libraries are designed. A degree of insufficiency is recognized, however, when this pattern of organization is required to serve a current research and development effort in science and technology, however broadly science and technology is interpreted. The reasons for this insufficiency are several.

THE LITERATURE EXPLOSION

The current circumstances of science information requirements are amply illustrated by quotation from an article in the *Washington Post* of August 11. Entitled, "Computer Software Is New Frontier," the brief text commences with the following propositions:

Of all the research and development work conducted by the human race since the dawn of history, about one half has been accomplished since 1950.

Of all the scientists in the history of the world, about 70 per cent are still alive.

In 1960 a total of $13 billion in research and development generated 60 million pages of technical reports requiring 55,000 journals in 60 languages for its total publication.

The rate of accumulation of scientific data is doubling every 8½ years. And the indexing of this data is falling behind the rate of accumulation.

It has been estimated that 10 per cent of all research is devoted to the search for information which actually is in existence but can't be easily located.

These paragraphs describe what has been termed a literature explosion which has seen acceleration of a research and development enterprise since World War II. Numbers aside, there are several intriguing aspects that can be recognized. The traditional "book" no longer serves the scientist. Some have stated that the articles in professional journals are too far behind the actual situation in research to serve as useful reflections of the current state of the art in given disciplines. The "research report" and the preprint of articles, as well as privately circulated mimeographed papers, serve as next best means for conveying current information. The best means still appears to be oral communication between scientists, and here the significant problem is one of identifying the individual who knows.

The crucial factors in this development, in the so-called information explosion, may be expressed in terms of the amount of information, the speed of its accretion and change, and the character of the vehicle. The journal articles, research reports (government, academic, industry), preprints, etc., represent a quantity of units which no existing library is staffed to handle in terms of traditional methods applied to books. The concepts and subjects with which these materials are concerned are more elemental (in the sense of scope) than the subjects of books, and because they are more current they are also more transient. Thus the underlying assumptions which design the pattern of subject analysis applied to books do not pertain to these materials, at least in certain respects. The retrieval requirement might still be to secure everything on and related to a given subject of inquiry. The request would have to be much more rigorously specified in order to prevent a deluge of material in response. The terminology applied to the documents for subject analysis would have to recognize the need to be more responsive to the speed with which new concepts and subjects are generated.

In passing, one may note that with minor exceptions libraries have not attempted to organize information contained in journals, research reports, etc. Periodical indexing services and scientific indexing services have been subscribed to by libraries as have similar services provided by various government agencies (Armed Services Technical Information Agency, Atomic Energy Commission, Office of Technical Services in the Department of Commerce, etc.). Libraries, for the most part, place these indexes at the disposal of their patrons and complete the cycle of their responsibility.

COMPUTER INSTALLATIONS

The efforts to cope with this newly significant corpus of informational material have gravitated toward computer installations, or, where the need could be justified, have invited such installations. The computer has provided the capability of operating with great speed in sorting and matching descriptive data designed to give reference to documents of the type described. Because these efforts have been and continue to be to a large degree in their infancy, they are described by a considerable variability. The major variations are of the following order: assigning a larger number of subject terms to a given document and searching for the useful documents on the basis of a predetermined logical arrangement of such terms; abstracting the contents of the document, followed by indexing and searching in the manner previously described; making micro-photographs of the documents together with the coded subject terms and searching the store of such coded micro-photographs. There are also variations in the particular methods of generating terms for the indexing or subject analysis function. The retrieval code is commonly the address of the document in the store, or the reproduction of the document from a micro-image. Based on the assumption that the titles of documents serve as adequate descriptions, computer programs have permitted permutation of the title so that each permuted form begins with another significant word, arranging the permuted list alphabetically by significant word. These are called quick indexes, and have a useful but transient retrieval value mainly for current awareness perusal.

More significant is the tenor of research and development which characterizes these efforts. Aside from experiments with further variations on known methods applying mechanical means to the retrieval function, the major emphasis has been focused on the language component of the subject analysis problem. In part, this effort is designed to provide consistency and reliability in machine operations, to secure the needed specificity of retrieval and eliminate irrelevant matter that nevertheless is responsive to the formulated request. In part, it is designed to cope with the problem of meaning of word combinations or semantics, in order to permit eventual automation of the indexing or subject analysis process. Since developments with respect to machine or computer speeds are approaching theoretical limits, interests are focusing on improvements in system components and relationships. A particularly significant problem pertains to communication with the system or computer memory, involving in the case of information retrieval the need to carry on a dialogue between the inquirer and the memory in order to secure the rigorous formulation of the question in terms which the memory can answer or resolve.

RETRIEVING INFORMATION AS SUCH

Although much can be said about these developments, the general condition is one of exploring the potential of the computer for application to subject analysis of documents. In the process of such exploration there is an inevitable interaction which results in the modification of traditional methods to permit the harnessing of the potential of the computer and similar electronic devices. For the most part, however, these developments have not escaped from their antecedents. The resulting information is not information in the pure sense. It is rather information that describes a document and its address in a store. It is mostly document retrieval rather than actual information retrieval. It is the same library in another form, applying the same organizational functions in another form, in order to secure the same end results in another form. In those few examples that exist of actual information retrieval, the sufficient conditions which permit the function are homogeneity of information, i.e., critical tables, chemical structures, etc., where the information itself is placed in the store and not information about its container, and a predictable pattern of inquiry or approach to the stored information by a relatively well-defined consumer.

Given the circumstances as described, a further development requires notice, namely that of the *information specialist*. Briefly stated, this is a condition in which the research team is aided by a member who is responsible for supplying pertinent literature or information from the pertinent literature to aid the research in process. This responsibility involves competence in the substance of the research problem and in the literature of the field as well as in peripheral fields. Whether the latter competence is associated with a specific discipline or not continues to be debatable. It has been demonstrated that a research effort can be enhanced by information provided in anticipation of need rather than through search after need has been determined. This differentiation assumes the greater value of time and effort devoted to research rather than to literature search.

NEW ORGANIZATIONAL FORMS
FOR DIVERSIFIED COLLECTIONS

The experience in the special retrieval situations in which computers have been applied more or less successfully is one in which the scope of collections and interests has permitted definition of boundaries. Although scientific research, even when devoted to subjects such as interest the Atomic Energy Commission, the Department of Defense, etc., cannot be rigorously bounded, the diversity of subjects embraced by the collections of their research reports pales in comparison to the subjects contained even in the most modest university library whose intellectual curiosity ranges from these very sciences to the immense variety of subjects in the humanities, the belles lettres, and other manifestations of the diverse cultures of the world in all known periods of recorded history, to the behavioral and social sciences, and others without end.

Given the large research library, with collections numbering in the millions of volumes covering the diversity of human knowledge and interests, with all the unpredictable features of changed uses of today's information as knowledge is reappraised and revised, the approaches to information retrieval that may be practical in the previously described computer installations will not serve in the research library. Although libraries need to expend greater effort to cope with the problem of the increase in current and transient information, they cannot relinquish their obligation to continue to bring order into the cumulative store of man's intellectual enterprise as reflected in recorded information. An important consequence of this reflection is that the present technology does not yet provide economical computer capacity required in the storage of the immense amount of information involved in the description of the units in the library's collections, as well as in additional files associated with its subject organization and other control apparatus that would be required in the process of automation. Further, the technology does not yet provide economical access that satisfies the requirement for speed and supports the dialogue requisite in the process of refining an original formulation to the point at which it matches the output capability of the information system.

This is not to deny that progress should not be anticipated. Computer memories or memories associated with computer control will become available in the requisite size, and means of querying these memories simultaneously by many individuals at proximate or remote locations with virtually instantaneous responses will also be realized.

Any such technological developments, which also assume rather drastic improvements in efficiency and speed of communication in digitalized form between remote locations, involve adjustments of present library organizational forms to newer, interdependent relationships in order to support the system requirements. These requirements relate not only to the hardware aspects but to the fact that their economic exploitation will be defensible only when based upon a rational merging of library efforts at many points of the spectrum of bibliothecal activities. Library co-operation is not new and has been realized in discrete experience in acquisitions, in cataloging, and in reference and informational service. The autonomy of individual libraries, much as in the case of the problem of international sovereignty, has not yet been put to question.

At the point when such developments become real rather than conjectural, the library system will more explicitly recognize the need to embrace the consumer as an integral aspect of the system definition. The scholar or the discipline representing the scholar will have to formulate the expression of the need to be served by the library in rigorous terms. In the contemporary library system, the librarian more often than not risks the creation and development of information service whose survival function frequently resembles the survival of business in a theoretical laissez-faire economy.

SUMMARY

The research library has a long tradition of acquiring, organizing, and serving materials from its collections, both when the required items are known and also when they are specified only with respect to a known subject or problem. The past decade has witnessed an explosion of literature in forms for which traditional library organization has not been designed. The development of novel methods of coping with the emergent literature has gravitated to, or has attracted the computer with its capabilities for speedy manipulation of large quantities of data. The resulting services do not differ in underlying function from traditional library methods. Their key difference is that they serve a relatively homogeneous body of information in response to a known user group with predictable requirements. They do provide services of document retrieval that are more responsive to current usage and needs than libraries can provide. The size and subject scope of research libraries requires computer memories together with rapid access capabilities which the present technology cannot now provide but which may soon be realized. Economic imperatives will require an integration of library functions to justify and support the economic costs of such developments. Concomitantly, the active realization of the improved library system will require a closer relationship to the user, the scholar and research worker, who will also have to accept the responsibility of expressing in explicit terms the requirements which the library must serve.

Images of the Future for School Libraries

J. LLOYD TRUMP

Associate Secretary,
The National Association of Secondary-School Principals,
and Chairman of Its Committee on Staff Utilization

School librarians inevitably will become involved in many changes now being urged on American schools. Never before have the proposals for change been so basic and comprehensive. They touch all aspects of the school—its organization of instruction, its scheduling of students, its staffing patterns, its curriculum, its facilities, and its use of educational funds.

Librarians cannot be neutral in the face of change. Nor does a negative attitude contribute to a constructive approach to the future. Librarians should encourage and spearhead the examination of new ideas in education.

ORGANIZATION OF INSTRUCTION

The school of the future will place much more emphasis on the development of individual student responsibility for learning and growth in intellectual inquiry. At the same time individual differences among students will be recognized as never before. Students will spend much more time in independent study outside of classrooms. Most high school students will spend about twelve hours per week *in school* in independent study. Independent study time will include reading, viewing, listening, writing, working on automated learning devices, and doing various things in different kinds of laboratories.

Books for student use will regularly be found in three locations in the school of the future. The largest collection will be in a room not unlike today's library with its general reading room and conference rooms for smaller groups of students. Reference books and materials for general use will be housed in open stacks to facilitate student use.

The second place where reading materials will be available are the laboratories. Materials especially appropriate in social studies, mathematics, science, language arts, and the other subjects will be housed in the several laboratories to be described later.

The third location of reading materials will be in the individual cubicles of students also described later. These materials will be checked out to individual students. Students need the material at hand to save the time and labor of carrying them from their lockers.

The same general arrangements for reading materials apply to the location of those for viewing and listening. Today's library places little emphasis on these avenues to knowledge. The school of the future will accord viewing and listening a status comparable with that accorded reading today. Some viewing and listening will be done by students in relatively large groups. Much more will be done by them in smaller groups in rooms located adjacent to the general reading room. Some viewing and listening will be done in individual booths. Facilities for viewing and listening will also be available in the laboratories. Students will be able to view and listen to some materials through push-button operation connecting them with central storage facilities.

Most student writing and some reading will be done in individual cubicles. These cubicles will be quite simple in construction, mainly consisting of a flat desk top, two by four feet in dimension, with lockable drawers, and partitions to the height of five feet on three sides. A school will probably need one such cubicle for each three students enrolled. This does not mean that all students will use the cubicles, or that each student will use the facility one-third of the time. This cubicle will provide a quasi-private place where a student may keep his materials between writing periods without having to go through the tedious task of assembling them each time he wishes to work. It is a home base for creativity.

The school will also provide a place for working with automated instruction devices (teaching machines). A variety of programs in all subject areas will be available. Students will be directed to these programs part of the time by their teachers and part of the time by their own discoveries of personal inadequacies and needs. Some of these programs will be studied by students in groups. Most of this work will be done on an individual basis. The exact nature of programed instruction is unknown at the present time. Some devices will be programed textbooks, cataloged by the library. Some of the electronic and machine devices will be located in the laboratory areas, while others will be assembled in group and individual spaces adjacent to the areas of the school reserved for reading, viewing, listening, and writing.

Separate student laboratories will be found in mathematics,

sciences, social studies, English language arts, foreign languages, fine arts, practical arts, and physical education. Whenever possible, much of the equipment in these laboratories will be portable so that it can be moved from one laboratory to another when a student is working on materials that cut across subject lines. Storage areas will facilitate continuation of projects over a period of time.

The library staff will be directly involved in servicing the independent study of students. As materials of instruction become more important, and as students have more time and reason to use the materials, the library staff is thrust deeper into the heart of the learning process. The derivation of the word *library* (from Latin *liber*, book) will be overlooked as other avenues to knowledge are recognized.

Today's teachers and librarians are overly concerned with books. Tomorrow's professional staff will see books in relation to many other avenues to knowledge. Librarians will play key roles in helping teachers decide how and when to use books along with a variety of electronic devices. Space does not permit an elaboration of the role of technology in education. As a matter of fact, the picture changes so rapidly that what librarians need now is a point of view rather than a compilation of devices.

The foregoing concept casts the librarian in the role of an expert on technology in instruction. These technological services must be provided both to teachers and students. Today's expert on books will need more knowledge in the school of the future. This may mean added personnel on the library staff.

STAFFING PATTERNS

Today's self-contained classroom limits the educational opportunities of students to the competencies of their particular classroom teacher. It also perpetuates the concept that one teacher should do everything, including subprofessional tasks, and it makes unnecessarily expensive and difficult the providing of educational services through modern technology.

Tomorrow's teachers will work in teams, each teaching in the areas of his interests and abilities. Thus students will benefit from contact with several personalities in a subject area rather than one. Librarians will be part-time members of teaching teams so their services can be more closely interrelated with the teaching-learning process. They will meet with teaching teams to plan and evaluate instructional programs.

Librarians, like teachers, will teach those phases of courses where their interests and abilities lie.

Tomorrow's school will provide teachers and librarians with a variety of assistants. One kind will be called instruction assistants. They will supervise many places where independent study is scheduled, and correct some parts of student efforts. For example, they will mark some of the mechanics of expression in an English theme, or factual details in a social studies paper, while the professional teacher evaluates the development of ideas. Instruction assistants will be carefully selected workers with college training equivalent to a minor in the subject area in which they serve. They will usually be part-time workers drawn from the ranks of housewives, college students, and part-time workers.

Other teacher and library assistants will be called clerks and general aides. Clerical tasks will be performed by clerks, and general aides will perform other nonprofessional duties throughout the school, for which specialized subject knowledge is not essential. Experience and study will have demonstrated how many of the three types of assistants the librarian will need and what their duties will be.

CHANGE IN THE IMAGE OF THE LIBRARY

Other changes proposed for schools have less obvious but significant relevance to the library role. Flexible schedules and curriculum changes will give both teachers and students more time to use expanded library facilities. The proposal that these facilities be open more hours and days in the year also suggests the need for more library staff. Some of the costs of the change in program will be offset by savings in instructing students in larger-than-usual groups part of the time, by using facilities more efficiently, by employing lower-paid assistants to do work now done by professional teachers, and by organizing the curriculum more effectively.

Today's libraries, and the librarians, are too much on the fringes of education. Tomorrow they will be in the main stream. It will be difficult to identify the library in the conventional sense, because its services will permeate the totality of education. The librarian is a teacher whose special competence is professional knowledge about the materials of instruction. In the library, as elsewhere in the school, time, space, and materials will be the servants of instruction rather than determinants of the pattern.

The Cheap Paperback Is No Country Cousin

VINCENT RICHARDS

Assistant Director,
Fraser Valley Regional Library,
Abbotsford, British Columbia, Canada

Over two years ago I was sitting in the airport at Mexico City waiting for a plane, which eventually arrived twelve hours late. The various passengers for this flight were amusing themselves in different ways. One man was sitting reading a 35-cent paperback western; printed on poor paper and with a gaudy cover, it was the type to make many librarians blanch.

The reader looked familiar to me, his photograph had appeared often in British Columbia's newspapers. Questioning another passenger, I was told: "It's Norman the Foreman." This was the students' affectionate term for the then President of the University of British Columbia, Norman A. M. MacKenzie, C.M.G., M.M. and Bar, Q.C., B.A., LL.B., LL.M., LL.D., D.C.L., D.Sc.Soc., F.R.S.C., etc.

There had been an international conference for university administrators in Mexico City. Presumably he had attended it and was now earning some deserved relaxation. For me the incident solved the perennial question of the provision of light fiction in public libraries. There *is* a definite justified demand for it. Why not meet it simply through the inexpensive paperback?

Librarians rightly put the emphasis on quality in books, but long experience only teaches that a person's reading is like his morals—in some ways a lot worse and in others a lot better than his friends suspect. Those public librarians who want to serve the "advanced" reader only are like those churches that serve only the "elect." The most successful libraries and churches are those which serve the ignorant and the intellectual, the sinners and the saints.

Unfortunately, there are still too many conservative librarians whose minds are always on "improvement" and "their mission," never on delight and pleasure. They are afraid of variety, contrast and controversy, they are out of touch with the roughness and sweatiness of human beings as they really are. They are always regretting public taste, usually overestimating the taste of those like themselves and underestimating the rest. Their book stocks reflect their own mediocrity.

Their contribution to librarianship is one of massive failure, they preserve our image of stuffiness and dullness. Avid for status and prestige, but so lacking in genuine charity for mankind, they never receive it.

Naturally these public librarians are the last to accept anything new. They pussyfooted for years about using what are now called "quality" paperbacks, sending around questionnaires about matters they should have been competent to decide. One librarian, Eli Oboler, was led to declare, "I don't care if a book is bound in human skin, as long as it's used!" The author of an article in a paperback trade journal certainly knew her library audience when she made the following statement: "To discuss paperbacks sensibly, 'cheap' and 'quality' paperbacks must be distinguished. Quality paperbacks begin at 95¢ and may cost as much as five or six dollars. Unlike their cheap cousins . . ."

This definition might be true, were physical appearance only considered; when applied to content the statement is fatuous. It is precisely because of the quality of content and very low price that these cheap cousins deserve attention. Early in 1962 the Fraser Valley Regional Library decided to use paperbacks costing under 95¢ and bought an initial total of 15,300. The great success of this experiment and the reasons for making it are worth studying.

College and school librarians are well ahead of public librarians in accepting the paperback revolution. The latter need waking up to some basic facts of life.

We know that we are in the middle of what has now become a cliché—the paperback revolution. It is one which the public and librarians (as individual readers) have accepted. The 300–400 million total of paperbacks produced and sold annually in North America is half as many books as U.S. public libraries circulate. There are now about 30,000 paperbacks in print in the U.S. and about the same in the United Kingdom.

The availability of cheap paperbacks in any community is self evident. They are to be found in varying places—supermarkets, stores, milkbars, church lobbies—but the one place where they are absent is the public library. Why shouldn't the public library have the biggest and best collection of paperbacks in the community? As a supplement to the regular bookstock of hardbounds and quality paperbacks, cheap paperbacks (PB's) are ideal. There is no good reason for ignoring them, except tradition and minor administrative details which cloud the issue. Cataloging is not a sacred ritual that must be applied to every book—it is only a means of getting books to work. PB's can be made to work in other ways. They must be considered as short-life, disposable items of great potency.

Other good reasons for the use of PB's by public libraries are:

(1) They are excellent value for their low cost (details later).

(2) They allow extension of the range of books provided, at low cost. This is especially valuable in regional and county systems with small branches.

(3) Their small size allows compactness of display, providing proper racks are used. Compact display is, again, of special importance in small branches.

(4) A display rack of PB's in the window of a branch with a store front has an irresistible appeal and brings in new readers.

(5) The preference many readers have for PB's. This is a commonplace fact: people will tackle a book published as a PB, which they would shy away from in regular format. This is one of the most important psychological weapons a librarian can use.

(6) The PB display rack acts as a bridge between juvenile and adult collections for those who rightly suspect the emasculated collections of Young Adult sections. Librarians who wonder why they lose so many teen-age readers should check more closely on the real reading tastes of young adults. One of the surprising results of the provision of PB's was the great use made of them by teen-agers. The collections (900 titles on a rack) were selected with adult tastes in mind. It would be correct to say that on a percentage basis the teen-agers had better reading tastes than the adults. The comparison of their actual tastes with the usual dismal lists of recommended books for young adults should cause much soul-searching amongst children's librarians. Unfortunately they are usually the arch-conservatives of librarianship.

(7) PB's are the delight of old people who find them easier to carry and hold than hardbound books.

(8) PB's are in great demand during vacations because they are space-saving.

(9) PB's help in providing light fiction at reasonable cost.

(10) Heavy requests for a particular title can be met easily by using a PB edition.

(11) The use of PB's helps to break down the image of

stuffiness and dullness which too many libraries deserve. Readers who reacted against a display rack full of PB's by saying it was undignified, soon admitted their prejudice was unjustified when they discovered the variety and quality available.

(12) The mixing of fiction and nonfiction titles leads some readers to different fields of reading.

COST AND LIFE OF PB'S

Before buying any PB's the average price was estimated at 34¢, including the standard 20 per cent discount. In actual fact 15,300 PB's were bought for an average cost of 32.7¢ each. Distribution and processing costs brought the average price per PB to 40¢. If anyone is not certain what the paperback revolution means, let him reflect that it costs most libraries as much, or more than 40¢, to *issue* a book only once. In many cases it would be more efficient to give a PB away than issue the hardbound edition.

A conservative estimate of the cost of adding one hardbound book to stock was $3.60, including cataloging and processing costs. Thus nine PB's can be added to stock for the price of one hardbound.

It was expected that a PB would average 10–13 issues: in actual practice 10 issues was the average, a depreciation of 4¢ an issue. The average life of an adult hardbound book was estimated at 30 issues, a depreciation of 12¢ per issue. This latter figure will vary from system to system and can be found by checking the average number of issues for a large number of discards (or books deserving to be discarded). Another method is to divide the total adult circulation by the adult bookstock and multiply the result by four—the four representing the number of years the average adult book survives repair, rebinding or obsolescence. The difference between 4¢ and 12¢ an issue is obvious.

This saving is lessened by the cost of every unnecessary minute spent in handling one PB. When handling 15,300 PB's one wasted minute a book becomes seven working weeks of unnecessary labor and expense. The moral is: keep handling costs to a minimum. Library systems vary so much that only principles can be outlined. These are:

(1) Use low-cost help.

(2) Under no circumstances catalog PB's, nor keep any records of titles.

(3) Keep processing to an absolute minimum. It was found

that all that was needed for each PB, was a date slip, book-card and pocket, which bore a matching number. This number is used for circulation purposes.

(4) Instruct those circulating PB's not to bother repairing them. Allow them to discard immediately when necessary. Decide what records of discards you need. A simple method is to retain the book jacket, destroy everything else.

(5) Establish a flat rate for lost books, say 40¢.

SELECTION AND DISPLAY

There is only one satisfactory way to select PB's: keep the number of people involved to one or two who know books thoroughly. Secondly, the selector must see each book, especially when buying large quantities. The reason for this is that the introduction of PB's into a library can be a delicate operation, especially in the United States where so many people are wandering around with "lists." Those citizens who think the worst sins are always committed after midnight are the same ones who think inexpensive paperbacks must be sordid ("They're O.K. in their own way, but would you want *your daughter* to read one?")! The selector of PB's must meet this possible criticism by picking a wide range of good books, and hence foil the drugstore book-sniffer armed with his list of objectionable books. Once the principle that PB's are not all lurid is established, a more normal course can be followed.

The best source of supply is the distributor responsible for supplying paperback outlets in the area where the library is situated. Just ask the nearest druggist who supplies his paperbacks. Visit the distributor and tell him the total you wish to buy. Expect a 20 per cent discount and stress that you must have at least one 112-pocket display rack, loaned free of charge for every 900–1000 books. PB's without a proper display stand are useless. In the Fraser Valley Regional Library racks are used in 15 branches. In two bookmobiles where shelves had to be used the use of PB's was a complete flop. Publishers and distributors of PB's know that they must be displayed in a certain way, and librarians who try otherwise will either revolutionize paperback display methods or make a gigantic mess of things.

No attempt will be made here to suggest what to buy. The procedure followed by the Fraser Valley Regional Library can be mentioned briefly as a guide. It was decided that a large display rack would be sufficient for displaying a collection of 900 PB titles, since a large number of these titles would of course be in circulation at any given time. A check of the PB's in stock with the distributor showed that a total of 900 suitable titles was available. Fifteen branches and two bookmobiles were selected as having room and being able to make good use of PB's. It was decided to duplicate the collection of 900 titles 17 times for a total of 15,300 PB's at a cost of just over $5,000.

The basic collection was made up of 450 nonfiction and 450 fiction titles divided as follows: science fiction, 40; mysteries, 40; western, 60; light romances, 60; classics, standard and contemporary fiction, 250. The 900 titles cost $294.30 and presented a dazzling variety. The first rack to go on display had readers of all ages jostling and elbowing, and even the man who muttered at paperbacks in the library sheepishly checked out six a little later. The general reaction was one of delight.

No attempt was made to differentiate between large and small branches. PB's wear out faster in large branches; therefore their replacement level is higher. The total number of PB's bought, represents about 15 per cent of the library's adult stock—in very small branches the percentage is very much higher.

SIX MONTHS LATER

After PB's had been in use for six months, their circulation stood at 68,393. Donations of PB's flowed in for a total of 3500, of which 2000 were of value. Six hundred and eleven PB's had been discarded.

In four small branches the circulation of PB's exceeded that of regular adult books. This was something of a surprise, since the adult stock was good, up-to-date and attractive. PB's accounted for 15 per cent of the total adult bookstock, and 30 per cent of the adult circulation. Branches reported that overall adult circulation was up 15 per cent. The complete success of the experiment has led to the decision to use some of the very low-priced preschool children's books marketed through PB distributors.

The great majority of public librarians can no longer afford to ignore inexpensive paperbacks. School and college librarians have put them to work with great success. Extensive use of the PB in public libraries is justified in theory, and in practice the results exceed expectations. Public acceptance of the cheap paperback is complete and enthusiastic. The generally condescending attitude of public librarians towards the cousin of the "quality" paperback is foolish. The cheap paper-back is no country cousin.

Freedom for Creativity: Data Processing in the Schools

DONALD KLEMER

Principal, the Middlesex and Mather Junior High Schools, Darien, Connecticut

The use of data-processing equipment for many clerical tasks presently handled by professional school personnel will be one of the major changes over the next decade in the public and private schools. Some 800 data-processing systems are in operation in school systems throughout the country. The industrial revolution has at last entered the clerical arena in full force. In the schools data processing has contributed to the natural desire to release teachers and administrators from clerical responsibilities that erode valuable professional time which could be focused on more important educational problems.

Data processing has recently been applied to attendance keeping, grade reporting, and the scheduling of pupil classes. Recording and analysis of such information as health data, physical education data and standardized test scores can release the school nurse, the physical education teachers, and the guidance counselors for the more productive and efficient use of their professional time. Harried school business managers are introducing electronic data processing for the writing of payroll checks, census taking, accounting, development of bus lists and a myriad of tasks that have grown to almost unmanageable size with the growth in pupil population and professional staffs.

THE DARIEN PROJECT

As a school administrator who has been involved over the past several months in the "piloting" of a data-processing program in a school system, I have observed the impact of this approach upon the school staff. The history of the Darien, Connecticut, program in data processing goes back to the summer of 1962. It provides a case history through the details of its application in the junior high schools, where, as a school principal working closely with other staff members, I initiated the first school applications in Darien. Superintendent Gregory C. Coffin was highly interested in the applications of data-processing procedures to the schools. In the summer of 1962 he contacted a local market research firm with the idea of handling the school census on the company's data-processing equipment. I suggested that we might also work on a plan to develop a pilot project for using data equipment in the Darien junior high schools. We explored the possibilities. The board of education fortunately had been associated, indirectly and directly, with modern business operations in the metropolitan New York area. Because these board members had some experience with such techniques, they felt that data processing had great possibilities for the school operation. Thus, from the beginning, Darien had data-processing equipment available, plus an administration and board of education equally interested in data-processing applications.

We decided to begin the use of data processing through both the development of pupil report cards and the keeping of attendance records in the junior highs (1200 pupils). From the outset, our approach was to begin on a small basis with the assumption that the system could be "de-bugged" and then expanded to areas beyond the junior high schools. It was important that the pilot nature of the program be emphasized to aid the transition and develop a staff attitude that anticipated "bugs" and accepted them as expected occurrences in a new program. We realized that, in the beginning, the new approach would be more of a strain on the staff than the customary approach. The "experimental" attitude set the proper climate for our investigation.

We planned the project in the summer of 1962 and the applications went into effect in September of 1962. The introduction of data processing has resulted in teachers being freed from clerical details to devote more of their energies to creative professional tasks. A description of the pupil attendance and report card procedure might serve as a good example of this.

GRADE REPORTING

Under the old system when report card time arrived, a teacher would compute his or her grades and then spend time laboriously recording the grades on a central card. This card was borrowed by several teachers during the school day. One can readily imagine the frustrations and chagrin of the teachers in getting these same cards if and when they were available. (The special-subject teachers had 200 to 300 grades to record instead of the average academic teacher's 125!)

Once the grades were recorded on the office copy of the report card, homeroom teachers then recopied each of their 25–30 pupils' grades onto the pupil report cards. At the same time the homeroom teacher recorded the pupil attendance record for the marking period by drawing it from his or her register. Pupil report cards were then distributed by the teacher and collected after they had been seen by the parent. Meanwhile, guidance counselors made copies for themselves of their counselees' grades.

A myriad of more than 100 separate operations that took many professional hours and endless amounts of nervous energy characterized the old system. Anyone who has taught in the public or private school system knows that the week that "marks came out" meant that the wheels of education were bogged down by the many clerical tasks that teachers faced in that particular week. Teachers often did not have the time to think of "that child in one group who showed a remarkable interest in the Etruscan tombs and needed some help in finding source material" or "the reason why the class in mathematics had failed to gain an understanding of the commutative principle."

In contrast, our data-processing application in the reporting of pupil grades requires one *single action* on the part of the teacher. He is given a package of alphabetically arranged IBM cards for each class. A grade for each pupil is recorded on that card. These cards are returned to the school office and the teacher is finished with his phase of the operation. We feel that we have saved a total of 1000–1500 man hours per year for the staffs (70) of both of our junior high schools.

PUPIL ATTENDANCE

Connecticut, as well as most other states, requires accurate records of pupil attendance. The state bases part of its distribution of financial aid to local communities upon pupil attendance. Connecticut wisely opened the door to the use of data processing for pupil accounting by making it possible for the Commissioner of Education to approve local plans as long as the basic data required by the state was properly secured.

Before the introduction of data processing in the junior highs, a teacher would record basic information concerning homeroom pupil attendance in a large register filled with narrow horizontal lines and designations for days and months. On a daily basis, absence and tardiness for each pupil were recorded in the register. The reader is invited to imagine the nerve-rattling experience of attempting to maintain bookkeeping accuracy while supervising a classroom of 28 youngsters, or attempting to record this information between a biology laboratory class and a study hall assignment. In addition, pupil registers had to be painstakingly balanced each month and each marking period so that the proper information could be transferred to the report card. At the end of the year, a final balance had to be determined and summarized by the principal for the central office.

Our present data-processing application for pupil attendance requires merely that the absence and tardy information is passed on each morning to the central office. From there on the process is out of the hands of the classroom teacher. Registers are no longer kept. It is estimated that a total of approximately 2500 hours a year are saved for 70 teachers.

PROBLEMS OF IMPLEMENTATION

Introduction of data processing to a school system involves not only the blessing of hours saved, but also definite problems, of course.[1] A great deal of time must be spent in carefully reviewing each clerical sequence to its very smallest segment. Most of us are unaccustomed to such a minute and careful analysis of the flow of clerical work. Introduction of data processing demands, ultimately, a redesign of other office sequences and forms. Introducing the data-processing approach without this kind of review is akin to grafting a peach tree branch to a cherry tree.

The clerical staff must also be retrained so that they understand the necessity of changing all of the basic data on all relevant cards if a change must be made. It is advisable to have the staff actually see the machines in operation and realize that the machinery has definite limitations. Otherwise, we have noticed that a kind of "machine mythology" develops. This mythology implies that the machine can accomplish any task—that it can take over all of the thought processes. The machinery, in this context, has replaced man and woman in their entirety. To shatter this illusion, it must be made clear what the machinery *cannot* do.

[1] It has been said that a solution to any problem creates additional problems!

In addition to the problem of misunderstanding the power of the machines and subscribing to the "machine mythology," there is a tendency on the part of some staff members to feel that this new process is endlessly complex and difficult to understand. Believing that they cannot possibly understand the system, they patently avoid attempting to learn how it works. This attitude might be called "fear of the unknown." It is a fixation that keeps the "unknown" unknown! Thus, a system that depends upon a broad basic understanding by all who use it becomes overly dependent upon a few for its proper operation. This calls for staff education and an explanation that adequately shows the basic simplicity of data processing. I say basic simplicity, because the data-processing operation must be reduced to a simple "yes" or "no" kind of a sequence. This binary simplicity is part of its complication. The real challenge in the development of the system is to reduce each operation to its simplest components. This is not radically different from the challenge facing an author of a linear program for programed instruction.

Another less serious problem is the healthy sort of Missouri skepticism on the part of some staff members. It was difficult at first for our teachers to believe that a report card would be produced through data processing. They could not imagine how the modicum of work done by the teachers could produce the result. This skepticism was mixed with a subtle sort of anxiety because of the change in routine procedures. This was an anxiety which suggested that the teacher's job was really of little real importance if a phase of it could be easily taken over by machines. What was, then, the importance of the job? This reaction calls for the administrative explanation that, far from minimizing the teacher's role, the converse was true. The teacher is viewed as more important than the machine because we have decided not to waste his or her valuable professional time on clerical tasks.

Data processing also has a certain dehumanizing effect due to the fact that pupils, teachers, guidance counselors, courses, and even schools are reduced to numbers so that they can be "punched" accordingly and "read" by the machines. The most interesting illustration of the reaction of pupils to the numbers was a Christmas card sent to a principal by a pupil. It was a humorous greeting in the form of an IBM number in very small print. Though clever and amusing, it also reflected a feeling of her loss of personal identification.

Data processing has reduced the number of uncreative

tasks required of the teacher. A careful analysis of the reduction in teacher clerical tasks shows that data processing has improved the opportunity for teachers to focus their energies on helping pupils. Thus more human individual contact with pupils is possible. There is a benefit here that offsets the dehumanizing effect of numbering pupils and teachers.

At the present time, we have provided funds in the school budget for further applications of data processing in our junior high schools and the central administrative offices. Future possibilities involve freeing office secretaries from some work. Data processing will be used for pupil scheduling, design of master schedules and the development of class lists. In previous years some two to three weeks of summer time were spent in the development of class lists by an office secretary. Use of data processing here will provide secretarial time for the development of curriculum outlines, lists of resource materials, evaluations, project designs, etc.

The school principal previously spent many days before a board with varied-colored cards, puzzling out a school master schedule that would hopefully have minimum conflicts. Now a master schedule can be put through a trial run and revised to make an ideal schedule in a maximum of three hours of rented computer time. Thus, the principal is no longer closeted for days with his "hook board" and is released to provide the kind of educational leadership demanded in today's schools.

In the central office, payrolls are now being produced by IBM equipment, thus freeing the payroll clerk to expedite the processing of requisitions and other materials. The entire school census has been reduced to a data-processing application. Further applications will be explored in the business phases.

The school nurses spend a considerable amount of time recording and summarizing the results of eye and ear examinations for state reports. In addition, listings are made of physical defects for teachers. Valuable professional nursing time is thus spent in clerical applications similar to the clerical applications of teachers in reporting and register keeping. Ways are being studied to apply data processing to this area.

Any data that has been recorded on IBM cards can be drawn out and studied in almost any number of combinations. This has already been done in the junior high schools with teacher grade distribution and will undoubtedly be done with other available data.

THE PROBLEM OF AVAILABILITY

Any school system contemplating the introduction of data processing will encounter some of our problems and probably some new ones. One critical problem is the availability of equipment on a local basis. Darien was fortunate to have a local business firm that was willing to handle our data processing on a service basis. Our beginning application did not justify our rental of the basic equipment and hiring of our own trained personnel to operate this equipment. Initially it would have been operating only in uneconomic "spurts." However, with a school system of approximately 5000 pupils, it is felt that a gradual expansion of the applications will ultimately result in our being able to justify the rental of our own equipment.

If we look at the nation in its entirety, it is clear that there are many school systems which have neither business data-processing equipment nor data-processing service bureaus nearby. These smaller systems would probably be unable to justify rental of equipment. Some regional pooling of resources might be called for if some local systems are to be able to apply data-processing procedures. Combining school use with local government utilization is another possible solution to the rental problem.

THE REDUCTION OF CLERICAL STAFF

Another factor that we considered was the possibility that data processing would eventually reduce clerical salaries. This is always the promise of data processing. However, we did not present the data-processing application in the junior high as a possible way to reduce clerical expenses. We presented it as a way to more efficiently use money invested in professional salaries to focus teachers' time on the primary task of the teacher preparing classes and evaluating pupil work. Thus, we felt, the return for dollars invested in education would be improved. On the other hand, in the central office, the Assistant Superintendent for Business saw data processing as a way to reduce the need for additional central office clerical personnel as the number of pupils and staff increased.

THE PROBLEM OF TIME AT THE BEGINNING

Any system that considers data processing should anticipate that the process of conversion will undoubtedly involve more time and effort on the part of some in the first year or two than was the case under the old system.[2] Thus data processing may appear to be more of a burden than a slave in the beginning. This is inevitable, since the entire system of handling clerical work must be reviewed, the staff retrained and the old routines reshaped while others are begun. Things done automatically in the past must be replaced by procedures that will have to be "thought through" from the outset until they too become part of a routine operation. To endure this painful period, the administrator must be fully convinced that the system will ultimately improve the entire operation.

RESISTANCE TO CHANGE

One factor largely ignored by the writers of textbooks on education, that we did not face in Darien, is the raw fact that educational systems feature tables of organization, lines of responsibility and divisions of responsibility and have well-established patterns for getting things done. This is another way of saying that some small local school systems or large city school systems are forms of bureaucracy that often have an automatic cynicism when confronted with the threat of change. More than likely this bureaucracy has not only cynicism but also a basic inertia. Some have preferred to describe this resistance to change as a sort of symbiotic, almost biological, interrelationship of parts that have learned to perform, to adapt, and to live in a given environment. The "organism" then prefers to keep things as they are rather than face an adaptation. Bureaucracies do not always show immediate response to suggestions for change, even though the change would be advantageous in the long run. This situation calls for a great deal of skill and imagination on the part of the administrator and a faith that he has chosen the right path. This is not unlike the faith of any innovator who must face public resistance and cynicism.

CONCLUSION

The industrial revolution has entered the school office. Much as the application of the flying shuttle in the weaving industry led to a need to develop other inventions, so data processing leads to the development of innumerable applications to provide more information faster for more intelligent decision making. It also leads to a redirection of the energies of the

[2] We used the quote: "Never do anything the first time," extensively in a half-joking (but really deadly serious) attempt to prepare the staff.

professional and clerical staffs. A mountain of paperwork has formed a bottleneck in school progress and has slowed down teachers and secretaries. The domination of forms and reports has created many victims of the tyranny of trivia. Data processing can help to free many from this burden.

The field of education today is faced with a number of changes in content of the courses of instruction, in redefinition of the purposes of the various levels, in methods of instruction and in the use of the professional staff. Just as such innovations as programed instruction mean a redefinition of the teacher's role, the application of data processing to the clerical tasks of the teacher offers great promise for giving teachers more time for the preparation and evaluation of their teaching. Called upon to face greater and greater challenge in his professional area, the teacher has very little time to devote to tasks better done by office personnel or data-processing equipment. Indeed, if a teacher is to be creative, time must be available for the teacher to carefully evaluate and plan the program of instruction. Arnold Toynbee once pointed out that civilization tended to thrive in cities where much leisure time was available for the exchange of ideas and re-evaluation of the old ways of doing things. A similar margin of time for creative thinking is needed for superior teaching. We can no longer afford to devote extensive time to non-teaching tasks if we are to move ahead in education at the pace needed today. Data processing is a welcome servant because it can and will make this time available.

Testing, Tests, and Testing Service Organizations

HENRY CHAUNCEY
President, Educational Testing Service,

ROBERT L. EBEL
*Vice President for General Programs,
Educational Testing Service*

TESTING

Those who believe that educational testing is essential to effective education are likely to welcome an opportunity to express their views on its current status and future prospects. At the same time they are likely to have some qualms about setting forth these ideas as contributions to "The New Technology of Education." For testing is not something radically new. In one form or another, tests are as old as man himself. Testing, in its broadest sense, refers to any method of observing and measuring human behavior in order to evaluate and compare individuals. And man has been sizing up his fellow man since he first drew breath.

Testing, in short, has always been a fact of life. What is relatively new is the systematic improvement of tests and their wide application—a development that has occurred largely within the last fifty years.

Modern testing is both an art and a science. It is the art of fashioning and using many different kinds of devices and techniques for sizing up human beings and trying to foresee how they will make out as students, workers, and members of the community. Behind these techniques and devices is a new science, a growing body of theory drawn principally from psychology and mathematics and known as psychometrics. Both the art and the science are imperfectly developed and constantly changing, a characteristic of all arts and sciences. But the rate of development and improvement in testing is remarkable, considering the relatively short history of a systematic, scientific approach to the problem of determining individual differences.

The increasingly wide demand for educational testing has encouraged the use of objective tests, which are especially well adapted for the efficient measurement of many important educational achievements. This, in turn, has encouraged the development of high speed machines to read and process the information students record on their test answer sheets. Objective testing began before the turn of the century, but high speed test scoring and data-processing machines are largely a development of the last decade.

These machines, amazing in their speed and versatility, are indispensable to modern wide-scale testing programs. But it would be as incorrect to say that these machines test people as to say that the linotype machine or the high speed rotary press writes the news. The technology of testing has provided many good answers to the question, "How shall we test?" but it has provided few answers to the question, "What shall we test?" Examiners must still work out their own answers to this question. The one advantage wide-scale testing programs have in answering it is that the sponsors of such programs secure panels of expert teachers to take time to consider carefully what to test.

Another common misconception about modern educational testing is encouraged by the use of terms like *mass testing* and *machine testing*. This is the misconception that mass testing, using standardized, machine-scored tests, contributes to uniform, lock-step, depersonalized education. The opposite is closer to the truth.

If one looks at educational testing in perspective and context, a good case can be made for the view that objective tests promote the democratic values to which most Americans subscribe. This country is a multitudinous, heterogeneous nation. We are dedicated to the principle of equal opportunity and we believe that justice should be done each individual according to his merit. We try to recognize and respect individual differences and we attempt to accommodate local and regional differences. We believe in change and we strive for progress. Because our present civilization is in part founded on it, we have faith in science and the wise application of technology. These are some of the traditional values that, along with historical, social, and economic factors, have contributed to the present character of American education—and of educational testing.

In a vast nation where talent may be anywhere, and where we advocate its right to be discovered and developed, large-scale testing that is reliable and efficient is a necessity. If it did not exist, it would have to be invented. Unlike the personal interview, the classroom test, or the teacher's subjective evaluation, the objective test is a *common* touchstone. It gives every student a chance to demonstrate his academic abilities. It gives all students who take it the same chance, asks them to run the same race—even though they have had different economic backgrounds, different educational, cultural, and social opportunities.

If these opportunities have been seriously inadequate, the student may do poorly on the test. But this very fact highlights the degree to which Americans have failed to provide equal educational opportunity for all children according to their abilities. It may even help more people to become aware of the fact that talent and ability are developed in direct proportion to the excellence of educational opportunity.

TESTS

Tests are essentially observations of certain types of student behavior under conditions designed to permit precise observation and efficient recording. They are not substitutes for teacher observations. They simply provide for more detailed observations under more uniform conditions than is possible otherwise. The history of education records successive refinements in this process of observing what a student knows and what use he can make of what he knows. Informal classroom observations were first supplemented by oral quizzes and examinations. These gave way, in part, to uniform written tests of the essay type. Essay tests, in turn, have been partly replaced by objective tests. Each change has been motivated by the desire to gain more information, and more precise information, about the student and his knowledge.

The advantages of multiple-choice tests are frequently thought to be that they can be scored clerically or by machine and that they are relatively inexpensive. These are only minor virtues. The important qualities are three. The first is that a hundred questions, more or less, can be asked instead of six or twelve. This permits a much wider sampling of the subject matter and the student's abilities. It means that if a student for one reason or another does not do himself justice on one, two, or even half a dozen questions, he will not seriously affect his score.

Secondly, a test can be planned, and each question prepared, with the greatest possible care. The first step in developing an achievement test, for example, is to draw up a "blueprint" for the examination, specifying the abilities to be measured and the content to be covered. These specifications may be stated in a variety of ways, depending on the nature and complexity of the test. Sometimes a two-way grid is prepared, which enables each question to be classified in two dimensions—the ability to be measured and the subject matter covered. Such a grid for the Advanced Sociology Test in the Graduate Record Examinations is shown in the illustration.

Those responsible for the test then decide approximately how many questions should be written to cover each ability in each content area. When the questions are written and classified, the number of questions falling into each classification is recorded on the grid. A completed grid thus indicates at a glance the score and balance of the test.

The third asset of multiple-choice tests is that they lend

Graduate Record Examination

Advanced Sociology Test

Specifications

SUBJECT MATTER	ABILITIES	Knowledge of basic facts, definitions and terminology	Knowledge of theoretical conceptions incl. authorship of works	Acquaintance with sources of information	Applications of principles to unfamiliar situations	Interpretation of data	Analysis of material into its constituent parts	Synthesis of patterns and structures from the individual elements in a situation	Evaluation of data according to stipulated criteria	TOTAL
Criminology										
Demography										
The Family										
Religion										
Other Social Institutions										
Industrial Sociology										
Race and Ethnic Relations										
Social Organization										
Social and Cultural Change; Ethnology										
Social Disorganization										
Social Psychology										
Collective Behavior and Social Control										
Small Groups and Sociometry										
Human Ecology										
Urban and Rural Sociology										
Social Stratification										
Political Sociology										
Economic Sociology										
Sociology of Law										
Theory										
Methodology, Statistics, and Techniques										
History										
TOTAL										

themselves readily to systematic study. Preliminary tests using newly developed questions are tried out to determine whether, in fact, able students generally select as the best answer the response that the teachers who prepared the question considered the best answer. This is the point at which elements of ambiguity that may make it an ineffective question are spotted. If a question is found to be ambiguous, or if it does not generally elicit from good students the intellectual skills and reasoning powers it seeks to measure, the question is eliminated, or it is revised before it is used in an actual test.

In any aptitude or achievement test, the objective is to get the best possible sample of a student's ability and knowledge. The larger the sample, the more representative the sample, and the better the individual questions, the better the test will be. But even the best test is subject to error—because all possible content is not sampled, because authorities may differ in their evaluation of responses, and because language itself is imprecise.

Those who prepare good multiple-choice tests recognize all three sources of error. They seek to reduce all three by the processes I have described: 1) they include many questions in the test, thus increasing the size of the sample; 2) they ask several outstanding teachers and scholars to come to a consensus in evaluating intended responses to any question; 3) they eliminate ambiguity of language as much as possible by trying out new questions and studying student responses before including the questions in an actual educational group or testing agency. In this case, the sponsoring group determines the policy and nature of the program, sees that tests are developed to serve the program's purpose, and arranges for administration of the tests on designated dates.

TESTING SERVICE ORGANIZATIONS

The functions of the testing service organizations, in relation to testing programs such as we have just described, are four-fold.

First, they provide personnel with special technical competence in educational measurement to advise the program policy makers on the questions and problems that inevitably arise, to work with them in the development of appropriate tests, and to analyze the test results.

Testing service organizations work in close co-operation with expert teachers in the preparation of educational tests. These teachers are seldom experts also in the techniques of measurement. A test which is a product of the joint efforts of specialists in subject matter and specialists in testing techniques is likely to be a better test than either kind of specialist could produce working alone.

A testing service organization is also likely to have specialists in the statistical analysis of test results. These specialists are responsible for equating scores on different forms of the same test, for developing adequate norms to aid in the interpretation of test scores, for making internal analyses of the quality of tests, and for studying their validity. Other specialists advise test users on how to cope with the problems they encounter.

Second, testing service organizations provide the special mechanical and clerical facilities needed for accurate and efficient administration of tests, scoring of answer sheets, and reporting of test scores.

A good testing program produces accurate test scores promptly. To do this on a large scale requires specialized data-processing equipment and specially trained clerical personnel. Most large testing service organizations have specially designed electronic test scoring equipment which operates in conjunction with high capacity computer systems. One such test scoring machine is capable of scoring objective test answer sheets at the rate of almost 100 per minute, and of obtaining scores on as many as six different tests simultaneously from each answer sheet.

In many admission testing programs, each student who wishes to take the test applies directly to the testing service organization and is give an ticket of admission to a testing center near his home. Thus the so-called mass testing is in reality composed of a large number of individual transactions between the student, the testing organization, and the educational institutions to which the student's scores are to be reported. Routines are developed to make these transactions as simple and as convenient as possible for all concerned, but individual cases that call for special handling are given special, individual attention. In a recent testing program, involving more than a million students, the records of 35 per cent of the students registered required non-routine handling. There were, in fact, nearly nine hundred thousand instances where it was necessary to give special individual attention to an application, a ticket of admission, an answer sheet, or a score report.

Third, testing service organizations supply an administrative secretariat for matching their testing services to the needs of the educational community, and for providing program continuity.

Most of the educators who initiate, support, and determine the policies of a testing program have full-time jobs as educators. The attention they give to the program is necessarily intermittent. Usually they receive no compensation for the time they devote to it. Hence, there is need for a continuing central office to prepare for the policy committee meetings, to translate policy decisions into program actions, and to provide a center for all program records, and for all inquiries regarding the program. This is the function of the office of the program director.

Testing service organizations provide program direction services. Usually the program director is a specialist in educational measurement who is also a skilled administrator. It is his responsibility to keep the policy committee informed of program progress and problems, and to help them use the advice of specialists in finding solutions to the problems. It is also his responsibility to co-ordinate the special services of test development, test administration, score reporting, statistical analysis, and research which make the program effective and efficient.

Fourth, the testing service organizations encourage and support basic research on testing problems.

Research provides one of the principal avenues of progress in educational testing as in most other endeavors. But research is often expensive and sometimes unproductive. Testing service organizations differ considerably in the extent of their involvement in research. Most of them do some research, but some limit their research to immediate practical problems and leave the more basic research to the college professors and their graduate students. One testing service organization maintains a large staff of specialists in fundamental research on educational measurement problems. Its expenditures for research amounted to about 7½ per cent of its total expenditures during a recent year.

The work of the testing service organization is important. Its staff members need to be competent and well trained. But its role is always that of an educational servant, not an educational master. What it does, or helps others to do, is almost always done in response to an educational need, identified by educational leaders who are not themselves test specialists. Educational testing is a useful tool for achieving educational objectives. It is not an independent, autonomous force. There is not the slightest danger that education will ever be taken over by "the testers." Testing can do no more to education, or for education, than the makers of educational policy want it to do and direct it to do.

PART THREE

THE NEW CURRICULA

The New Mathematics Programs

EDWIN MOISE

*James Bryant Conant Professor of Education and Mathematics,
Harvard University*

One of the handicaps of school mathematics in our generation has been the gulf between the professional mathematicians and the schools. Another has been a general lack of sympathy for mathematics in the popular culture. Not long ago, and perhaps even now, there were some circles in which mathematics was regarded as an activity which might be all right for certain eccentric and spiritless adults, but which surely ought not to be inflicted on helpless children.

In the last few years, for reasons that are not entirely clear, both of these tendencies have been reversed; and one result of the changes has been a remarkable development of new programs. Most of these have been developed by collaborations between professional mathematicians and professional school teachers; and they have gotten—from schools, teachers, and students—a more favorable reception than most of us dared to hope for.

In this article, I shall try to explain the spirit and the meaning of these developments, as I understand them. For two reasons, I ask the reader's patience.

First, of all the sciences, mathematics is notoriously the least intelligible to non-specialists. Nevertheless, it would make no sense at all to try to discuss changes in curriculum and methodology without giving concrete mathematical illustrations of what these changes mean.

Second, the sheer volume of new programs and experimental text materials is by now overwhelming. The publications of the School Mathematics Study Group (SMSG) now fill over three linear feet on a bookshelf high enough to hold them in a vertical position; the productions of the University of Illinois Committee on School Mathematics (UICSM) are quantitatively less, but still impressive; and if we add those of the Maryland group, the Ball State group, and others, it is plain that a full critical survey of this literature would require a book rather than an article. The most that I shall try to do here is to describe the leading features of the programs that

seem to me to be the most important and to explain the ideas
that underlie them.

In 1955 the College Entrance Examination Board set up a
Commission on Mathematics to study the problem of the curriculum in Grades 9 through 12 and recommend reforms. It
may seem a little strange for such an initiative to be taken
by an organization whose primary function is to design and
administer examinations. But in its context, this initiative was
natural. Any agency that writes examinations influences the
curriculum, whether it wants to or not; and the board was
quite rightly afraid that it was freezing the mathematics curriculum at a time when changes were needed. It therefore
sought the advice of the mathematical world. In fact, the
commission was rather large and rather broadly representative, both of the universities and of the schools.

The commission's report appeared in 1958. The basic
thesis of the report was that high school courses needed to
be recast to bring them into harmony with the methods and
spirit of modern mathematics. This idea is fundamental in all
the new programs. Later, we shall examine how the idea
applies to the presentation of particular topics. We should,
however, understand at the outset what it does not mean: it
does not mean that recently discovered theorems should be
taught early and often. In fact, the program recommended
by the commission did not include, in Grades 9 through 11,
a single topic that was not well understood in the year 1800.
(It is true that the idea of a set, or collection of objects, was
to be presented in the ninth grade; but this idea is not new,
in mathematics or even in common speech.) As far as I know,
none of the new programs in the United States includes such
topics before the twelfth grade. This does not convict anyone
of being unmodern. The point, rather, is that mathematics,
uniquely among the sciences, does not fall into fundamental
errors; much of the best mathematics that we have has been
with us for a long time; and we should not be surprised if
rather old material turns out to be adequate and suitable for
the first three years of high school.

On the other hand, mathematics is constantly being re-
formulated; its language and its conceptual apparatus change
faster and faster as time goes on; some ideas and methods
lapse into relative insignificance, while others move into central roles. For example, the value of Horner's method (for
the numerical solution of algebraic equations) has by now
sunk to absolute zero; everything that can be done with it

can be done better without it. Meanwhile, the idea of a set, which was hardly made explicit by the mathematicians of Horner's generation, has become part of the basic apparatus, even at the most elementary level.

The commission's purely curricular recommendations are far easier to summarize. Following is an outline of their outline:

Ninth grade. An introduction to algebra, as far as quadratic equations with real roots. Novelties: the idea of a set (at the start of the course); a proof that 2 has no rational square root; descriptive statistics (optional); numerical trigonometry of the right triangle (optional).

Tenth grade. Introduction to geometry, including plane and solid synthetic geometry and a short introduction to co-ordinate geometry. Co-ordinate systems are introduced somewhat after the middle of the introduction to plane synthetic geometry; and the unit on solid geometry appears at the end.

Eleventh grade. This is a course in algebra, analytic geometry, and trigonometry. The main topics are basic properties of the real number system; linear functions; radicals; quadratic functions; quadratic equations, in the general case, allowing complex roots; systems of two or three linear equations in two or three unknowns; exponents and logarithms; arithmetic and geometric series including infinite geometric series; subfields of the real and complex number systems; plane vectors; co-ordinate trigonometry, using vectors; trigonometric formulas, including addition formulas and the laws of sines and cosines; complex numbers in polar form.

Twelfth grade, first semester. This was to be a course in "elementary functions." Main topics: sets and combinations; permutations; mathematical induction; functions and relations; polynomial functions; solution of polynomial equations; exponential and logarithmic functions; trigonometric functions; the inverse sine and tangent.

For the second semester of the twelfth grade, the commission proposed two possible courses: introductory probability with statistical applications or an introduction to modern algebra. For the first of these courses, the commission published a book, entitled *Introductory Probability and Statistical Inference* (1). As a text, this book is very original and is remarkable in many ways. The technical mathematical apparatus is held to a minimum, as it would have to be at this level. But the probabilistic and statistical concepts are presented in a quite modern and rather abstract form. A television course of this type taught by Frederick Mosteller in the spring of 1961 on "Continental Classroom" was very well received. A new textbook to accompany the course has been written by Mosteller, Rourke, and Thomas (2).

The proposed course in modern algebra dealt with groups, rings and fields, including permutation groups. It presents a treatment of the real number system considered as an ordered field in which every bounded set has a least upper bound.

The differences between this scheme and the old curriculum are rather striking. Solid geometry, which commonly has a semester to itself in the twelfth grade, now appears merely as a unit at the end of the tenth grade. Trigonometry has disappeared as a separate course. Algebra appears as a branch of mathematics, dealing with the properties of various number systems, rather than a collection of manipulative tricks. There is a similar reform in the treatment of trigonometry, stressing the kind of trigonometry that is going to get used in later studies and omitting the long and almost useless calculations that used to appear as the grand climax of the twelfth-grade trigonometry course. In the same spirit, the twelfth-grade course includes material on the functions that are going to be studied in calculus.

A student who finishes the first three and a half years of this program is amply prepared to start his college work with analytic geometry and calculus. In fact, many schools teach calculus in the twelfth grade; and the experience of the last few years shows that this is quite workable, if qualified teachers are available. But the *if* is important. High school calculus courses have become status symbols, pursued, in some cases, without proper regard to staff resources. It is fortunate that the commission avoided accelerating the latter trend by recommending calculus in twelfth grade as an immediate national objective.

The commission's program is radical in some ways and conservative in others. Probably the most imaginative of the commission's contributions was the twelfth-grade probability course, and the least imaginative was the tenth-grade course, which was formed by fitting together portions of existing conventional programs, with innovations and improvements merely in matters of detail. Many people, including the author, dissent from a number of the commission's judgments, both philosophical and curricular. But there would be small profit in discussing these dissents here. The commission was not writing, or trying to write, a bible. They asked that their program be regarded as a "point of departure." Thus, their report is the sort of document which, if successful, is superseded by events; and one measure of the commission's success is the fact that their report has been superseded in this way.

We have already pointed out that the commission's policy on twelfth-grade calculus was a response to practical considerations governing the near future. The same considerations applied, in less simple ways, to their program as a whole. Their program was designed to be feasible in this decade; and it was supposed to require only the sort of additional teacher-training which in practice is available. Fortunately, such additional training is now available on a fairly large scale, in summer institutes and academic-year institutes sponsored by the National Science Foundation. The importance of these institutes can hardly be overestimated. Without them, the sort of reforms that we have been discussing could proceed only at a small fraction of their present pace.

Even this advantage, however, would not have been enough. In practice, high school courses—and for that matter, most college courses—are taught out of books; and the commission's ideas were not carried out, even approximately, in the textbooks that were available. It is even doubtful whether the feasibility of a really new program can be judged until books have been written for it. It is well known that almost any course works well in the classroom if it is taught by its inventors or by a few of their highly trained converts. This principle helps to account for the fact that so many enthusiastic innovators have fired shots heard round the immediate vicinity. To get a valid test of feasibility, you must turn over the program to teachers who are a fair sample of the people who would be teaching if it were adopted on the scale for which it is intended. For these reasons—either of which would have been compelling—the natural next step was the production of experimental textbooks.

The School Mathematics Study Group started its work at Yale University in the summer of 1958, under a grant from the National Science Foundation. The director is E. G. Begle, formerly of Yale and now at Stanford University. At the start, the total writing team included some forty people, about half being from the schools and the other half from the universities. This arrangement reflected a policy that has been fundamental in the School Mathematics Study Group ever since: all its work has been carried out in collaboration between mathematicians and experienced classroom teachers; and this policy is now formally stated in its bylaws.

The exact relation between the School Mathematics Study Group and the commission is not easy to determine. It was agreed, at the first writing session at Yale, that the commission's program would form a provisional outline. The immediate purpose of this arrangement was to permit a division-of-labor scheme, with one writing group for each of the four high school grades. But surely this scheme would not have been used if the group as a whole had not been in general sympathy with the commission's program. Within the limits of its assigned grade, each writing team made its own policies. (There was, of course, enough consultation between the teams to avoid serious duplications and incongruities.) The members of each group, moreover, were not selected for their adherence to particular viewpoints. At the outset, disagreements were extensive, and the discussions were vigorous and prolonged. As a member of the tenth-grade team, I can testify that the 1958 session was educational in a number of ways; everybody in the room was teaching everybody else, by the Socratic method; and this process took so long that after four weeks we had arrived only at a course outline and a few pages of sample text. It seems, in retrospect, that one of the main results of our first session was a common understanding that formed the basis of the rest of our work.

In the summer of 1959 all four of the groups met again at the University of Colorado, with many recruits, and finished four textbooks. Each of these was tried out at about seventy experimental centers throughout the country. Consultants were available to help the teachers, but the teachers had no special training to prepare them for the job (except, of course, those few who had participated in the writing project). In fact, they had not even seen the books until the week before the opening of school. On the basis of these reports, all the books were revised at a writing session at Stanford in the summer of 1960 and were put on the market for use in the academic year 1960–61.

The response of the schools was favorable beyond all expectations. At first, about fifty thousand copies were ordered from the printer; after a few weeks, the order was doubled; and a few weeks later it was plain that this was still not enough. In 1961–62, the total circulation of these books approximately tripled. This was especially significant in the light of the fact that none of them had been adopted in any state. Thus every SMSG book that was ordered for school use had to be paid for in some awkward fashion.

In addition to its high school work, the SMSG has also produced books for use in the elementary schools. The problems involved here are rather peculiar. Just as a student who can ever learn calculus can learn it in the twelfth grade, so a student who can ever learn algebra can learn it in the eighth grade or the seventh. But in most schools, it is not practical simply to move high school courses downward. Few teachers are trained to handle them. Moreover, a large proportion of elementary school pupils are headed for courses in "general mathematics" rather than ninth-grade algebra courses; and such students need frequent fresh starts. For these reasons, much of the new elementary school writing is in the form of short units, largely independent of one another. The need for new programs in the seventh and eighth grades is especially acute. By this time, an able student has learned all the arithmetic that he needs to know; and marking time for two years is not only wasteful but demoralizing. It is a sad fact that most of the mathematics that gets taught at this level is disliked for the excellent reason that it deserves to be disliked.

Some of the most novel and most interesting of the new text materials are designed for use in the early grades. I mention these briefly, because I am not qualified to discuss them fully. It is obvious, however, even from a distance, that young children can learn much more and much better mathematics than is ordinarily taught to them. The possibilities shown by some of the recent experimental teaching in the early grades are a great challenge both to course design and to teacher education.

In addition to publishing textbooks for students, the SMSG has published a rather large amount of material for the use of teachers. The manuals accompanying the textbooks go much further than is customary in discussing the mathematical backgrounds of courses. Some of them include short essays on various related topics. The SMSG has published a series of separate books, including several new ones, some reprints, and one translation from the Russian. It has also promoted the preparation of a series of mathematical monographs intended for independent reading by superior high school students. Recently it has begun a study of the possibilities of programed instruction in its own courses.

All this work has been remarkable, not merely for its quality and its variety, but for the speed with which it has been carried out. The starting point, we recall, was June of 1958.

The SMSG is now beginning a different sort of work. Its "crash program" is finished; and it is expected that its high school books will be withdrawn from circulation in another two or three years, when similar books become available through commercial publishers. From now on, the main job of the SMSG will be long-range experimentation with courses and programs that are not necessarily suitable for wide use in the near future.

In the discussion of federal aid to schools, warnings have been given about undesirable side effects, notably the possibility of federal interference with the traditional state and local control. In the case of the SMSG, this danger seems remote: its work has consisted in the development of programs that various school systems can adopt if they want to. The influence of the organization has of course been great, but it has worked by example and by positive contributions rather than by any attempt to exercise authority. It would be easy to name individual authors who have exerted a similar influence on the teaching of college calculus by making the sort of positive contributions that the SMSG has made.

Obviously the volume and speed of the SMSG's work have been in some ways wasteful. One wag has suggested that its whole style of operation is based on a misinterpretation of a "word problem" in algebra: "If one man can do a job in three years, how many men does it take to do the same job in half an hour?" It would be fairer, however, to say that the style of the SMSG's work has been based on the idea that the teaching of school mathematics is so large and expensive an enterprise that if you save even a single year in making an improvement, you have justified a large budget.

The shift in choice and order of topics is by no means the most important aspect of the new programs; it is merely the easiest to explain. To see the sort of issue that is involved in the reform of ninth-grade algebra, let us start with a simple example.

Most teachers of college freshmen fight an annual war against the supposed algebraic identity

$$\sqrt{x^2} = x.$$

Annually, thousands of students arrive on college campuses with the firm conviction that this formula is a universal law of nature. They have seen it as a displayed formula in textbooks. Some books enclose it in boxes. And sometimes it appears in color.

In fact, the formula is about as valid as the statement that on a checkerboard all the squares are red. We recall that if y is positive, then $\sqrt{y}$ denotes the positive number whose square is y. Thus $\sqrt{4} = 2$, $\sqrt{64} = 8$, and so on. If we want to describe the negative number whose square is y, we write $-\sqrt{y}$. Thus every positive number y has two square roots: $\sqrt{y}$ (which is positive) and $-\sqrt{y}$ (which is the corresponding negative number). Of course, $\sqrt{0} = 0$.

Thus, if you substitute 2 for x, in the above displayed formula, you get

$$\sqrt{2^2} = 2,$$

which means that

$$\sqrt{4} = 2.$$

This statement is true. But if you substitute -2 for x, in the supposed universal law, you get

$$\sqrt{(-2)^2} = -2,$$

which means that

$$\sqrt{4} = -2$$

or

$$2 = -2,$$

which is surely false. In fact, the formula

$$\sqrt{x^2} = x$$

is right about half of the time: it is true when x is positive or zero, and false when x is negative. Hence our analogy of the all-red checkerboard. The correct formula is

$$\sqrt{x^2} = |x|.$$

Here $|x|$ is defined by two conditions:
If x is positive, then $|x|$ is x.
If x is negative, then $|x|$ is the corresponding positive number. (Thus $|2| = 2$ and $|-2| = 2$.)

If this seems an overabstract fine point, the reader should bear in mind that it is never practical—for mathematicians, physicists, engineers, or anybody else—to get the wrong answer. Some years ago, there was a sad case in which an engineer's Master's degree was delayed for a year because he was unable to get his experiments to agree with his theoretical predictions. The trouble with his "theory" was that he thought that the formula

$$\sqrt{1 - \sin^2 x} = \cos x$$

was a trigonometric identity. This is merely an elaboration of the error that we have just been discussing: the correct formula is

$$\sqrt{1 - \sin^2 x} = |\cos x|.$$

It may seem a simple matter to correct such errors. But to many of us who have struggled with them, such trifles as this seem like the tip of a dragon's tail, sticking up out of the sand: they are small symptoms of a large problem. When I have pointed out to college freshmen that the supposed identity $\sqrt{x^2} = x$ is false for $x = -2$, repeatedly I have gotten the impression that the students felt that they were being tricked. They seemed to think that I had changed the subject from algebra to arithmetic; arithmetic deals with particular numbers (like 2 and -2), while algebra deals with "general numbers" like x, y, and so on. Perhaps the equation $\sqrt{x^2} = x$ fails for certain particular numbers, such as -2 and -3, but it holds for "general numbers," such as x and y.

Now these ideas are, in a literal sense, nonsense. There is no such thing as a general number; and the idea suggested by the phrase is incapable of rehabilitation. Expressions such as

$$\sqrt{x^2} = x$$

or

$$x^2 + 5x + 6 = 0$$

are not statements about general numbers. In fact, they are not statements at all. To get statements, you must substitute numbers for x. An expression of this kind is called an *open sentence*. In an open sentence, the letter x merely marks the spot where a number is to be inserted. Some numbers, when substituted for x, may give true statements; others may give false statements. The set of all numbers which give true statements is called the *solution set* of the open sentence. For example, the solution of the open sentence

$$\sqrt{x^2} = x$$

is the set of all non-negative numbers; and the solution of the open sentence

$$x^2 + 5x + 6 = 0$$

is the set whose only members are -2 and -3.

If you think of algebra in these terms, then you see that algebra is the study of numbers; it is not the art of manipulating letters like x, y, and z. The pursuit of this idea to its logical and pedagogic conclusion is (in my opinion) the main basis of the revolution that is now being carried out in the teaching of algebra by the SMSG, the UICSM, and others.

It should be understood that the issue involved here is not one of logical rigor in the sense that mathematicians attach to the term. The question is one of intuitive understanding versus mystical illusions and gross misconceptions. The most radical response to the problem that I know of is that of the UICSM; and the UICSM is firmly committed to the doctrine that in mathematics teaching, logic is not enough.

Far from relying on logic alone, the UICSM takes the position that mathematical knowledge need not always be verbalized at all and that at some stages the student learns better if he is not asked either to produce or to read verbalizations. If this seems odd, let us recall that in the first year of its life, a baby learns to interpret, three dimensionally, the two-dimensional images received by the retina. Thus, a one-year-old understands, in an important sense, the laws of perspective. This is probably the most striking example of the efficiency of nonverbal learning. And it does not stop with childhood. Adults have an understanding of human nature; but few of us can formulate, explicitly, a single valid principle of behavioral psychology.

It may well be that this principle has been overstressed by UICSM. But the stress laid on it serves, at least, to exonerate UICSM of naïve reliance on abstract preachments. One striking illustration of the UICSM's approach is the treatment given to multiplication in the general case, where each factor may be positive, negative, or zero. The problem is to explain why the product of two negative numbers is positive. From the standpoint of purely deductive mathematics, the problem is trivial: in one style of treatment, the statement is part of the definition of the product, so that no question of fact appears to be involved at all; and in another style of treatment, the statement appears as a very easy theorem. The UICSM, however, has set itself the task of furnishing an intuitive foundation for statements of this sort by supplying concrete interpretation of them. The concrete interpretation furnished for multiplication in the general case is rather complicated. It involves a tank of water; a pump, which can pump water either into or out of the tank; a movie camera; and a projector, in which the developed film can be run off either forward or backward. Max Beberman, the founder and the leading spirit of UICSM, is fond of telling about this device. It is obvious that he feels proud of it and considers it important. Some critics of the UICSM program have said that it stresses the deductive aspect of mathematics at the expense of everything else. These critics have quite misunderstood the situation. No doubt the program has its faults, but this does not happen to be one of them.

I have stressed that the issues discussed so far are independent of the question of deduction and logical rigor. If this is plain, I may now add that all the new programs in algebra stress the deductive structure far more than the conventional ones do. (Indeed, it is rather hard to see how they could stress it any less.) Usually there is a fair amount of intuitive material, discussion of special cases, "discovery exercises," and so on. But at some point the basic laws governing numbers are made explicit, and later statements are based on them, in somewhat the style that is familiar in geometry.

While the objectives of the SMSG and UICSM ninth-grade courses are similar, the methods used are different. Much of the terminology and notation in the UICSM course is novel, and the pedagogy is of a special type. (The teacher's manual is about as long as the book; and there is, essentially, only one way to teach the course.) For this reason, the program has a practical disadvantage independent of its essential merits: it is far less flexible and calls for much more special preparation on the part of the teacher.

In geometry, other issues are involved. To understand the history of the teaching of geometry, we must begin with the history of geometry itself. Nearly all elementary books are modeled on Euclid's *Elements* or on adaptations of the *Elements* (notably the famous textbook of Legendre). In the context of modern mathematics, Euclid's book is very peculiar indeed. It is impossible to do justice to this topic in a general article. For a fuller account of the matter, see the section on geometry in a book soon to be published by the SMSG (3). Here we merely cite two facts, which may suggest the sort of thing that is going on. First, in Euclid, there is no such thing as the length of a segment. Second, in Euclid, there is not even such a thing as the ratio of the lengths of two segments.

Instead of these ideas, Euclid used the idea of *same-length* (or "equality") between segments, and the idea of a four-term proportionality of the form

$$AB : CD :: EF : GH.$$

This has a meaning; it says that "*AB* is to *CD* as *EF* is to *GH*." Thus we have the idea of *same-ratio*, but not the idea of ratio: in Euclid, the expression *AB* : *CD* has no meaning at all if it stands alone.

The root of these delicacies and oddities was the fact that lengths and ratios are real numbers, and Euclid did not profess to know anything about the algebra of the real numbers. Later, of course, the real number system came to play a central role. Algebra is now commonly taught before geometry. And algebra appears, as it should appear, in geometry courses. Segments are labeled with numbers, in figures, to indicate their lengths; and proportionality is treated by equations between fractions, with real numbers in the numerators and denominators. As far as I know, there is only one high school in the country (the Priory School at Portsmouth) where students are taught the Euclidean theory of proportionality. Nevertheless, nearly all the existing textbooks state Euclid's postulates and describe, in some fashion, Euclid's conceptual apparatus. These Greek vestiges are hardly more functional than the Roman togas that are sometimes worn at meetings of high school Latin clubs.

The first policy decision of the SMSG geometry group was that Euclid's postulates should be replaced by metric postulates describing the connections between geometry and algebra. Under such a scheme, the postulates describe the mathematical system which in fact is going to be studied and suggest the methods which in fact are going to be used.

(The reader is reminded that as a member of the SMSG geometry team, I am not a neutral on this subject. You may attribute to me special prejudice, special knowledge, or both, according to your taste and mood.)

This scheme in elementary geometry was first proposed by the late G. D. Birkhoff, of Harvard, and was used in a textbook written by him and Ralph Beatley, over twenty years ago (4). Aside from its basic advantage of directness and candor, the book vastly simplifies the logic of the subject. A logically accurate treatment, in the Euclidean spirit, is so complicated that people seldom even try to present it in the tenth grade. (The only plausible recent attempt is in the book of Brumfiel, Eicholz, and Shanks (5); it uses a metric treatment of proportionality.) In the Birkhoff scheme you do not start from scratch; you need deal only with the transition from algebra to geometry. This head start vastly reduces the number of pedagogic compromises that you need to make with the logic of the subject, to get a course that moves at a proper speed and is intelligible to the student.

The reader is warned that this topic is—or recently was—highly controversial. I am not qualified to summarize the opposing views, because I have not been able to understand them. Meanwhile, once the SMSG had written a book on metric geometry, the idea spread with rapidity. The UICSM, which had tried three other schemes during the preceding few years, and professed dissatisfaction with all three, is now trying the metric scheme. Presumably because the tenth is the most controversial of the high school grades, the SMSG set up, last year, a new writing group to produce an alternative geometry book. The new book includes important innovations but retains the metric scheme.

It remains to discuss the pedagogic ideas behind the first (and presumably the second) SMSG geometry book. In connection with algebra, we have mentioned disagreements on the extent to which the learning process should be verbalized. It is clear, however, that the ability to verbalize must be, at some point, an objective in itself. The alternative is mathematical illiteracy. Here by a mathematical illiterate we mean a person who can neither read mathematics nor write it. The phenomenon is not rare: a very large number of mathematics students make no attempt to read their textbooks; they rely on classroom discussions to prepare them to do homework, and beg for assurances that on written examinations they "will not be held responsible for the theory."

To avoid this sort of thing is no easy job. The mathematical theory must be simple enough that an explicit formulation of it is intelligible to an immature student. (This was one reason for the choice of the metric theory.) The verbalizations must be introduced by intuitive discussions that indicate what they are driving at. (In fact, the process of transition from intuitive ideas to exact formulations is one of the things we need to teach.) The formulations must be valid. (All too often, authors write definitions so loosely and inaccurately that students learn by experience not to waste attention on them.) Finally, the verbalizations must be put to work; if they are not used, they are not learned and are not worth learning. For example, it is useless to say, as Euclid says, that "a line is length without breadth." At no point are we going to infer anything about lines from this supposed definition. In fact, the only real purpose of Euclid's first page of definitions is to suggest—falsely, of course—that all the terms used in geometry are defined.

Obviously the present article is not a contribution to scientific literature. It is, rather, an attempt to describe an enterprise; and any valid description of the enterprise in question must be full of the sort of subjective judgments that we have been discussing. The point is that the design of new mathematics programs has not been guided by scientific research in any commonly understood sense of the term. The only science involved has been mathematics itself, and pedagogy has appeared as a practical art, learned by experience. A study is now being made of the operation of the SMSG programs, from the viewpoint of cognitive psychology. During the first year in which they were tried, standard achievement tests were given before and after. These have not been published. Roughly speaking, they indicated that the SMSG students did approximately as well, on tests based on traditional courses, as they would have done if they had taken the traditional courses. Valuation by traditional tests is the handicap that new programs are expected to accept and overcome; and if the shift in objectives and emphasis is great—as it was in these cases—the handicap is correspondingly large.

All the new programs are in process of growth, and most bibliographic references would soon be out of date. It seems better, therefore, to refer the reader to sources of current information on the publications of the SMSG and the UICSM. The UICSM textbooks are published by the University of Illinois Press, Urbana, Illinois. Those of the SMSG are published by the Yale University Press, New Haven, Connecticut. Lists of current SMSG books are given in its *Newsletter;* requests for this should be addressed to SMSG, Stanford University, Stanford, California. We have already mentioned the forthcoming book of the SMSG (3). The best source on the spirit of the UICSM program is Max Beberman's Inglis Lecture at Harvard (6).

The task of surveying this literature, and judging its merits, involves a number of hazards, some of which may not be obvious. Some of these hazards are as follows:

Innovations in the treatment of mathematics, or in the

language used to explain it, are usually confusing to a reader who is accustomed to something else. From this it does not follow that the innovations are harder for the student; for the student, both the subject matter and the language would be new in any case.

Much of the current theorizing on mathematical pedagogy is intellectually subtle and may often seem obscure. It does not follow that the resulting textbooks are equally subtle or equally obscure to the student. The whole purpose of hard thinking about pedagogy is to make the student's work simpler and easier, and this purpose is often achieved.

The new books seldom explain the reasons behind the methods that they use. (Such explanations belong in the teachers' manuals. To put them into the text usually represents a lapse from intellectual discipline.) Often the reasons are far from obvious. For these reasons, many passages in the new books, considered in isolation, may seem at first to be actually silly. Sometimes, no doubt, they are; to err is human. But most of the time, they are not.

The new books try very hard to convey mathematical concepts. From this it should not be inferred that they are addressed solely to the superior student. In fact, nearly all of them are intended for the same students who now study the corresponding conventional courses. There is even some fragmentary evidence which suggests that the advantages of the new courses are greater for mediocre students than for brilliant ones. If this turns out to be true, we should not be surprised. It is the mediocre students who need the most help in grasping concepts; the brilliant students are more likely to figure things out for themselves.

A brief and casual inspection of the new books may convey the impression that they neglect the traditional material, including the material useful in science, and replace it by "modern" mathematics which is of interest only to research mathematicians. This is not true. Some of the changes are curricular, but most of them are merely changes in style of treatment. All the new programs lead to analytic geometry and calculus, in the usual four years. At the laboratory school at the University of Illinois, the students begin algebra in the eighth grade. With this head start, they take a twelfth-grade course that covers more than half of the calculus textbook now being used at Massachusetts Institute of Technology.

These possibilities for misunderstanding are due basically to the fact that the ideas underlying the new programs are not intellectually trivial. They are the results of long, hard work, at both mathematics and teaching. I cannot believe that anybody has found the final answer to any of our problems; I cannot even believe that such final answers exist. But the progress made in the past few years forms the basis of a long overdue revolution in mathematical education, and I am convinced that even better work is soon to come.

REFERENCES

1. *Introductory Probability and Statistical Inference.* New York: College Entrance Examination Board, 1959. (Generally known as the Gray Book.)

2. Frederick Mosteller, Robert E. K. Rourke, and George B. Thomas, Jr. *Probability: A First Course.* Reading, Massachusetts: Addison-Wesley Publishing Company, Inc., 1961.

3. This book will be published by the School Mathematics Study Group. Title and date of publication not yet known.

4. G. D. Birkhoff and Ralph Beatley. *Basic Geometry.* New York, New York: Chelsea Publishing Company, 1958.

5. Charles F. Brumfiel, Robert E. Eicholz, and Merrill E. Shanks. *Geometry.* Reading, Massachusetts: Addison-Wesley Publishing Company, Inc., 1960.

6. Max Beberman. *An Emerging Program of Secondary School Mathematics.* Cambridge, Massachusetts: Harvard University Press, 1958.

Forces Redirecting Science Teaching

RALPH W. TYLER

Director, Center for Advanced Study in the Behavioral Sciences, Stanford, California

Science teaching has taken on new life and vigor. More developments are under way in this field than in any other school subject. The National Science Foundation has spent or committed thirty million dollars to support the work of committees of scientists and teachers in developing modern courses for the high school and is beginning to work out appropriate content for the elementary school. The federal government has spent or committed more than two hundred million dollars to support summer institutes where science teachers can increase their training in modern science. Under the National Defense Education Act, federal funds are available to states on a matching basis, to build and modernize high school science laboratories.

The public interest in science is not only providing more moral and financial support for the efforts to improve science teaching but the public attention and concern have profoundly influenced the career choices of the ablest of high school students. Ten years ago, the most popular career choice of the ablest students was the field of medicine. At that time the American medical colleges had seven times the number of qualified applicants than they had room to admit. Last year, there were only about one and three-fourths as many qualified applicants as could be admitted. A number of the less well-known medical colleges had fewer qualified applicants than the available places. This drop in popularity of medicine among the ablest students has been paralleled by a great increase in the popularity of science. Among the National Merit Scholarship winners last year, physics and mathematics were by far the more frequent choices.

TECHNOLOGICAL REVOLUTION

The current increased interest and concern for science is commonly interpreted as the American reaction to Russian scientific achievements, and, no doubt, this is a factor. But an examination of the figures on employment and on career choices of high school and college graduates over the past fifty years makes clear that development of and interest in science and technology have been growing for a long time as a natural result of the technological revolution. Fifty years ago, scientists and engineers represented one-third of one per cent of the labor force of America. According to the 1960 census, scientists and engineers represented three per cent of the labor force. In fifty years, the proportion of people working in these fields has increased nearly tenfold. This illustrates the changing character of our economy and our society. Science, technology, and education are now the chief means by which modern industrial societies increase productivity, reduce death and illness, and provide wider opportunities for goods and services. Public recognition of this has greatly influenced science teaching.

A second major influence on science teaching is the closer working relationship between the university and research scientist and the teacher in the schools. Only a few years ago, the scientist had no first-hand contact with science teachers in the schools, and no understanding of the problems faced in teaching science to the "children of all the people." Frequently scientists blamed the teaching of science in the schools for the alleged inadequacy of college and university students, but they made no effort to help develop better courses and instructional materials, or to aid the teacher in getting a more adequate education in the sciences. In fact, most university scientists advised their good students not to go into science teaching.

The growing public concern with science led to a more comprehensive and objective appraisal of the condition of science in the schools. The shortage of qualified science teachers and the lack of authentic, up-to-date books and other instructional materials were emphasized in this survey and, in increasing numbers, highly competent scientists are responding to the need and the opportunity. The committees supported by the National Science Foundation working on new courses and teaching materials for the schools include topflight scientists as well as teachers. Summer institutes and academic year institutes for the further training of science teachers are involving an increased number of able scientists. And, although slowly, scientists are recognizing the need to encourage competent science students in the universities to go into school teaching rather than to urge them to establish careers in the research centers. This closer working relationship is redirecting science teaching by getting the best thinking of scientists into the development of the school program. The result is an expansion of the horizons of many science teachers regarding the nature of science, the kinds of educational objectives to which science can contribute, and the possibilities in new instructional materials. This relationship is also providing a new sense of confidence to the science teacher as he appreciates through this relationship his own unique and important contribution to the development of science in working with children and youth.

A third important influence on science teaching is the rapidly expanding explosion of knowledge. Although science is always advancing, the common view from 1900 to 1950 was that the basic principles and important facts of physics, chemistry, and biology had been discovered and were central to all further elaborations of these subjects. In the schools, children would learn these basic principles and important facts and they would be properly grounded in science no matter how much more research might uncover. Except for the addition from year to year of new illustrations of the applications of science, the textbook content of these subjects barely changed from 1910 to 1950. No wonder that most students and many of the teachers thought the learning of science was the memorization of the basic principles and the important facts. But new developments in science have sharply shaken this view.

The "explosion of science" is not just adding more and more details to a stable basic outline. Scientific inquiry is continually examining basic definitions, assumptions, principles, and relationships; and the results of scientific research frequently require a reconstruction of the basic ideas as well as the addition of details. If students are to understand science and contribute to its intellectual development, they need to understand it as a process of continuing inquiry and reconstruction of knowledge. As this becomes recognized by science teachers, it results in considerable influence upon their work. A science course becomes an introduction in "learning how to learn" science, an effort to start the student on a lifelong endeavor to make sense out of his experiences with the material world and the observations made of natural phenomena, as well as environment.

A fourth kind of influence which is redirecting science teaching is the increased understanding on the part of science teachers of the wide range of pupils in school—range in general and special abilities, range in interests and purposes, and range in home and community backgrounds and experiences. When science was thought to be of primary significance only to those planning to be scientists or engineers, the really basic concepts and methods of science could be developed in courses elected by senior high school students who were interested in science and well prepared to cope with the subject. Now science is conceived more broadly both as an intellectual discipline and as a means of understanding modern society, its achievements and its problems. As such, science is essential not only for those preparing for careers in science and technology but also for all citizens. Faced with this need, science teachers are realizing that the varied nature of the whole range of elementary and secondary school pupils poses problems for science teaching which have not yet been solved.

Currently, the effect of these four major forces is to bring into focus several important and difficult problems which must be solved if science teaching is to achieve its goal and carry out the responsibilities associated with this task.

TEACHING SCIENCE AS INQUIRY

There is the general problem in all science courses of ably teaching science so that it is an "introduction to learning how to learn" rather than teaching it as a collection of today's answers to questions which will be answered differently tomorrow. The tradition of teaching and learning in most school subjects is that of memorizing important facts. To change this tradition involves developing a new attitude on the part of students and teachers so that learning becomes an experience in inquiry. It must become a process in knowing how to raise questions which are relevant to science and how to carry on investigations of these questions; it must include investigations which keep broadening and deepening the student's understanding of the questions themselves and also considerations that need to be taken into account and finally the adequacy and incompleteness of possible answers. To teach science in these terms requires a change in the notion of what has to be covered, a change in the kinds of learning experiences provided, a change in instructional materials used, a change in the tests, examinations, and other evaluation procedures. This is a problem on which science teachers and educators will need to work for a long period.

A more particular problem for science teachers to solve is to provide adequate depth in the learning experiences and sufficient variety to care for individual differences in the various courses offered for the competent student who has a major interest in science. The new course-content projects supported by the National Science Foundation are developing useful materials and ideas to meet this problem.

A second particular problem is in teaching competent students whose major interests are elsewhere. Many of these boys and girls consider science as irrelevant to their purposes and as having little connection with their own lives. The teaching problem is to aid these students to perceive science as an area which is vital in their own lives and which involves intellectual efforts which are rewarding in themselves.

A third particular problem is probably the most difficult of all. It is the problem of reaching the student with more limited scholastic aptitude who has had little or no background in systematic thinking and problem solving. In the past, courses have been provided for such students which did not involve inquiry, but emphasized descriptions of common and interesting applications of technology; for example, describing the operation of an electric refrigerator. Sketchy memorization was the kind of learning expected. These students rarely gained any notion of what science really is and no insight into science as an intellectual enterprise. Their notions of the marvels of science were more like beliefs in magic than in science. This approach did not prepare them to cope with the modern scientific world as citizens. Thinking, inquiry, and exercise of intelligence are possible for most if not all children and youth, but the development of intellectual potential for children with limited and inhibiting experiences in their homes and community environments requires new approaches, new materials, and new skills on the part of teachers. This is one of the important unsolved problems needing attention.

CONCLUSION

Can we expect that these difficult teaching problems can be effectively attacked? There are three kinds of resources on which science teachers may draw to counter these problems. The first of these is a more adequate knowledge of how learning takes place. Recent studies of the acquisition by children and youth of more complex mental processes provide suggestive guide lines for improved learning and teaching. The second is the number of rapidly developing devices for aiding teaching and learning; for example, new cartridge motion picture projectors for quick presentation of phenomena difficult to observe; simple laboratory equipment which can be used at home; teaching machines and programed instructional materials which permit progress in learning at one's own rate; new printing processes which make economically feasible an individual science library; team teaching which can bring a range of teaching talents to bear on each student; co-operative work experience to extend the student's perception of meaningful science activities; and educational television which can bring additional teachers, demonstrations, etc., into the classroom or the home. Some of these devices are already being adopted and adapted by science teachers who are attacking difficult problems of teaching and learning.

To my mind, however, the one most important resource we have in improving science teaching and in solving the serious problems of this age is the science teacher. It is my opinion that we shall move forward in developing a comprehensive program of science instruction which is effective in meeting the present task because of the degree of intelligence, ingenuity, and concern among the science teachers of America.

The Physical Science Study Committee

GILBERT C. FINLAY
Professor of Education,
University of Illinois

The Physical Science Study Committee was formed in 1956 as a group of university and secondary school physics teachers working to develop an improved introductory physics course. The committee is developing interrelated teaching materials for physics in the secondary school. Materials intended for direct instructional use include a textbook, laboratory apparatus and a laboratory guidebook for students, motion picture films, and a set of ten achievement tests. Supporting materials include a four-volume teacher's guide and resource book, and a series of paperback books that provide authoritative science literature for students and adults.

To help teachers who are considering the use of these materials, the committee has encouraged the development of instructional programs that enable teachers to study the new course in detail.

For its various activities, the committee organized teams of university and secondary school physics teachers. These teams blended teaching experience at several levels with deep insight into the nature and meaning of physics. The materials developed by these teams were used in classes and subjected to close scrutiny by the teachers who used them and by the committee's staff observers. The course materials were tried, evaluated, and revised for three years before they were released for general use in the fall of 1960.

The committee, in the course of its work, thought it wise to establish a permanent organization to provide for revision and related development. A nonprofit corporation, Educational Services Incorporated, was formed. This corporation now administers the program of the Physical Science Study Committee.

Science is becoming an increasingly consequential factor in the affairs of man. There are the practical goods: the hand-in-hand advance of science and technology continuously increases human potential for producing, transporting, communicating, healing. The attendant problems of social control and adaptation are pervasive and complex. In business, legislation, and statesmanship, the scientist increasingly is called upon to help unravel the social and economic implications of science. But beyond its technological goods and meanings, science as a humanistic study stands on its own terms as a dynamically stable system with its own ends and procedural styles. As a form of human expression, it is one of the triumphs of the intellect. It lends perspective and direction to other aspects of life. It is a system one can ill afford to ignore if one is to become a whole man in a world of whole men.

Physics, as a parent discipline, stands close to the center of our scientific milieu. What instruction in physics is appropriate for secondary school students in the mid-twentieth century? The work of the Physical Science Study Committee is an attempt to answer this question operationally.

As an initial target, the committee chose to design a new course to fit into the current pattern of school curriculums. Physics is usually offered as a separate, elective subject for students in the eleventh or twelfth grade. In terms of prior measures of ability, these students are drawn mostly from the upper half of their classes, with the distribution of their abilities skewed toward the top levels. Some of these students will follow careers in science or science-related fields, and further work in science will be a part of their higher education. However, the careers of many secondary school physics students will be in fields other than science, and they will do no further formal work in physics. The committee judged that the needs of both groups of students could be served with a single course.

The committee chose to plan a course dealing with physics as an explanatory system, a system that extends from the domain inside the atom to the distant galaxies. The course tells a unified story—one in which the successive topics are chosen and developed to lead toward an atomic picture of matter, its motions and interrelations. The aim was to present a view of physics that would bring a student close to the nature of modern physics and to the nature of physical inquiry. Finally, the committee sought to transmit the human character of the story of physics, not simply an up-to-date codification of the findings. The student should see physics as an unfinished and continuing activity. He should experience something of the satisfaction and challenge felt by the scientist when he reaches vantage points from which he can contemplate both charted and uncharted vistas.

Achieving these aims in a one-year course meant that coverage of the field of physics had to be sharply restricted in favor of a deeper development of ideas that are central to a comprehension of the fundamentals of contemporary physical thought. This deeper development meant carrying key concepts to higher levels than have been ordinarily reached in secondary school courses. Deeper development also meant a more extensive exploration of the substructure of experiment and thought that underlies the basic physical principles.

The student is expected to be an active participant in this course. The textbook, laboratory experiments, and films were developed in a way that reflects this expectation. The course materials do not assert the ideas of physics, then illustrate their utility by exemplifying them in problems and in laboratory exercises. Instead, the student is expected to wrestle with a line (or with converging lines) of inquiry, including his own laboratory investigations, that leads to basic ideas. The power of the fundamental ideas is brought out partially in the student's work on carefully chosen end-of-chapter problems, but more important, the intellectual thrust of the basic ideas is brought out sequentially through using those which are introduced early to illuminate other ideas in a chain that comprises an introductory view of the structure of physics.

As one examines the changes that have occurred in secondary school physics courses during the past few generations, one is likely to get the feeling that modern technology has found its way into the courses almost to the exclusion of modern physics. Such modern physics as has been worked into many courses is often limited to statements of some of the conclusions. There is little other choice without a preceding development of such subjects as dynamics, wave behavior, and fundamental electricity, that is sufficiently penetrating to permit seeing modern physics as a logical synthesis of ideas emerging from a related structure of experiment, principle, and theory.

No one-year course can give an adequate account of both an expanding physics and the related technology. Planning a course that concentrates on either of these subjects still poses a selection problem of large proportions. As the magnitude of what might be learned grows rapidly, it becomes increasingly clear that the school at any given level, indeed in its entirety, can do little more than provide a base for further learning. The development of a mind is never ending. The function of the school is to provide a fertile start—such a start that the end of formal schooling does not mark the end of further learning.

The central problem is to transmit those ideas and styles of thought that have the broadest applicability, the greatest power for further thought and activity. To this end, the Physical Science Study Committee judged it wise to shift the emphasis in secondary school physics away from technology toward a deeper exploration of the basic ideas of physics and the nature of inquiries that can lead to these ideas. This choice was based on the premise that, for the future scientist as well as for the non-scientist, an introductory course that provides a grasp of the central ideas of physics and the kind of thought that lies behind them is more useful and rewarding than a course that emphasizes a somewhat more ephemeral technology. Technological applications have not been eliminated from the course. But they have been cut back sharply from the role they play in many secondary school courses. While the course was not specifically developed with college preparation in mind, the course is regarded as providing a sound base for further work in physics.

In this course, experiments—whether they are performed by the student, analyzed in the textbook, or shown on film—are not used simply to confirm an earlier assertion. The laboratory experiments are designed to supply firm rooting for the growth of ideas by providing direct, nonverbal contact with relevant data. Hence, the most common use of laboratory experiments is to introduce a topic or to contribute to the early stages of its development. The student's laboratory guidebook keeps specific instructions to a minimum, directing the student's attention to key points by raising questions. The student is responsible for thinking out the nature and the meaning of what he is to do. The purposes of the experiments vary. Some are qualitative and give general familiarity and introductory experience with a set of phenomena. Many experiments are quantitative but differ extensively in the degree of experimental accuracy that is sought. Students should understand that prior knowledge and experimental purpose influence the precision required to secure new knowledge. Experimentation is a great deal more than establishing the third decimal place. In all cases, students are encouraged to establish or approximate their experimental error.

Clearly a student can have direct laboratory experience with only some aspects of physics. Careful selection of experimental activities can advance the student's understanding of the more important physical ideas. Moreover, presenting these activities in the spirit of experiments rather than as exercises should enhance the student's ability to analyze and appreciate experiments that he reads about or sees on film. Still further, the emphasis in the course on experiment and experimental style is meant to foster insight into the role of experiment in the generation and refinement of physical ideas. While some demonstrations are suggested, more emphasis is placed on experiments performed by students. The apparatus and the laboratory guidebook provide for more than fifty experiments, many of which include optional extensions to provide for variability among students and classes.

A great deal of what might ordinarily be called demonstration is provided by the films produced by the committee. Basically, the films are built around experiments. Films are used to bring to the classroom certain key experiments and a range of experiments that are likely to be too difficult, too time consuming, or too costly for students to perform or for teachers to demonstrate. For many experiments, films can bring the purposes, techniques, data, and analysis more directly within the students' purview than any other approach can. The films are planned with attention to the general aims of the course and to the particular choices that have been made in the development of related ideas in the students' laboratory and in the textbook. Because the films articulate closely with these resources and because most of the films assume that the viewer is familiar with earlier parts of the course, the scheduling of the films is a matter of consequence. The films are intended as take-off points for teachers and students. They are not intended to replace a teacher. As of October, 1961, forty-four films were available, and sixteen more were being completed.

Some films—such as those on the Millikan experiment, the Rutherford atom, and the Franck-Hertz experiment—are concerned primarily with the presentation and the interpretation of a complex experiment. Other films are more general in purpose and may use a dozen or more experiments or models to develop a set of related ideas. Such films are intended to help integrate and summarize a field of study. Films on crystals, on the relation between mechanical and thermal energy, and on frames of reference are examples. Finally, a few films are intended as introductions to major areas of study. Such films are meant to give the viewer perspective by taking stock of the array of phenomena that require explanation and by suggesting some of the central questions.

The films do not glitter. There is no background music,

and there are no elaborate stage settings. They are frankly teaching films. It should go without saying that the experiments presented are scrupulously honest. The films are not impersonal, neither are they stylized in a personal sense. They present a number of real scientists, speaking in their individual ways to students, directing their attention to key points. In this quiet way, the films bring students into closer contact with a group of scientists as persons.

As supplementary sources of authoritative, scientific information, the committee is developing a series of paperback books. These books are appearing as the "Science Study Series." Some deal with individual topics in science or technology. Some are biographical, some historical. As of October, 1961, twenty books had been published in the series. More than thirty were in preparation, and others were planned. An interesting side light on the pedagogical application of these books is the occasional use of some of the foreign-language translations of the series as reading material for science-oriented students in language classes.

The content of the course of the Physical Science Study Committee has been described in somewhat greater detail in other sources (1, 2, 3). The course is divided into four parts. Part I is an introduction to the principal actor in the physical drama—matter—and its setting, time and space. The course begins with a consideration of the dimensions of time and space and how they are sensed. Through laboratory work the student sees how his senses can be extended by instrumentation and begins to develop a perception of the role, nature, and limitations of measurement. This perception is extended through films that go beyond the usual facilities for measurement available in school laboratories. Familiarity with techniques of defining intervals of space and time leads to a study of motion through space in the course of time. The student learns the relation between distance, velocity, and acceleration and how to move from one to another through graphical differentiation and integration. The use of vectors to represent these quantities completes this introductory view of the descriptive tools of physics. The course then turns to an introduction to matter, the substance of the universe. Here, the ideas of mass and conservation of mass are considered. The student examines experimental evidence for the existence and the size of atoms. In the laboratory he establishes an upper limit for the size of a molecule and sees how extensions of his experiment can lead to determining the size of an atom. The combination of atoms in molecules is studied, and the ideas of atomicity are extended through a consideration of the arrangement of atoms in solids (crystals) and in gases. A beginning on the molecular interpretation of a gas makes it possible to deal specifically with the idea of a physical model.

In Part II the student begins the process of observation of, and abstraction from, a family of physical phenomena; in this case, light. The natural development of the subject leads to an examination of a particle theory of light. This section of the course illustrates how models are abstracted from experimental observation, how they illuminate further investigation, and how they are established, modified, or rejected. Study shows that a simple particle model does not fit the behavior of light, and the course turns to another model, waves. Extensive laboratory experience with waves—first in one dimension on ropes and springs, then in two dimensions on the surface of water—shows similarities between wave behavior and light. A detailed study of interference establishes the wave nature of light.

Part III returns to motion, this time from a dynamical point of view. Again depending heavily upon laboratory work, and extensively reinforced with films, the course moves through the relation between force and motion, the story of the discovery of universal gravitation, and the conservation of momentum and energy. The generality of the conservation laws is stressed. The use of the conservation laws in situations where detailed observation of the motion is not possible (as in the molecular turmoil in gases) and emphasis on two-body interactions lay groundwork for exploring the atom in Part IV.

The atomistic character of matter is introduced in Part I and carried further in the kinetic theory of gases in Part III. Part IV develops the nature of electrical forces and energy; begins to bind together dynamics, electricity, and waves in a consideration of electromagnetic radiation; and returns with all these tools to an exploration of the structure of matter, atoms. Analysis of scattering experiments establishes a simple Rutherford model. Some of the inadequacies of this model are pointed out. The particle-wave nature of both light and matter is shown. Experiment discloses the internal energy states in atoms. The energy levels are explained in terms of standing wave patterns, and the course comes to a close with a quantum mechanical view in which both wave and particle characteristics are essential to an understanding of the structure of matter. In this part of the course, because of the difficulty of many of the relevant experiments, films carry a large share of the burden of presenting experimental evidence.

The logical unity of physics has been emphasized in this course. As an alternative to covering the various fields of physics at the same level, the course employs earlier material to clarify that which follows. For example, ideas about waves and particles recur, each time to be carried further in a higher synthesis of ideas. This characteristic plus the exploration of concepts that are clearly unfinished, the tightly related student laboratory, the investigative approach in the films and the frequent analysis of experiments in the text all contribute to a perception of physics as a continuing search for order in a picture of the universe. This coherent, searching character of man's approach to building an explanatory structure of the physical world is one of the course's principal aims and chief pedagogical characteristics [1: 292].

The Physical Science Study Committee had its beginning early in 1956 in exploratory discussions, held first at the Massachusetts Institute of Technology and later at other centers. These discussions, led by Jerrold R. Zacharias of the Massachusetts Institute of Technology, established the desirability of rethinking the secondary school physics program and made it clear that an adequate number of able secondary school and university physics teachers would be willing to join in such an effort. In November, 1956, an initial grant from the National Science Foundation marked the official beginning of the project. The National Science Foundation has provided the principal financial support. The Ford Foundation and the Alfred P. Sloan Foundation have contributed to the support of the program.

By the time of the initial grant, informal groups had been established at Cambridge, Massachusetts; the Bell Laboratories in New York; the California Institute of Technology; Cornell University; and the University of Illinois. Several of these groups developed tentative outlines for a new physics course. A meeting of most of the people who had participated in these groups, together with other interested individuals, was held in December, 1956 (4). The proposals of the several groups were presented and discussed. General agreement was reached on a broad outline and on the major pedagogical characteristics of the course. Following the December meeting, several of the centers began to prepare detailed outlines and preliminary drafts for a work conference to be held during the summer of 1957 at the Massachusetts Institute of Technology.

About fifty people participated in the 1957 summer work session. Most of this group were high school and university physics teachers. In addition, there were specialists in such fields as testing, film-making, educational administration, and editorial production. Work was begun on all parts of the project: textbook, laboratory experiments, films, tests, teachers' guides, the "Science Study Series," and instructional programs for teachers. The textbook and the laboratory programs were given priority so that enough material would be ready by the end of the summer to make it possible to use a preliminary version of the course in a few schools during the following year. Early use of the course in schools permitted an almost immediate application of classroom feedback to the problems of revising existing materials and helping to shape materials yet to be developed.

During the 1957–58 school year, eight teachers used preliminary versions of the course with about three hundred students. These teachers had participated in the committee's summer project, and they and their schools were in a position to work closely with other members of the committee in evaluating their teaching experience. During that first year, it was possible to supply teachers with printed versions of Parts I and II of the course, mimeographed copies of Part III, and the materials from which preliminary designs of the laboratory apparatus could be built. Formal materials for Part IV of the course were not available that year. Because of the newness and the tentativeness of the materials, few classes moved fast enough that year to get into Part IV. For those that did, the teachers improvised from their knowledge of the plans for Part IV.

This first year of experience in teaching the course was extremely fruitful. Because the number of classes was small, the committee's staff was able to work intensively with the teachers. In some cases modifications of approach were discussed and tried out on the spot. The over-all evaluation was highly favorable. Teachers and students found the course stimulating and were enthusiastic. The close relation between the laboratory and the textbook and the premium on student initiative in the laboratory were well received. The results of the preliminary achievement tests used that year indicated that students attained the desired levels. The desirability of revising the textbook and the laboratory program was pin-

pointed at various places in Parts I and III. Part II was judged
as markedly successful. In that part of the course, teachers
found that the mutual reinforcement of the textbook and the
laboratory program enabled them to bring students to a deep
understanding of advanced ideas on wave behavior. The
year's experience also suggested the desirability of a change
in the way in which the committee had expected schools to
acquire laboratory apparatus. Originally the committee hoped
that the use of simple designs of apparatus to concentrate on
fundamentals would not only clarify the subject but make it
possible for schools to acquire most of the necessary laboratory material locally with construction to be done by students.
While the local acquisition of materials and local construction
of apparatus were shown to be possible and instructive, shop-
ping and construction time was costly. This excessive time
burden on students and teachers was confirmed in the following year, and the committee turned to the development of
easily assembled kits of pre-formed apparatus.

During the summer of 1958, five universities offered institutes on the course. The institutes were from six to eight
weeks in duration. These institutes were organized under the
National Science Foundation's regular program of support to
institutes for teachers of science and mathematics. The institutes enrolled a few more than three hundred teachers. As a
part of the experimental development of the course, the preliminary course materials were supplied without cost to any
of these teachers who wished to use them during the following
year, 1958–59. The course was used by about 270 teachers
and 11,000 students.

The course materials available for that school year were
not complete, but represented a considerable advance over
the year before. The preliminary textbook included a partially
revised version of Part I, and the textbook extended through
the first half of Part IV. The committee was able to supply
preliminary laboratory guidebooks and apparatus for Parts I,
II, and III and a partial laboratory program and apparatus
for Part IV. A preliminary edition of the teacher's guidebook
was distributed for all portions of the course except the latter
half of Part IV. A complete set of ten achievement tests was
used. Although a number of films had been completed during
the year, only a few were available for use in the schools at
the most appropriate times.

The feedback from the larger number of schools benefited
all parts of the program. Intensive feedback relations were

maintained with a few schools. From the rest, information was derived from periodic reports, questionnaires, and regional meetings. Results from the administration of the series of achievement tests also contributed helpful information. In one school, a few students who had gone through the first three parts of the course in the previous year studied Part IV in the fall. This experience contributed several key ideas to the further development that winter of Part IV, which was used by a large number of students in the spring.

During the summer of 1959, about seven hundred teachers studied the course in fifteen institutes. For the 1959–60 school year, the course materials were provided at cost to schools that wished to use them and whose teachers had already taught the course or had studied in one of the institutes. That year about 560 teachers used the course with 22,500 students. Some of the teachers who had taught the course during the year before had moved to administrative positions, enrolled in graduate study, or had otherwise withdrawn (in many cases temporarily) from physics teaching. Of those who continued to teach physics, 96 per cent elected to continue with the PSSC course.

Except for the films (about thirty were available for use at the appropriate showing times), a complete set of preliminary materials was on hand. Feedback arrangements were the same as for the 1958–59 school year. The information gleaned from the use of the course in earlier years had already been used as starting points for some revisions of the textbook and the laboratory experiments, and these were tried out and studied. During the 1959–60 school year, the committee's major effort was directed to a complete revision of all printed materials and the design changes appropriate to the commercial production of kits of laboratory apparatus. By the fall of 1960 the textbook, laboratory guidebook, apparatus, tests, films, and teacher's guidebook had been turned over to commercial suppliers and were available generally.

The institute programs have continued to provide opportunity for teachers to study the course in detail. During 1960–61, the course was used by about 1,100 teachers with 44,000 students. As of October, 1961, a conservative approximation of the number using the course in 1961–62 was 1,800 teachers and 72,000 students.

Evaluation of the course has several aspects. The committee's own evaluations are directed toward the improvement of the course, not comparisons with other courses. The course differs sharply from most secondary school physics courses both in selection of content and in style of development. Comparison with other courses is not a matter of evaluating the relative merit of different methods of teaching toward the same objectives. Rather, such a comparison involves questions as to the choice of the objectives themselves. Close scrutiny of the courses is enough to confirm this fundamental difference. Further confirmation comes from the few instances in which standard examinations have been given to PSSC students and PSSC examinations have been given to students in standard courses. The results show that the students have studied different courses. The sharp difference between the PSSC course and other courses has been recognized by the College Entrance Examination Board, which has provided separate examinations in physics for PSSC and non-PSSC students. Certainly it is possible to design an examination on which matched groups of PSSC students and students from other physics courses would achieve equivalent score distributions. This procedure would hardly provide a comparison. It would prove only that such an examination can be prepared. Comparative evaluation requires common objectives—common with reference to fundamentals of substance and intellectual style.

In terms of its own objectives, the committee judges that its present course is successful in the sense that it provides a context for teachers and students through which students have reached the desired goals. Evidence comes from several sources. Performance on the PSSC achievement tests speaks of the students' understanding of content and their power to handle ideas, to apply them broadly. In preparing the achievement tests, the level of difficulty was set so that an average performance of answering half the questions correctly would be regarded as satisfactory achievement. This goal was attained. On the qualitative side, the preponderant testimony of teachers and students who have used the course indicates that it sharply stimulates the development of more powerful styles of inquiry.

The difficulty of the course and its adaptability to students of varying abilities have been the subject of a great deal of discussion by those who have used and/or studied the course and by some who have not. The results of the analysis of achievement test performance by students from various levels of academic aptitude, as measured by conventional aptitude tests, clearly suggest that success in handling the ideas of the

PSSC course is not limited to a narrow band of what, by traditional measures, might be called high-aptitude students. The testimony of a majority of the teachers who have used the course supports this view. Most teachers who have used the course feel that it is appropriate for the range of student abilities that typically has been enrolled in physics. Some teachers make the point that, for the less facile student, an exposition based on experiment rather than assertion is especially helpful. Of the teachers who have used the course, a clear minority feel that the course is too difficult for average students and prefer to restrict the use of the course to high-ability students. On the difficulty of the course, the committee is inclined to agree with the student who wrote that "the course is not for those who have difficulty tying their shoelaces." The course was intended to provide a challenging experience. Students and teachers say that it does. Most of them also say that it is highly rewarding. The committee feels that the course is close to the intended mark. Certainly other course structures could be developed that would provide a satisfactory secondary school physics course. The present course is simply a stage in the development of one satisfactory course. Indeed, through Educational Services Incorporated, the committee expects to give continuing attention to the improvement of secondary school physics.

The committee fell a bit short of reaching its objective of providing a one-year course. The course as it stands was prepared so that teachers could omit several sections without seriously undermining the material that follows. These are, however, omissions that most teachers will make only with regret. Without cutting, many teachers feel that the course should extend for more than a year. This problem is being met in various ways. Some teachers are making the possible cuts. Some schools are lengthening the time given to physics by teaching it for more than two semesters or by giving it more class time during the year. Some schools are trying early parts of the course in earlier science courses. The development of improved science courses at lower levels will be one of the factors influencing revision of the current PSSC course.

The committee has a number of ongoing projects. To get information on what and when revision should occur, study of the use of the course continues. In this connection, it is now apparent that improvements in laboratory experiments for Part IV will be sought. The "Science Study Series" is being extended at the rate of nearly a book each month. The film studio of Educational Services Incorporated is continuing its work on the series of films that are a part of the course.

Another current activity is the preparation of a second battery of achievement tests to augment the existing series. In the development of these new tests, techniques are being investigated that are expected to extend the information that can be obtained on the nature as well as the over-all quality of student performance.

In the general area of evaluation, other studies are planned. While the course was not planned specifically as preparation for college work in physics, it is natural to look at students' performance in college physics for one source of evidence on the effectiveness of the course. With growing numbers of students completing the PSSC course in secondary schools and continuing physics in college, it will be possible to look more definitively than before at their performance in college physics. To the extent that certain college courses and the PSSC course share common goals, such studies should be helpful in reflecting the contribution of the secondary school work. There have been a few preliminary studies of this kind, necessarily with small numbers of students. These studies indicated that PSSC students were at no disadvantage and in several respects (grades in one study; flexibility of thought and procedure, particularly in the laboratory, in another) were at an advantage.

Another kind of investigation that is being formulated uses the extensive element of design in the PSSC course (over-all story line with closely related textbook, laboratory, and films) to provide a context for a clinical study of learning over a year-long span. Among other things, this plan contemplates the development of nonverbal as well as verbal measures of performance.

The PSSC course was planned to fit a pattern in which physics is offered as a one-year course during the eleventh or twelfth grades. The achievement of adequate depth in a one-year course required the omission of many topics that logically could have been included and for which the course as it stands lays a powerful base. Some schools are able to offer a somewhat more advanced course either because of the time they give to physics, the ability of their students, the teaching of some of the earlier parts of the PSSC course in earlier grades, or a combination of these reasons. For such courses the committee is developing supplementary textbook material, laboratory experiments, and films for a series of advanced topics.

In the development in the PSSC course of an atomic model, some teachers have found a convenient structure for moving toward the integration of their work in chemistry and physics. Several schools have developed an integrated, two-year sequence in physical science using the PSSC course and a chemistry course, either one of their own devising or one of the chemistry courses recently developed with the support of the National Science Foundation. These activities are worth further effort and support.

The development, including trial and evaluation, of a course such as that of the Physical Science Study Committee naturally leads to suggestions on the kinds of educational experiences that might logically precede and follow such a course. A number of related activities, some of them partially stimulated by the work of the Physical Science Study Committee, have come into being. Some of those who shared in the PSSC project are now working with the Commission on College Physics, which is concerned with the improvement of physics teaching at the college level. Some are working in individual university centers on the improvement of the physics courses taught at their university. Some are turning to the problems of science instruction in elementary and junior high schools.

A great deal of interest in the work of the committee has been shown by science teachers and scientists from other countries. From the beginning, many foreign visitors have come to observe and discuss the project. This interest has led to the translation of the "Science Study Series" into other languages. Publication rights have been granted in eighteen countries. The books are now appearing in seven languages other than English. As the course materials neared completion, the interest of other countries in the use of the course (in some cases translation and use) quickened. By special arrangement, several dozen educators from abroad have attended some of the regular summer institutes of the Physical Science Study Committee. During the summer of 1961, staff members of the committee accepted three invitations to conduct intensive institute programs in other countries. These institutes enrolled secondary school teachers, university teachers, and, in some cases, science supervisors. Two of these institutes, in Israel and in New Zealand, were national in character. One, in England, enrolled teachers from half a dozen European countries. One outcome of these institutes was that the course will be used soon in several countries. Also, during the past summer, a planning conference was held in Japan to consider the problems of translation and use of the course in that country. At the invitation of the Australian College of Education, a staff member of the committee recently spent a week in Australia discussing the course with teachers who were convened for that purpose. Similar visits have been made to India and to some of the African and South American countries. These various explorations of the applicability of the course in other countries have been supported by the governments of New Zealand and Israel; the United Nations Educational, Scientific and Cultural Organization; the Carnegie Foundation; the Asia Foundation; the Organization for European Economic Cooperation; the Office of Information Services; and the Organization of American States.

The course of the Physical Science Study Committee has proved to be rewarding to a large number of teachers and students. Clearly, its applicability is not confined to highly selected students or to a particular culture. The several hundred men and women who have contributed directly to the course have derived a great deal of satisfaction from that work. The committee looks forward to continuous improvement of the course.

REFERENCES

1. Gilbert C. Finlay. "Secondary School Physics: The Physical Science Study Committee," *American Journal of Physics,* XXVIII (March, 1960), 286–93.

2. Physical Science Study Committee. *Physics,* pp. v–vi. Boston: D. C. Heath and Co., 1960.

3. Stephen White. "The Physical Science Study Committee (3) The Planning and Structure of the Course," *Contemporary Physics,* II (October, 1960), 39–54.

4. This conference was reported in "Physical Science Study Committee, A Planning Conference Report," *Physics Today,* X (March, 1957), 28–29.

Chemistry—An Experimental Science

J. A. CAMPBELL
Director, Chemical Education Material Study,
Harvey Mudd College

There are many ways to teach chemistry. Past courses have been enormously varied, present courses explore many methods, and future courses are being planned with considerable care in many localities. Yet widespread discontent exists among secondary school chemistry teachers, even those who are giving the most thought to planning improvements in their courses.

Some sources of discontent are apparent to the teacher, but many are not. Discontent may stem from a course full of contradictions of which the teacher is not overtly aware. Discontent may arise from historical approaches that terminate in a period remote to the student. The course may emphasize memorization of data rather than comprehension of concepts. The course may present a static picture of chemical systems rather than offer opportunities to discuss the dynamic processes that lead to chemical reactions. The laboratory work may require attempts, generally unsuccessful, on the part of the student to prove what he already knows, rather than provide opportunities to discover new ideas.

Examples of each of these sources of discontent are easy to come by. It is common to suggest that diffusion accounts for the rapid spread of odors throughout a room, and the explanation may be offered even after a conclusive demonstration with ammonia gas and hydrogen chloride that diffusion actually occurs at the rate of a meter an hour. Small wonder that the student is confused. Most historical developments of the atomic theory end with a description of a modified Bohr atom, which was first presented in 1913 and replaced some ten years later. Hardly a recent idea. Teachers are more likely to stress memorization of valence tables than an understanding of how these data originate or how they are tied in with the detailed structure of the atoms. Long hours are spent balancing chemical equations with no discussion of the mechanisms by which the reaction occurs or the nature of the processes by which one set of chemicals can be converted into another. Laboratory notebooks typically contain blank spaces to be filled in by the student. Generally, 50 to 90 per cent of the entries require only perusal of the textual material with no reference to laboratory work. In the laboratory the student is encouraged to get the "right answer" rather than to investigate a system with some freedom of experimental design. Under such circumstances discontent and frustration are difficult to avoid.

Clearly such deficiencies, whether or not they are overtly apparent to the instructor and the student, are intuitively felt by both, to the detriment of a satisfactory course. No single course can ever remove all the deficiencies or attack with equal success any large number of them. Consequently there is a widespread feeling that a national effort needs to be made to deal with as many of these problems as possible.

The Chemical Education Material Study, more commonly known as the CHEM Study, grew out of suggestions by a committee headed by A. B. Garrett, of Ohio State University. In 1960, Nobel laureate, Glenn T. Seaborg, now chairman of the Atomic Energy Commission but at that time chancellor of the University of California at Berkeley, obtained a grant from the National Science Foundation and assembled a staff to investigate what could be done to produce the most effective high school chemistry course possible.

The general history of the study and an outline of its major areas of operation have been presented in some detail in the newsletters published by the CHEM Study. In the summer of 1960 a group of well-known chemists assembled at Harvey Mudd College in Claremont. As a result of their labors, a textbook and a laboratory manual were prepared and tried in twenty-four high schools during the 1960–61 academic year. Some thirteen hundred students were involved in the tryouts. Close contact was maintained between the staff of the study and the teachers. The results of this trial were then given to a second writing group in the summer of 1961 at the University of California in Berkeley. This group produced a second trial edition of the textbook and the laboratory manual and a complete teacher's guide.

In both sessions the writing groups were composed of distinguished high school, university, and industrial chemists. It is a tribute to these groups that, though the initial textbooks and the laboratory manual were written in only six weeks, no insuperable difficulties were encountered during the first-year trial. Some students did poorly, and others did well. But in general, the evidence showed that the students were interested, and student attrition was no greater than usual. In fact, drop-out rates for the courses were remarkably low, considering the level of the material in comparison with the level of more conventional courses.

The CHEM Study administered four tests and a final examination to all students taking the course. The results were compared, on an individual and a school basis, with performance on the Co-operative School and College Ability Tests. There was no evidence that students of lesser ability, as indicated by their scores, had unusual difficulty with the CHEM Study materials. Indeed, preliminary results indicated an unusual number of these presumably less able students did well in the CHEM Study course. At the same time, an appreciable number of students whose aptitude was supposedly high had considerably more difficulty with the course than would have been anticipated. Similar results have been noted in most of the major curriculum studies. Apparently, the studies are measuring criteria other than those normally associated with the present definition of *ability*. Further studies are under way to determine why such variations occur.

During the 1961–62 school year the test program expanded to include one hundred and thirty high schools scattered across the United States. Some thirteen thousand students in these schools are studying CHEM Study materials. This sample should provide much more definite evidence on the limitations and the strengths of the course. The results will be reported in the newsletters.

Additional experimental schools were brought into the study during the 1962–63 academic year. During that year an appreciable number of schools tried out the materials at their own expense—a total of 700 teachers and 45,000 students. In 1963–64, over 100,000 students used the materials.

The first permanently bound version of the textbook, the laboratory manual, and the teacher's guide are available for use in schools. These materials are published in collaboration with the W. H. Freeman Company of San Francisco and are available to any school or school system that wishes to adopt them, on the same basis that other commercially available courses are obtained. In addition to the materials mentioned, the study has produced a set of twenty-six motion pictures, some special equipment, wall charts, and a series of chapter and review tests and two programed instruction pamphlets in mathematical skills.

Perhaps the greatest deviation from courses now in common use is the strong emphasis on laboratory experimentation and on the use of concepts to tie together chemical information that the student observes. The course is heavily based on laboratory work. It is hoped that high school students will spend more time in the laboratory. It seems unfortunate that many schools have felt it necessary to change from the double laboratory period common in the past to the single laboratory period found in the majority of schools in the present. Successful laboratory work normally requires an extended period of preparation and observation, and most teachers agree that double periods are more than twice as effective as single periods. Several schools in the first year of their work with CHEM Study were so attracted by the laboratory work that they rescheduled their programs to allow double laboratory periods. Each school that has tried the double laboratory periods plans to continue them.

The importance of laboratory work is emphasized in many ways. One is that the student normally does the experiment before he reads about the material in the textbook or before the material is discussed in class. The student is allowed to discover many of the fundamental ideas and relations himself and to discuss them in a laboratory context with his classmates, rather than to read about them or merely hear them described as things that can be observed.

The student is sent to the laboratory the first day of school, and he works there about seven of the first ten days of school. He is not given his textbook until the fourth day of school. This approach so intrigues the student that he comes to look forward to laboratory days. He realizes that chemistry is indeed an experimental science, not a subject that can only be read about in a book or talked about in class.

The first set of experiments involves a fairly extensive set of observations that center on a candle. The student begins by writing down as many observations as he can make in a short period of time. He then compares his list, which normally contains ten or twelve observations, with the list of a professional chemist, which contains fifty-three observations. The disparity in the number and the quality of the observations comes as a shock and an eye opener to most students. The student then studies melting-point behavior, investigates the chemical changes that occur when a candle burns, identifies the product of the reaction. He also analyzes the intermediate steps that must occur during the reaction. He measures the heat of combustion of candle wax and the heat of fusion of the wax, compares the two and relates the magnitude of these two energy terms to the operation of a candle. In the process the student is encouraged to generalize on the relative magnitude of the energy changes associated with chemical reactions and those associated with phase changes.

The first section of the textbook and laboratory experiments introduce most of the fundamental ideas with which a chemist deals. The second section investigates chemical reactions in terms of the concepts found useful in interpreting reactions. The subject is discussed in greater depth than is now common. The third section, normally started just after the opening of the second semester, deals with chemical bonding and structural relationships. The final section deals with systematic chemistry, involving a study in some detail of certain elements and compounds. In this last section considerable emphasis is placed on interpreting chemical behavior in terms of the conceptual ideas developed earlier in the course.

About three-quarters of the laboratory experiments are quantitative in nature, but the level of mathematical ability required to handle the results is not too demanding for students at this level. A good comprehension of seventh- and eighth-grade arithmetic will enable the student to perform practically all the operations. Occasionally algebra is required, and it is certainly true that only a student with some comprehension of algebra could do outstanding work in the course.

Many experiments involve unknowns, and a considerable number of the experiments give the student options in methods of performing the experiment or in continuing beyond the discoveries that the majority in the class will make. The intent is to encourage students at all levels to carry on a serious investigation and to discover effects that they were not familiar with. The equipment is kept simple in design and low in cost. Any school with a reasonable laboratory budget should have no difficulty in introducing these experiments into its program.

A description of the first experiment in the overview section might be profitable. The student weighs a piece of copper wire and places it in a solution of silver nitrate. Beautiful crystals of metallic silver begin to form, and the solution slowly turns blue. The aesthetic appeal of this experiment to the students should not be underrated. The reaction is watched for a while and then put away so that it can come to equilibrium. The residual copper is weighed, as is the silver that has been formed. From the weights of the copper used and the silver formed, the student calculates the ratio of moles of copper to moles of silver in the chemical reaction. He then is asked to write a simple chemical equation in terms of moles of reactants and moles of products, applying the conservation laws concerning numbers of atoms, elements, and mass. Next comes the question, "If atoms of one of the two elements form ions of unit positive charge, what charge will the ions of the other element carry?" This is the first contact the students have had with ions, yet they seem to have little difficulty in realizing that the silver ion will have a single charge and that the copper ion must then have a double charge.

In the next experiment the silver is dissolved in nitric acid, precipitated with hydrochloric acid, and the resulting silver chloride is weighed. Analysis of these data enables the student to calculate the formula of silver chloride. He is then asked to use the data from the two experiments to predict the empirical formula of the chloride of copper. Remember, he has no prior knowledge of what a reasonable formula for this chloride might be. This type of quantitative experimentation seems to intrigue the students, without proving overwhelming to the less capable ones.

The introductory section of the textbook outlines the importance of an experimental approach and the tentative nature of the conclusions that will be reached. The importance of expanding the conclusions and of building a more inclusive model is developed from the beginning so that the student realizes that scientific observations are uncertain and that the resulting theories contain uncertainties. Here as well as in the overview section the atomic theory is presented as something that the student has learned about from past education in science and as a theory he can use in understanding chemical observations.

This first section of the textbook gives a brief introduction to the electrical nature of matter, mole concept, kinetic theory, the idea of dynamic equilibrium, structural properties, energies associated with phase changes, the periodic table, and systematic variation of chemical properties with atomic number. In each case a minimum experimental basis is laid, but the full experimental treatment is deferred until later sections of the book. The purpose of this section is to acquaint the students with the general principles within which chemists operate.

It seems to us that just as a painter first sketches on a blank canvas the general areas that he will use in treating his subject, so a teacher should sketch out for his student the general areas he will be studying and give him a framework into which further details can be fitted. The framework can be nebulous, but it should be adequate and, even at this level, it should be tied in with as much experimental evidence as is essential for the framework to hold together.

This section of the course has given us the greatest difficulty so far. It is difficult for an experienced and competent teacher to defer detailed treatment of some of these ideas until the over-all framework has been constructed. However, it has also been the experience of the teachers who have completed the course that the approach has merit. The second time through considerably fewer problems seem to arise. One result of the approach is that the conceptual treatment and the bonding treatment seem to flow smoothly for the student. He has a comprehension of how they fit together even before each one is developed in detail. He has also developed a desire to understand general concepts in more detail, since he has seen that they do indeed fit together and give a coherent over-all picture.

The more intensive treatments in the third and fourth sections are strongly dependent on the laboratory work that the student is performing. In addition, reference is often made to experiments that the student may not have had the time or the opportunity to perform in his own laboratory work. A strong emphasis is placed on the dynamic nature of chemical systems, on the energy changes involved in reactions, and on the mechanism of approach to, as well as the nature of, chemical equilibrium. Particular attention is given to acid-base and oxidation-reduction systems as examples.

The discussion of chemical bonding is based heavily on the electrical forces that operate. A chemical bond is treated as existing because of the simultaneous attraction of a given electron or set of electrons by more than one nucleus. The development of ideas concerning atomic structure is traced up to the contemporary quantum-mechanical atom. It is pointed out that the position and trajectory of electrons are unknown but that it is possible to describe a general distribution of charge in space in terms of orbitals and their energy. These are related to experimentally determined energy levels. The formulas, structures, and shapes of chemical molecules are then correlated with the distribution of these orbitals in space and with the differences in energy of the available energy levels.

It is our feeling that the student finds this treatment more satisfying, less naïve, yet not too sophisticated compared with the more conventional Bohr treatment. It also seems to leave him with fewer misconceptions about atoms and molecules.

The final section of the textbook consists of a set of chapters from which teachers may select a suitable number to conclude the course. Teachers who are conducting more extended courses can cover all the material. Few new ideas are introduced in this section. Rather it was designed to give the student an opportunity to apply to specific situations the ideas learned in a more general context. He is encouraged to predict chemical properties and to check his predictions with experimental results. He is encouraged to perform experiments and to interpret them in terms of the concepts he has learned. He is led to consider relatively simple systems, such as the alkali metals, and more complex systems, such as those found in biochemistry, and to reach the conclusion that the fundamental principles that apply in both kinds of systems are identical. It is hoped that the student will find in this section ample justification for the study of chemistry and a feeling of success in using the powerful ideas he has discovered earlier in the course.

The teacher's guide parallels the laboratory manual and the textbook. For each chapter in the textbook there is a section pointing out the intent and approach, the outline, new concepts, schedule of related material, development, supplementary material (including a full discussion of each laboratory experiment), background discussion, and answers to exercises and problems for that chapter. The intent is to provide the teacher with the knowledge that he will find useful in interpreting the course and to ease mechanical duties, such as setting up laboratory experiments, working out answers to problems, grading papers, and making daily assignments. Preliminary comments from the participating teachers indicate that the guide is filling a long felt need and is most useful.

The purpose of the films is to enable the teacher in the classroom to illustrate experiments and concepts that would be difficult to illustrate in any other way. Filmed experiments can easily be carried out on a large scale or on a small scale or under conditions that meet special safety requirements. With the films the teacher can present concepts that require special equipment or animation techniques that are difficult to reproduce in a typical classroom. The purpose of each film is to supplement what the teacher can do by providing him with a means of doing what he wishes could be accomplished.

For example, the film "Catalysis" shows three experiments in which catalysis occurs and then illustrates in full detail the mechanism of the catalyzed reactions, showing the role of the catalyst and how this role can vary with conditions. The three reactions are the acid catalyzed decomposition of formic acid, the platinum catalyzed reaction between hydrogen and oxygen, and the enzyme catalyzed reaction of benzidine and hydrogen peroxide.

The film "Nitric Acid" illustrates a second approach. The textbook and the laboratory manual make little mention of nitric acid, its properties, or its preparation. The intention of the film, which is to be shown at the end of the section in which chemical concepts are introduced, is to allow the student to see that he can understand the chemistry of a fairly complicated substance, such as nitric acid, in terms of simple concepts that he has learned for other systems. It is our feeling that even though the student has not studied nitric acid, a twenty-minute film will allow him quickly to learn and comprehend the main properties of nitric acid and its preparation. He will do this in terms of the general concepts of acid-base, oxidation-reduction, equilibrium, and reaction-rate theory that he has learned in a more general context.

The films on catalysis and nitric acid are being produced in co-operation with the Manufacturing Chemists' Association. In making the films the CHEM Study staff is collaborating closely with outstanding experts in the field discussed in the film. All of the CHEM Study Films are now available for sale or rental from Modern Learning Aids, New York City.

I shall not give the details of our production of special equipment and wall charts or the preparation of other special materials that can be used with the course. Suffice to say that as suggestions arise, the staff of the study gives them careful consideration. Whenever feasible ideas are presented, the staff designs materials to fit the need and makes them available to secondary schools.

The main purpose of CHEM Study, then, is to experiment with as many means as possible of making a high school chemistry course highly effective. CHEM Study has tested its materials in experimental schools and uses the feedback to improve the course further. CHEM Study encourages any school system to look over the textbook, the laboratory manual, the teacher's guide, the motion pictures, and the other materials it produces. It is not the intention of the study to press for the adoption of these materials, but rather to see that every high school has a chance to compare its own needs with the CHEM Study course.

The staff of the study does not plan to send visitors to individual schools. At the invitation of a school, the staff of the study is usually able to provide someone who can discuss the course and its adaptability to local needs.

The emphasis on the principles of chemistry—discovered, learned, and applied in an experimental context—is an important part of the CHEM Study course. The evidence we have to date seems to warrant belief that this approach stimulates students of a wide range of ability.

Renascent Biology: A Report on the AIBS Biological Sciences Curriculum Study [1]

BENTLEY GLASS

Chairman, The Biological Sciences Curriculum Study,
University of Colorado

The American Institute of Biological Sciences is an association of forty-seven professional societies with an aggregate membership of eighty-four thousand. During my term of office as president of the American Institute of Biological Sciences, a committee to study educational problems was established. The members of this Education Committee, chaired by Oswald Tippo, had long been concerned about the insufficient supply of new biologists and the resistance or inertia preventing the introduction of sound modern biology courses in college and high school curriculums. In 1959, noting the excellent steps taken by the Physical Science Study Committee and the School Mathematics Study Group to meet similar deficiencies in science and mathematics teaching in American schools, the committee resolved to set up a curriculum study in biology. Although recognizing the great inadequacies of college courses in the subject, the members of the committee felt that effort should first be directed to the improvement of biology teaching in the secondary schools. For it is in the high schools that most students make their first acquaintance with science and its methods of exploring nature and discerning truth. At this level most students make a choice of occupation; far more future citizens are enrolled in high school biology courses than ever attend college. Finally, much of the difficulty experienced at the more advanced levels in interesting students in biology derives from the failure of high school biology teaching to awaken interest commensurate with the importance of this subject or from the quenching of that interest and curiosity in the nature of living things which is nearly universal at younger ages. I was asked to serve as chairman of a Biological Sciences Curriculum Study, to be established in the light of these needs.

Having secured substantial financial support from the Na-

[1] This is a condensed version of the original article which appeared in *The School Review,* Spring, 1962.

tional Science Foundation, the Biological Sciences Curriculum Study has moved forward rapidly since its initiation early in 1959. Under its director, Arnold B. Grobman, a professional staff was assembled at the headquarters of the study, on the campus of the University of Colorado in Boulder. A Steering Committee of some thirty persons was formed so as to include not only college and university biologists known widely for their researches as well as their interest in educational problems, but also high school teachers of biology, writers of textbooks and teachers' handbooks, and high school administrators. This Steering Committee met several times during 1959 and early 1960, and formulated a general plan of procedure. The members discussed various ways of attacking the problem posed by the antiquated biology curriculum in the secondary schools and considered what means might be used to thread the great biological themes and concepts through the entire fabric of whatever materials might be prepared for students to use.

There was general agreement on several major issues:

a) The biological sciences are now advancing so rapidly that with every ten to fifteen years there is a doubling of our significant knowledge. This fact makes imperative a frequent reappraisal and wholesale revision of existing curriculums. It also makes it increasingly difficult to cover in any satisfactory way all that is significant and all that a general citizen should know about these sciences. The biology actually being taught in the schools today is twenty years behind the advancing front of science, and in important respects is a full century in arrears. We were unanimous in our resolve that no opposition on the part of well-meaning but uninformed persons and groups would prevent an appropriate scientific treatment of such supposedly controversial biological subjects as organic evolution, the nature of individual and racial differences, sex and reproduction in the human species, and the problems of population growth and control.

b) Even worse than the failure to teach up-to-date biology is the prevalent sin of teaching the life sciences (as well as all others) as essentially a body of information established as true, together with concepts and laws of nature assumed to be unchangeable, irrevocable, and prescriptive. That our knowledge in real fact consists of limited observations, that our supposed laws are but summations of experience, and that as it develops, science is continually adding new observations and consequently modifying or even replacing its one-time "laws," or that change in existing conceptions of what is true must be expected, are principles honored in the breach. Science is consequently presented to students as if the knowledge of nature were static and crystallized, or was rapidly becoming so. The conception of science as a body of methods of inquiry by means of accurate and confirmable observations, quantitative and mathematical analysis, and controlled experimentation is given lip service but fails to enter into the current experience of the student of biology at the secondary school level. So-called laboratory work, in particular, has become a travesty of genuine science, having degenerated for the most part into mnemonic exercises that stress only the names of structures and processes and textbook definitions and explanations.

c) The life sciences are so diverse, both in point of view and in methodology, that there is no single best way to organize a high school course in biology. In point of view, there is a vast distinction between the analytical, physicochemical approach of a biochemist or biophysicist and the organismal approach of the student of behavior and the supra-organismal view of the ecologist who deals with communities and ecosystems. Even within a single field, such as genetics, there is an extraordinary difference between the point of view of the geneticist who undertakes to explore the chemical basis of heredity and the geneticist who is concerned with the effects of evolutionary processes on the genetic composition of populations. In consequence, it is valid and necessary to explore a variety of approaches and types of organization of the subject matter to be taught.

d) Whatever approach and whatever type of organization is used, the essential character of scientific activity and the great biological themes must permeate the treatment. This principle means that, on the one hand, the nature of science as an increasingly important aspect of human history—including the development of science through the correction of past errors, discovery of new evidence, and synthesis of new concepts—is to be stressed. The principle means, on the other hand, that the biological themes of the interdependence of structure and function, regulation and homeostasis, the genetic continuity of life, its evolution, the diversity of type together with unity of pattern, the biological roots of behavior, and the relation of organism to environment must be treated at all levels of organization, from the molecular level to the ecosystem, and at all stages of process, from the chemical reaction through the growth and development of the individual to the ultimate evolutionary changes with time. To do this is most difficult and has never really been attempted. But to achieve it is fundamental to a modern view of the life sciences.

e) As George Sarton, our greatest historian of science, has said, "It is not at all necessary that the average man should be acquainted with the latest theory of the universe or the newest hormone, but it is very necessary that he should understand as clearly as possible the purpose and the methods of science. This is the business of our schools, not simply of the colleges but of all the schools from the kindergarten up."

A rapidly changing society whose ways of life are continually disrupted and transformed by the advances of science and scientific technologies, and a democracy in which ultimate policy depends upon the enlightenment of the average citizen, must provide for the general citizen an education that makes possible adjustment to changing conditions, as well as some degree of foresight—an education that provides an understanding of the very nature of the scientific process that makes inevitable the gravest decisions. Is science friend or foe of mankind? We were agreed that the boy or girl in school cannot comprehend the nature of science by learning facts about nature. Instead, real participation in scientific inquiry, and as full a participation as possible, should be provided. Only by engaging in the steps of scientific inquiry may a student become able to discern the true difference between sound experiment that provides evidence and complex instrumentation that offers a show—between evidence and authority, between science and magic. This conclusion called for a thorough and radical change in the character and emphasis of most current science teaching.

f) A sound biological understanding is the inalienable right of every child who, when adult, will need to cope with individual problems of health and nutrition; with family problems of sex and reproduction and parenthood; and with the citizen's problems of wise management of national resources, the biological hazards of nuclear agents in peace and in war, and governmental support of science as the primary source of national strength and well-being in the scientific era. Consequently it seemed that the placement of biology in the high school curriculum ought to remain at a level where it will be studied by the great majority of students; that is, at the tenth-grade level as at present, rather than in a sequence following the study of physics and chemistry. Granting that modern biology cannot be taught without a considerable understanding of the physical sciences, we nevertheless felt that rather than postpone biology to the terminal year of high school, when it would very probably be elected by no more than 20 per cent of all high school students, it would be far better to undertake a thoroughgoing improvement of the science curriculum at the junior high school level. If a sound foundation in the basic concepts of physics and chemistry could be provided in those earlier years, biology could be taught in effective and modern terms at the tenth-grade level to almost all high school students. We therefore set as an objective the preparation of course materials for all high school students, irrespective of their future choices of occupation or their intention to go to college. This primary goal would not prevent experimentation with biology courses designed for selected groups, either at an earlier or a later period of secondary education.

The first major working committees to be established and to develop programs were a Committee for Innovation in Laboratory Instruction, under Addison E. Lee of the University of Texas, and a Committee on Course Content, under John A. Moore of Columbia University. The first of these two committees was to grapple in particular with the problem of real student participation in scientific inquiry. The second committee was to start the task of organizing subject matter and laboratory programs in the light of all the foregoing objectives. These two undertakings have proceeded in relative independence, the former developing the "Laboratory Block" program and the latter preparing several distinctive versions of subject matter and correlated laboratory exercises.

Discussion brought out the possibility that, in aiming both of these programs at the generality of high school students, those students who are particularly able, gifted, and capable of highly original and individual work in biology might be neglected. A third working committee was therefore established, to prepare materials for the guidance and use of especially gifted children. This committee worked under the chairmanship of Paul Brandwein, whose past leadership in this field is well known.

The Committee on the Gifted Student conceived the idea of soliciting from research biologists a variety of problems, still unsolved, that might be suitable for highly gifted students to use as subjects of individual research. The response was almost overwhelming. Hundreds of research problems were received and screened. A special task force was assembled to edit these problems carefully and to prepare an initial volume of one hundred of these during the summer of 1960. This plan was carried out by a team working for several weeks at Boulder, and the result was a volume entitled *Biological Investigations for Secondary School Students,* which was issued early in 1961 (1).

To start the major task of preparing several versions of course materials embodying different approaches to the life sciences, it was decided to draft the services of a considerable number of high school biology teachers and college and university specialists in different fields. During the summer of 1960 sixty-nine writers—together with a corps of typists, illustrators, and clerical personnel—were assembled in Boulder for seven weeks. The writers, according to their main interests, were grouped into teams to work on three versions— known as Yellow, Blue, and Green—to emphasize respectively the genetic and developmental, the biochemical and physiological, and the ecological and evolutionary approaches to biology. Each team of writers had a supervisor: John A. Moore for the Yellow Version (2), Ingrith Deyrup of Barnard College for the Blue Version (3), and Marston Bates of the University of Michigan for the Green Version (4). Each college biologist was paired with a high school colleague, so that the one might provide expertness on content, the other on level and manner of presentation. Half of the writers were assigned to the preparation of laboratory exercises intended to be closely co-ordinated with the respective textbook versions and to exemplify, in so far as possible, the quantitative treatment of the data and the use of controlled experiment in biological work. These teams were under the writer's supervision. As experiments were prepared, each one was given a preliminary testing by twenty select high school students working under the direction of two high school teachers. These students also read and criticized many portions of the text of each of the three versions.

In spite of what seemed an insuperable task, of differences of opinion and of some confusion resulting from lack of foresight and co-ordination in this unprecedented venture, the three versions, together with their laboratory accompaniments and teacher's guides for laboratory work, were drafted within seven weeks. Moreover, the first of three parts, into which each version was divided, was revised and printed in time to be used during the last week of August in a briefing session held for the prospective teachers. The remaining parts were completed, printed, and distributed in November, 1960, and January, 1961, in time for use by classes selected for the preliminary trials during 1960–61.

When Louis Agassiz and Thomas Henry Huxley introduced the teaching laboratory in biology, about a century ago, they had one primary purpose in mind. Their insight was a simple one: seeing is believing. In teaching science one must appeal not to the authority of a teacher or book; one must look squarely at the facts, at the infinitely varied phenomena of nature. The first function of the laboratory in teaching, then, is to present the evidence from nature that supports our biological concepts. This might be called the *illustrative function* of the teaching laboratory.

The illustrative function has been heavily emphasized in the past—often to the exclusion of everything else. Students have come to spend most of their time watching demonstrations, looking through the microscope, dissecting dead animals or plants, learning names, labeling drawings. Even when they were given a so-called experiment, all too often there was nothing in the least experimental about it. They have repeated, step by step, some well-worn procedure, perhaps illustrating a classic discovery of one or two, or even three, centuries ago. They have known in advance, from textbook and discussion, exactly what they were supposed to discern and conclude. It has been sheer cookbookery, a ritual of recipes. Small wonder that interest was often deadened. Little wonder that in this day of advanced audio-visual aids many educators have thought that large classes might see all that needed to be seen, and in much more effective fashion, if well-prepared motion pictures and sound were substituted for the routine of the laboratory.

But there is another function of the teaching laboratory and fieldwork, a function that cannot be replaced by audio-visual aids, demonstrations, or museums, no matter how excellent. To understand the nature of the scientific process one must participate actively in it—one must investigate some problem, the answer to which is unknown. If the paramount aim of science teaching in general education is to prepare citizens—most of whom will be non-scientists—to participate intelligently in the affairs of a scientific age, then the investigatory function of science teaching seems more important than any other. As the Foreword in each BSCS laboratory manual puts it: "No matter how much you learn about the facts of science, you will never quite understand what makes science the force it is in human history, or the scientists the sorts of people they are, until you have shared with them such an experience. The laboratory and field are the scientists' workshops. Much reading and discussion are essential in scientific work, but it is in the laboratory and field that hypotheses are tested."

Properly to do this, the experience must involve real, not make-believe, scientific investigation. One must approach the frontier of existing knowledge and deal not merely with what is unknown to the student, but with what is likewise unknown to the teacher and to the scientists who have prepared the teaching program—to everyone, in fact. Is that an impossibility, in the advanced stage of modern science? Perhaps in some sciences it is indeed. Fortunately, in the biological sciences one deals always with sufficient variables to render the outcome of a particular procedure uncertain. For example, one may know that a given concentration of thyroxin will accelerate the development of leopard frog tadpoles, but not what it will do to bullfrog tadpoles. It may simply kill them. Or one may know how a mutant called *dumpy,* in the fruitfly *Drosophila melanogaster,* is inherited—say, as a simple recessive, on chromosome 2. But a new mutant, although possessing a very similar phenotype, may turn out to be dominant and located in some different chromosome.

Even so, the investigatory experience must be provided in some depth, far exceeding what is ordinarily possible with brief exercises that are planned to accompany the study and discussion of a textbook day by day. To meet this hitherto largely neglected need, the laboratory block program has been devised. If the primary aim is to lead students to understand scientific methods of investigation and to appreciate the spirit and the outlook of a scientist, then it matters little what particular area is chosen. It is more important that the students have an opportunity to move step by step, from acquiring the necessary skills and preliminary acquaintance with the problems involved, toward the frontier of knowledge, where they can explore together a bit of the unknown and learn that by patience and carefulness, persistence to the point of obstinacy, precision in measurement, and accuracy in observation they can sometimes experience the joy of discovery. They must learn to ask the right questions, that is, to frame testable hypotheses. They must learn to draw valid conclusions from their data and to determine the significance of their findings. They must learn that science frequently advances through the correction of the errors and inadequacies of earlier science. And all of this takes time.

In past patterns of instruction, something of this sort has occasionally been provided for the gifted student by assigning him an individual project. Only too often, however, the student is left to flounder because the teacher lacks time and energy to supervise a number of individual projects over and above the heavy load of large-sized classes which are all too common in our schools. What the Biological Sciences Curriculum Study has sought, therefore, is a plan of instruction that would involve each entire class, yet provide real depth of investigation. The solution seems to have been found in the laboratory blocks. Each of these blocks deals with a circumscribed area of biological problems, within which considerable homogeneity of materials and methods may be utilized. Each block is planned to occupy a six-week period during which all other activities of the class (textbook assignments and discussions, regular laboratory exercises, etc.) are suspended. By careful planning, it is possible to have several independent experiments going on simultaneously or overlapping in time. The class is divided into squads which replicate each experiment; and each squad may be divided into teams that perform a particular part of the experiment. For example, one team may handle the control group of organisms, another team the organisms under a first set of experimental conditions, a third team those under a second set of experimental conditions. High group morale and personal responsibility develop as each student realizes that his own part is indispensable to the good results of his team and his squad. Time is allotted in the program for assembling the results, for quantitative handling of the data, and for comparison and discussion of the results as a whole. There is insistence on keeping clear and accurate records and on reporting the total experiment in scientific fashion.

Already four of these blocks have been prepared, pretested in a single school, and thereafter tested on a larger scale, each in two geographical centers and by six or seven teachers in each center. These blocks deal respectively with Microbes: Their Growth, Nutrition, and Interaction (8); Animal Growth and Development (9); Plant Growth and Development (10); and Interdependence of Structure and Function (11). As was mentioned previously, the laboratory blocks were received by teachers and students with enthusiasm. In spite of the arduous work involved on the part of teachers in preparing materials for such a program, and in spite of the extra assignments that required students to spend time out of school to make continuous observations, students and teachers alike expressed reluctance to return to the more conventional patterns of instruction. Typical student comments were of the following sort: "What are we learning? We're learning how scientists discover things." "This is hard but it's fun." "Our results don't come out the way we expected, and then we try to find out why."

Additional blocks have been completed in preliminary form on the topics: Ecology of Land Plants and Animals (12); Regulation in Plants by Hormones (in press); and Animal Behavior (in press). Other blocks are in preparation on the subjects of Physiological Adaptation in Animals and of Genetic Continuity. Possibly others will be prepared dealing with such subjects as radiation biology, light and life, evolution, and nutrition. The full plan is to have a sufficient number and variety of laboratory blocks, say at least a dozen, to permit every teacher to select for his classes one that is consonant with his own preparation and is adapted to the locality and the student body. It will be best to introduce each laboratory block in the year's program after the class has made some preliminary study of the biological information basic to the use of that block. If this is done, the unavoidable curtailment of the rest of the biology course, which must occur whenever a six-week laboratory block is used, will be minimized, especially since most of the regular laboratory program dealing with the same subject can then be omitted. But whether or not this saving is possible, the sacrifice of time that would otherwise be devoted to the general coverage of biology seems well worth while, if the block, no matter what its particular subject matter, can generate understandings of the nature of scientific inquiry that conventional teaching methods are quite unable to do.

Teachers may want to use different blocks in different years, or even in different classes during the same year, although the latter choice would involve excessive time and labor in preparation. Several teachers are now trying out the idea of making up an advanced biology course by using three or four laboratory blocks in sequence, with suitable connecting studies. It is also worth noting that a committee appointed by the Biological Sciences Curriculum Study to report on the feasibility of and the need for college biology curriculum studies that might be co-ordinated with the BSCS program reached the following conclusions. First, the revolution in biology at the high school level makes it imperative to rethink and replan both the introductory college biology course and the courses for teacher training. Second, while plenty of good college textbooks exist, and at present there is no need to prepare more of them, the program of the teaching laboratory, as commonly taught, is stultified and almost deadening. Third, the best means of redirecting laboratory teaching toward the goals thought to be most important is through preparation of laboratory blocks, comparable to those being used successfully at the high school level, but more advanced.

Finally, let it be said that the laboratory block program is somewhat more expensive than alternative ways of teaching biology. The program will generally require that the teacher carry a lighter class load and that classes be reduced toward an optimum size of about twenty-five. A laboratory assistant may also be required for each group of classes, to help prepare for the experimental work and to help in the checking of the voluminous data sheets and reports. The program will require, particularly the first time a given block is taught in a school, some outlay, both for permanent equipment and for expendable materials such as glassware and chemicals. It is a notable fact that schools which have participated in the BSCS laboratory block program thus far, while helped through loans of equipment from the Biological Sciences Curriculum Study, have also found the program a reasonable and sufficient basis for requesting, and getting, certain types of equipment from the school administration. For example, the experience is helping to make routine the provision in each classroom-laboratory of sufficient gas, electric, and water outlets, sinks, and storage space. A refrigerator is now recognized as necessary. Provision of enough binocular dissecting microscopes to equal the number of the compound microscopes conventionally provided is recommended as being among the best possible uses of funds available under Title 3 of the National Defense Education Act. The associates of the Committee on Innovation in Laboratory Instruction have devised many simple, homemade types of equipment that may satisfactorily be substituted for the far more expensive commercial instruments.

To conclude, the laboratory block program, as developed thus far, gives promise of being this generation's most exciting innovation in the methods of teaching science. Every report thus far received agrees that, whatever the expense and the added burden in time and energy, almost no teacher who has once included a laboratory block in the biology course would go back to the old way of teaching and almost every student who has participated in such a course regards the laboratory block as the high point of the year.

In sum and substance, what is the BSCS program that past efforts to improve the science curriculum of the secondary schools were not? One might say two principal things in reply. For the first time in the history of American education we now see a large number of research scientists, from the colleges and universities, taking part in a co-operative effort with high school teachers of science and science supervisors to replace an antiquated body of scientific knowledge and outlook with subject matter and perspective that are truly current. The Physical Science Study Committee and the School Mathematics Study Group, the two curriculum studies begun earlier, moved in this direction. But I believe that only in the Biological Sciences Curriculum Study has this fruitful collaboration been fully realized. The result is as astounding to the research biologist as to the high school teacher. How nearly fatal that until so recently no one seemed to realize that this must be the way—the only way, in an ever accelerating pace of scientific advance—to provide the well-oriented education in the sciences that modern man must have.

That is one answer to the question. The other is this. For the first time, I think, education in the natural sciences, at least at the secondary level, has assigned the acquisition of scientific information and concepts a place of lesser importance than the understanding of the very nature of scientific inquiry and of the scientific enterprise in which modern man is embarked. As I wrote on an earlier occasion: "The aim of the Biological Sciences Curriculum Study is to place biological knowledge in its fullest modern perspective. If we are successful, students of the new biology should acquire not only an intellectual and esthetic appreciation for the complexities of living things and their interrelationships in nature, but also for the ways in which new knowledge is gained and tested, old errors eliminated, and an ever closer approximation to truth attained."

REFERENCES

1. *High School Biology—Biological Investigations for Secondary School Students.* Boulder, Colorado: American Institute of Biological Sciences, Biological Sciences Curriculum Study, Committee on the Gifted Student, 1961.

2. *High School Biology—Yellow Version: Text, Parts One, Two; The Laboratory, Parts One, Two, Three; The Laboratory (Teacher's Guide), Parts One, Two, Three.* Boulder: AIBS Biological Sciences Curriculum Study, 1960–61.

3. *High School Biology—Blue Version: Text, Parts One, Two, Three; The Laboratory, Parts One, Two, Three; The Laboratory (Teacher's Guide), Parts One, Two, Three.* Boulder: AIBS Biological Sciences Curriculum Study, 1960, 1961.

4. *High School Biology—Green Version: Text, Parts One, Two, Three; The Laboratory, Parts One, Two, Three; The Laboratory (Teacher's Guide), Parts One, Two, Three.* Boulder: AIBS Biological Sciences Curriculum Study, 1960, 1961.

5. *High School Biology—Blue Version: Text, Revised Edition, Parts One, Two, Three; The Laboratory, Revised Edition, Parts One, Two, Three; The Laboratory (Teacher's Guide), Revised Edition, Parts One, Two, Three.* Boulder: AIBS Biological Sciences Curriculum Study, 1961, 1962.

6. *High School Biology—Yellow Version: Text, Revised Edition, Parts One, Two, Three; The Laboratory, Revised Edition, Parts One, Two, Three; The Laboratory (Teacher's Guide), Revised Edition, Parts One, Two, Three.* Boulder: AIBS Biological Sciences Curriculum Study, 1961, 1962.

7. *High School Biology—Green Version: Text, Revised Version, Parts One, Two, Three; The Laboratory, Revised Version, Parts One, Two, Three; The Laboratory (Teacher's Guide), Revised Edition, Parts One, Two, Three.* Boulder: AIBS Biological Sciences Curriculum Study, 1961, 1962.

8. *High School Biology—A Laboratory Block on Microbes: Their Growth, Nutrition and Interaction.* Developed by Alfred S. Sussman. Teacher Edition, Student Edition. Revised Teacher Edition, Revised Student Edition. Boulder: AIBS Biological Sciences Curriculum Study, Committee on Innovation in Laboratory Instruction, 1960, 1962.

9. *High School Biology—A Laboratory Block on Animal Growth and Development.* Developed by Florence Moog. Teacher Edition, Student Edition. Revised Teacher Edition,

Revised **Stu**dent Edition. Boulder: AIBS Biological Sciences Curriculum Study, Committee on Innovation in Laboratory Instruction, 1961, 1962.

10. *High School Biology—A Laboratory Block on Plant Growth and Development*. Developed by Addison E. Lee. Teacher **Edition, Student** Edition. Revised Teacher Edition, Revised Student Edition. Boulder: AIBS Biological Sciences Curriculum Study, Committee on Innovation in Laboratory Instruction, 1961, 1962.

11. *High School Biology—A Laboratory Block on Interdependence of Structure and Function*. Developed by A. Glenn Richards. Teacher Edition, Student Edition. Revised Teacher Edition, Revised Student Edition. Boulder: AIBS Biological Sciences Curriculum Study, Committee on Innovation in Laboratory Instruction, 1960, 1961.

12. *High School Biology—A Laboratory Block on the Ecology of Land Plants and Animals*. Developed by Edwin A. Phillips. Teacher Edition, Student Edition. Boulder: AIBS Biological Sciences Curriculum Study, Committee on Innovation in Laboratory Instruction, 1961.

13. *Guidelines for Preparation Programs of Teachers of Secondary School Science and Mathematics*. Washington: National Association of State Directors of Teacher Education and Certification, and American Association for the Advancement of Science, no date.

14. *High School Biology—Teacher's Commentary (All Text Versions)*. [Part One, but no additional parts were issued.] Boulder: AIBS Biological Sciences Curriculum Study, 1960.

15. *High School Biology—The Teacher's Handbook (All Text Versions), Revised Edition, Parts One, Two, Three*. Boulder: AIBS Biological Sciences Curriculum Study, 1961, 1962.

16. Paul DeHart Hurd. *Biological Education in American Secondary Schools, 1890–1960*. Boulder: AIBS Biological Sciences Curriculum Study, 1961.

17. *BSCS Newsletter*, Numbers 1–10, September, 1959–December, 1961.

Learning a Modern Language for Communication

NELSON BROOKS
Yale University

If a principal objective of learning a modern foreign language is to make contact, through the spoken or written word, with those for whom that language is a mother tongue, many changes are called for in the traditional practices still observed in most language classrooms in American schools and colleges. These changes are necessary not only for the improvement of language competence, but also for wider acquaintance with and deeper insight into cultural and literary studies. These changes must be reflected in the activities of both teacher and students in the classroom and the language laboratory, in the materials that are used for practice and study, and in the tests by which learning is measured.

A statement of what is involved in a program of language learning for communication may be made clearer and briefer by first listing what it does NOT include.

It is not the direct method. The direct method rejects the use of the learner's native language, translation, and the study of formal grammar. In the program here recommended, some use of all of these is prescribed. But in the classroom, English is used only to make meaning clear and to give brief directions or explanations.

No single method is preferred. Many different methods are found to be effective, with this important proviso—objectives must remain constant. A method that inhibits the student's advance by encouraging wrong learning cannot be recommended.

It is not the matching of an isolated word in one language with a word in another. This is the province of the dictionary-maker and is not an activity appropriate to the early levels of language learning.

The learner's advance is not measured in terms of his knowing x number of words. At first, the most important advances in learning a new language involve structure rather than vocabulary. Only after the learner has an adequate control of sounds, order, and forms, does the increase in vocabulary become an important objective. Words and expressions are learned in context and not in isolation.

It is not the learning of lists of names of persons or places memorized out of context. Anyone who knows geography can name many places, and anyone who knows music can name many composers. Unfortunately, the converse of these statements is not necessarily true.

It does not permit the student to use the mother tongue whenever he wishes. Strict rules are enforced concerning the use of English by the learner. Although he may occasionally *hear* English in the classroom, he does not use it as a speaker or writer.

It does not permit the student to have constant recourse to a printed script. The separate functions of ear and eye in language learning are fully recognized, and the ear is trained to respond to the new sounds without having at the same time a written transcript of these sounds before the eye. The theory that the more senses involved, the better the learning, does not hold in the early stages of second language learning.

It is not the exhaustive explanation of rules of grammar. Grammar rules are of some help to some students in understanding how the new language works, but they easily inhibit advance in the use of the new language. In all languages, the audio-lingual skills (hearing and speaking) can be and constantly are learned without any explanation whatever. Grammar rules should be restricted to the limited area in which they are clearly useful.

It does not include endless talk ABOUT the language instead of talk IN the language. No amount of discussion about the pianoforte will enable the learner to play the instrument; the fingers must touch the keys. The tongue must speak the foreign language.

It is not the chanting of paradigms. Language in use does not contain paradigms any more than arithmetic problems contain numbers in series. However helpful the systematic arrangement of possible forms and the use of memory devices may be, such aids in no way resemble language as it occurs in communication.

It is not an attempt to decode a foreign language into English. The foreign language is not studied as something from which English is to be extracted, like sugar from a beet. It is considered as a system fully adequate for communication in its own right, without recourse to English or any other language.

It is not an insistence upon talk in complete sentences. The sentence is a creature of the printed page, but it is not the unit of communication by word of mouth. Rather, the unit of talk is an utterance. Insistence upon speech in complete sentences does violence to the normal modes of communication.

It is not the practice of unbroken series of spoken questions and answers. Oral communication between speakers takes place only to a very limited degree in the form of question and answer. Communication is for the most part in the form of utterance and rejoinder: "Beautiful morning!" "Yes, indeed!"

It does not include practice by students in reading aloud from a printed text for long periods. Desirable as it is that the student eventually learn to read aloud, unless this activity is consistently and adequately modeled by the teacher, little more than wrong learning can result.

It is not x number of solo hours by the teacher. It is of the utmost importance that the teacher model what the student is expected to learn. But two other steps are equally important. Communication must be established between teacher and student, and as soon as possible between one student and another. The objective of language learning for communication is not reached until the teacher can withdraw from the process and observe.

It is not the transfer of the teacher's entire knowledge to the student. Much technical knowledge about language and language learning that is essential for the teacher should not be required of the student. One goes to the ski instructor not to learn to be a ski instructor, but to learn to ski. Students come to the language class to learn to communicate in the new language, not to become teachers.

Having stated what the program of language learning for communication is NOT, let us now state what it IS:

The program of language learning for communication is based upon broad professional agreement about objectives, methods, materials, tests, and outcomes. A number of documents now in print reflect the degree of agreement on these points, the FL Program Policy statement (PMLA, Part II, September, 1956), the Qualifications for Secondary School Teachers of Modern Foreign Languages (endorsed by sixteen national or regional language organizations), Modern Foreign Language in the Comprehensive Secondary School (The Bulletin of the National Association of Secondary School Principals, June 1, 1959), Modern Foreign Languages and the

Academically Talented Student (The National Education Association, 1960), among others.

The initial objective is to learn to understand and speak the language as it is used in its culture. In these terms the role of English, translation, grammar rules, and the book is reduced to very modest proportions, comparable to the part they play in the language behavior of native speakers.

At the start students are given exact information about objectives and how they are to be reached. The first period of every course should be devoted to an explanation in English of the nature of the learning problem and the procedures that will be followed.

In learning, great importance is attached to the model and to the reward. Since books cannot talk and machines cannot react to what the learner says, the teacher is irreplaceable as the model from whom oral communication is to be learned. The shorter the time span between the learner's performance and his knowledge of whether or not he has been successful, the better the learning.

The cultural objective. The search for the meaning of language leads to the culture itself. The point of view from which the new culture is to be approached should be that of a member of the culture who is of an age and status similar to that of the American learner.

The literary objective. Since language is the chief element of which literature is made, the development of language competence cannot fail to strengthen the understanding of literature. In suitable proportions, selected samples of good literature are important in language programs from the beginning, to be studied for their own sake and for the characteristics that lift them to the level of fine art.

Language is something you understand and say BEFORE it is something you read and write. This principle should be applied not only at the beginning level, but also at later levels.

Language learning for communication involves the learning of all the skills: hearing, speaking, reading, writing—and in that order. These are not engaged in simultaneously from the start. A period of at least some months (or in college, weeks) in which the student only hears and speaks must precede the introduction to reading and writing.

Language is three parts grammar and one part vocabulary. There is a grammar of sound, of form, and of order, and relationships. These are finite and learnable within a relatively short time. They should receive the principal emphasis at the start. Vocabulary is almost infinite, and can never be completely learned. Vocabulary becomes a principal objective once reasonable control of structure has been established.

Emphasis upon the learning of structure at early levels is made to coincide with the norms of language as used in communication. Materials are prepared in different modes, for example dialogues, which contain communication that is authentic in a selected situation, and pattern drills, which contain utterances that differ only slightly from one another and *could* be used in communication. Model sentences and short, simple narratives are also used.

All the student's efforts at language learning are integrated. He is asked to work in a classroom, in a language laboratory, and at home. Activities in all three places are part of a single, co-ordinated sequence of learning.

The stream-level concept is used for the programing of materials and learning. It is recognized that language learning begins at a number of widely different points, the elementary school, the junior high school, the senior high school, and in college. It is essential that materials be appropriate to the age of the student and to his previous learnings. A stream may originate at any one of the four beginning points. A level contains two dimensions: what can appropriately be learned, regardless of age, especially with regard to situation and structure, and what is appropriate to the age and advancement of the learner, especially with regard to vocabulary and ideas.

Mechanical aids are employed to the full extent that their limitations permit. In simplest terms, what is to be learned is first presented and modeled by the teacher, then repeated and overlearned in the language laboratory, and finally reviewed and perfected in class.

Language learning goes beyond audio-visual aids. Whatever use may be made of pictures, machines, and *realia*, the learner must eventually participate in the normal use of language for communication. This is a person-to-person activity and, for the most part, does not relate to what is present in the immediate environment.

Tests are designed to aid learning. There are tests that enhance the learner's progress; there are also tests that deflect his progress away from desired objectives to the point of negating the learning that is desired. Accurate measurement is just as possible with tests that aid learning as with those that negate it.

There are five critical points in classroom procedure. Any class or any course in second-language learning will succeed or fail according to what is done about the following: the use of English, translation, the explanation of grammar, the use of the open book, and tests.

The Language Laboratory

GEORGES L. BRACHFELD
Professor of Romance Languages,
New York University

One of the most striking features of our changing times is the unprecedented and rapid growth of the means and arts of verbal communication. Viewed in the broad perspective of the coming centuries, if it may be assumed that man does not explode his planet, it will certainly result in the reduction of all world languages into a single tongue, with regional differences in pronunciation and usage perhaps less marked even than those presently existing between the various forms of English. Before this happens, and in order to help bring about this inevitable outcome, we must first learn many of the languages now spoken throughout the world. The time has passed when an educated elite studied Latin, Greek or French as an intellectual exercise, aiming at best for an ability to read the foreign literary masterpieces. In the United States, and in other leading countries, world-wide commitments impose the necessity of learning foreign languages for effective communication.

ACCENT ON SPOKEN LANGUAGE

Changing needs beget changing attitudes and methods. A set of basic assumptions now governs the new approach to language teaching, all predicated upon the belief that the spoken form of the language is to precede, if not to take precedence, over its written counterpart. In order to assure correct pronunciation, the sounds of the language are learned without interference from their orthographic transcription. Thus a word like *monsieur* need not be at the outset distorted out of oral recognition. Language learning being a process of overlearning, constant repetition is required until responses become nearly automatic, as in one's native tongue. Grammar is not taught deductively, by stating a rule then illustrating it, but inductively, by repeated drills on new structures, which are first assimilated, then explained. The sounds and structures of the new language are committed to the auditory memory of the student and, as it were, to his organic, muscular memory, as his speech organs contrive to form and emit unaccustomed sounds. The language laboratory is an essential teaching tool in the implementation of these objectives.

APPARATUS AND PROCEDURE

Obviously, the language laboratory is not a laboratory. Students do not experiment with the language, they experience it. It is a language practice room, somewhat like a library in which words are stored in their spoken instead of their written form. The simplest language laboratory may consist of an audio source-phonograph or tape recorder—and a number of earphones connected to it. It is considered a lingually passive laboratory, since the student has no opportunity of hearing himself or recording what he says. An adequate, fully audio-active laboratory comprises a number of semi-soundproof booths, which are the student positions, each equipped with a dual-track tape recorder, a microphone and earphones. It also has a console equipped with several playback sources that may be channelled to any of the student positions and from which an instructor may monitor and communicate with any of the students in the booths.

The language laboratory may function according either to the broadcast or to the library system. In the broadcast system, students come in at an assigned hour, in a class group, and a program is channelled to them from the console. They follow instructions, do their exercises, but have no control over the program source. The library system, more flexible, allows the student to come in at any time that the laboratory is open. The student picks up the tape, which has been pre-recorded for his particular course, and proceeds to do his work at his own speed. On his dual-track tape recorder the master program cannot be erased. When he has finished, he returns the tape to its place, and the next student erases the practice track as he listens to the master program. In the library system the student may interrupt the program, and repeat parts of it as often as he wishes.

THE TECHNICAL EXERCISES

The language laboratory is a place where students practice what they have learned in the classroom. Whereas it is im-

possible for the instructor to devote sufficient time to the
drilling of each one of his students, the laboratory exercises
he has prepared will fulfill that function with tireless patience.
Since these exercises are intended to develop the student's
listening comprehension and speaking skills, the most constant
activity in the laboratory is vocal repetition. Students should
repeat everything they hear in the foreign language. While
the ear and the vocal organs are getting attuned to the
foreign language, the mind strives to solve structural problems, until it assimilates the new structures to the point that
a given stimulus will automatically elicit the correct response.

The basic structural exercise is a pattern drill, requiring
either substitution or transformation of the variable in the
given structure. As an illustration of the substitution drill let
us suppose that the structure to be drilled is, *je veux qu'il
parte,* corresponding to the English, *I want him to leave,*
where the use of the subjunctive after a verb of volition is
practiced. After a model problem sentence and response have
been given, the student proceeds on cue: *Sortir—je veux qu'il
sorte; courir—je veux qu'il coure;* etc. In a transformation drill,
intended in this case to practice the future tense, the student
may be asked to express an indirect statement in direct form,
thus *il dit qu'il viendra* should be rendered as *je viendrai;*
and *il dit qu'il parlera—je parlerai,* etc.; the persons may vary:
il dit que nous sortirons—vous sortirez; the negative form may
be practiced: *il dit que nous ne fumerons pas—vous ne
fumerez pas;* questions may be elicited: *il demande si nous
écouterons—écouterez-vous?* These may also be negative.
In the case of each drill, the student has practiced a pattern
ten to twelve times, then he goes to a slightly different and
more complex one, until all the possible aspects of a structure
have been practiced. On the tape itself, he hears the problem
sentence, stops his tape, repeats to himself the problem and
formulates the answer, then starts the tape; he hears the
correct answer as recorded by the instructor, and repeats it
as he records it in the space provided on the tape. When
he has finished the exercise, he should rewind the tape to
review the problem studied and compare his answers with
the original: he would then hear the problem, the instructor's
answer, and his own answer. By comparing these answers he
may be capable of correcting his pronunciation, rhythm, pitch
and intonation. Specific exercises may be designed for these
particular purposes. Thus in order to distinguish between
vowel sounds, minimal phonetic pairs will be repeated: *pain—*

peine, vin—veine, lin—laine, sein—saine, rein—reine. Proper intonation may be practiced by the repetition of statements and questions: *je verrai—verrez-vous? J'écouterai—écouterez-vous?* etc. The types and numbers of laboratory exercises are limited only by the ingenuity of the instructor. In addition to pattern drills and phonetic exercises, the laboratory lends itself to dictations, simultaneous interpretation or translation, memorization, listening of literary readings, songs, and also testing.

THE NEW ROLE OF INSTRUCTORS

It is clear that the language laboratory multiplies the action of the instructor—will it eventually displace him? On the contrary, and thanks to the language laboratory, the language instructor is able to devote more time to teaching, rather than to drilling. As a larger number of lingually qualified students enter college, literature studies achieve their due importance. The language laboratory facilitates a long delayed expansion in the study of languages, and so far the increasing demand for language instructors has been ahead of the available supply.

Where instructors are nearly unobtainable, as in the case of the more exotic languages of Asia and Africa, the language laboratory may be used in conjunction with programed learning to substitute for the missing teacher. The program presents inductively the explanations and examples that would otherwise constitute the classroom activity, in synchronization with the tape, whenever needed. In fact, the program may be studied through a microfilm viewer in the student's booth, and the student may activate a tape at times indicated on the program, to hear the examples. After certain structures have been explained, they may be practiced on tape by means of pattern drills and other exercises. When they have been learned, the student returns to the next frame on his program. This method will not replace the teacher. Will then a private television screen at each student position with a microfilm viewer and a tape recorder finally relegate the instructor into the growing category of the obsolete? By that time language learning will be so effective and enjoyable, that teachers will be needed more than ever, to produce better programs in greater numbers. The language laboratory is only one manifestation of the changing techniques of language instruction.

The Emerging English Curriculum

J. N. HOOK

Past Executive Secretary,
The National Council of Teachers of English
and Co-Ordinator, Project English,
The U.S. Office of Education

Greater ferment exists today in English teaching than has been observable at any other time in the history of this relatively young subject. The ferment is attributable to a number of causes. Among them these may be mentioned:

1. A growing awareness of the economic significance of English. For example, a typical business letter now costs about two dollars. About half the price of a new automobile is paid for words.

2. Increasing awareness of the cultural importance of English. Sterling M. McMurrin, former U. S. Commissioner of Education, has said, "Those who suppose that great music or great poetry or a knowledge of classical literature is not essential to not only the quality but even the survival of a nation and its culture are quite unaware of the lessons of the past."

3. Greater interest of college English professors in the curriculum of the lower schools. In the past, most such professors ignored the elementary and secondary schools, except to bemoan the inability of their graduates to read and write well. Responsibility for preparing teachers was handed over to professors of education. Today the realization is growing that college subject-matter specialists and professional educators both have a share in the responsibility for what goes on in the pre-college years.

4. Increasingly vigorous leadership from the professional and scholarly organizations. The National Council of Teachers of English, the Modern Language Association, the Association for Supervision and Curriculum Development, the American Council of Learned Societies, the National Association of Secondary-School Principals, the International Reading Association, and the College Entrance Examination Board are representative of the organizations that have strengthened or recently initiated efforts to improve English instruction.

5. Applications of the findings of scholarship. Although

much scholarship in literature and in rhetorical theory is now being translated into classroom application, linguistic scholarship has aroused still greater interest and, sometimes, controversy. Modern linguists constantly emphasize the need for teaching truths about the language as it actually is, not a distorted, Latinized English grammar that never was except in textbooks.

6. Technology. Although most English teachers still believe that a child, a book, and a teacher are the indispensable trio, much experimentation has been going on involving supplements to the book and a new role for the teacher. Some of the experiments involve educational television, motion pictures, filmstrips, overhead projectors, teaching machines, and language laboratories. Some involve new concepts of classroom design or variations in pedagogical organization such as team teaching, use of lay readers, or use of other lay assistants.

PROJECT ENGLISH

A symptom of the ferment is Project English, begun late in 1961 in the U. S. Office of Education. Project English involves a co-ordinated attempt to upgrade English instruction on all academic levels. Through research studies, curricular experimentation, conferences, and demonstrations, and perhaps later through institutes [1] and other means, Project English will assist schools, colleges, and State departments of education to find new answers to old questions and to effect easier exchange of information. While specifically eschewing federal control, it will provide federal financial support for important activities now inadequately provided for.

What is the shape of the English curriculum that will emerge as a result of the ferment? The risks of prophecy are well known; the future may be very different from what our most informed guesses suggest. Nevertheless, it seems reasonably safe to posit four statements.

The emerging English curriculum will have a shape. Today's curriculum is almost shapeless. For instance, some information about language, such as the definitions of the parts of speech, is repeated in eight or ten grades, while other and more valuable information, such as the importance of word order in the English language, may never be mentioned. Or,

[1] Teacher institutes under Project English would be authorized if the Congress should enact the President's bill S. 2826, "The Improvement of Educational Quality Act of 1962."

for example, different schools today may teach such a selection as "The Rime of the Ancient Mariner" or "Rip Van Winkle" in any grade from the sixth through the fourteenth. Some schools do have a well-planned curriculum, but in others curricular anarchy exists, with each teacher teaching whatever he feels like at the time he feels like it.

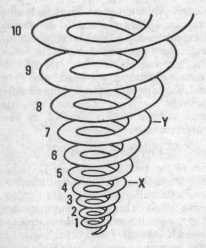

The probable shape of the English curriculum may be visualized as a spiral in the form of a cone, point down. In the primary grades the level of difficulty of material presented is low, the level of accomplishment is low, and the coverage is narrow. As the children grow older, they are introduced to more difficult material, they do more with it, and they cover more of it. Hence curriculum coverage rises and broadens simultaneously.

Different children of the same chronological age will be at different places on the cone. If the differences are not great, they may be accommodated by simple adjustments in the quantity of material presented. (In the illustration, for instance, less able children who are on the sixth ring of the spiral may be visualized as being on the inside of the cone, covering a limited amount of material of sixth-ring difficulty; their more able classmates will be on the outer edge, covering more material.) But when the differences between children of the same age are considerable, when two children are at widely separated points on the spiral, they cannot be expected to master identical work. Of two ten-year-old children, for instance, one may be at point X on the spiral, the other at point Y. Through varied assignments, grouping, or a rather drastic revision of our usual concepts of grade level, it is possible to provide for each child what he needs at the particular point he has reached on the spiral.

In the past the great difficulty in curriculum planning has resulted from the fact that two kinds of sequence are involved: sequence in subject matter, and varying abilities and rates of development among children. If all children were of equal ability and could progress at the same rate, it would be a relatively simple matter to decide upon a subject-matter sequence that would be logical. But since children (happily) are not identical, they are not all ready for the same learnings at the same time. The spiral cone concept provides for sequential progress in subject matter without ignoring variations in children.

Under way in Project English are six curriculum study centers, at Carnegie Institute of Technology, Hunter College, Northwestern University, and the State Universities of Minnesota, Nebraska, and Oregon. These are federally subsidized at about $250,000 each. Over a period of approximately five years, each of these centers is expected to develop a sequential English curriculum for specified grades and emphases. At the end of the five-year period each center will make its findings and recommendations available for use by any schools that wish to take advantage of them.

The emerging English curriculum will be devoted almost exclusively to language, composition, and literature. A quarter of a century ago a professor made a list of all the aims of English teaching that he could find anywhere in print. He discovered a total of 1,481 aims, ranging from "Improve character" through "Teach appreciation" down to "Teach the evils of alcohol." If the listing were to be brought up to date, it would probably now include several hundred additional aims. Particularly in the secondary schools, English has become a catch-all subject. Whenever community pressure is brought to bear to add something new to the total curriculum —anything from consumer education to sex education—everyone sees that it is possible to read and write about the proposed new material. Hence someone says, "Why can't we include this in the English program?" A too acquiescent English department consents, and part of the real job of

English is tossed out in favor of something peripheral. As a result, some secondary English programs devote more attention to the peripheral than to the central.

Today, however, elementary and secondary and college teachers of English are approaching agreement that their task is threefold and that they should concentrate on an integrated program of instruction in the nature and peculiar characteristics of the English language, the improvement of written and spoken composition, and the reading of the best materials that children at a given point on the spiral cone are able to comprehend. The twenty institutes sponsored by the College Entrance Examination Board in the summer of 1962, for example, were devoted entirely to this tripod.

Modern linguists have repeatedly shown the deficiencies in traditional grammar, and to take its place they are developing scientifically accurate descriptions of the language as it actually is. The public has misinterpreted some of their recommendations. Reputable linguists do *not*, for example, state that "ain't got none" is as acceptable as "haven't any"; they describe both constructions because both exist, but they point out that for social reasons, or because of historical accident, the one construction is ordinarily to be preferred. Nor do the majority of present-day linguists confine their study to the spoken language. They do state that the spoken language came first, that written language is based upon speech, and that writers may profit from detailed knowledge of the spoken language. Many errors in usage, for example, may better be corrected through oral drill than through workbook exercises.

Instruction in language in the new curriculum, then, will include such things as study of language as a social tool, the history of English and its relation to other languages, semantics, and an accurate, sequentially arrayed description of English. It will not ignore such matters as spelling and punctuation, but it will be conceived of as a cultural and not merely a practical subject.

In composition, the new curriculum will place increased emphasis on content and on organization. In some schools today a paper is given a high mark if it has the sole virtue of correctness. Correctness is important, but no more so than having something to say and arranging the parts in an intelligent manner. Basic principles of content and organization may be taught in the primary grades and elaborated upon as children mature.

Principles of rhetoric, a word that has become sadly debased in its connotations, will also be stressed in composition. The curriculum study centers at Northwestern, Nebraska, and Oregon are investigating, among other things, that which is still useful in classical rhetoric and that which has pedagogical implications in the numerous studies of rhetorical theory in the twentieth century. One result of this emphasis, it is hoped, will be writing that is not only significant in content, logical in organization, and correct in mechanics, but also effective in diction and presentation.

In reading and literature, much attention will be devoted to helping each child to read material of the highest quality possible for him. Although necessarily the first task of the elementary school is to teach the child how to read on a very basic level, curriculum makers are rebelling against unnecessarily long-continued exposure to selections about Webby the Duck and our friends the firemen. Some poems and stories with literary value may be introduced even in the lower elementary school, and the proportion may be steadily increased as children grow older. And pupils' attention may be drawn not only to what-happens-next and to analysis of the characters depicted but also to what it is that gives a selection literary value: such things as the over-all structure, diction, imagery, or the use of paradox.

A curriculum is developing in which information essential to the understanding of literature will be introduced gradually from the elementary grades on. This information relates not only to the terminology useful in discussing literature (*metaphor* and *dramatic monologue*, for example), but also to such background as often-mentioned Biblical stories or Greek, Roman, and Scandinavian mythology.

Curriculum planners are giving more and more thought to the question of what literature should be presented in the schools as common elements in our cultural heritage, elements that everyone should know. Vanished are such once-standard requirements as Burke's "Speech on Conciliation" and Webster's "Reply to Hayne." Today we are wondering about the cultural significance of a weaver named Marner, an assassin named Brutus, or a one-legged man named Silver. Perhaps Marner, Brutus, and Long John will remain, but if so, it will be for considered reasons, not historical chance. What *should* be the common ingredients in our culture other than the current television shows? What literature suitable for young persons is so timeless and yet so contemporary that it speaks

to today and will speak to tomorrow as it spoke to yesterday?
What literature from non-English speaking lands should we
know to reduce our provincialism? How can we avoid the
present overemphasis on literature that depicts only the middle and upper classes? What great fiction, drama, poetry,
biography, and satire should everybody know regardless of
his probable future occupation? How can pride in our American heritage be combined with informed respect for the
cultures of other peoples?

In addition to reading in common, the new curriculum
will pay much attention to individualized reading. It will
systematically encourage students to explore the world of
books, to dip in here and there, to read intensively in a few
areas, and to acquire what, hopefully, will become a life-long
habit of reading.

*The emerging English curriculum will make increased use
of technological devices.* For years many teachers of English
have employed record players, tape recorders, motion picture
and filmstrip projectors, tachistoscopes, and the like to enrich
or reinforce their instruction. Today educational television
programs are being viewed in more and more schools, and
millions of copies of paperbound books (improved in format
and durability as the result of technology) are supplementing
or sometimes replacing hardcover volumes. Tomorrow teaching machines and language laboratories promise to help in
routine learning tasks and especially in the individualizing
of some parts of instruction.

Technological and other innovations in English will neces-
sitate careful consideration by planners of school buildings
and by makers of students' class schedules. If teaching
machines are to be made available, should they be in each
classroom or in special rooms? Where should the language
laboratory be and how may a schedule be worked out for its
optimum use? With what devices should each English classroom be equipped: overhead projector, television, radio,
record player, tape recorder, movie and filmstrip projectors?

A recent guide to programed instructional materials describes 22 such programs in English available for general
use in September, 1962. These include both programed books
and material usable with certain machines. Among them are
programs for grammar, usage, punctuation, capitalization,
spelling, beginning reading, remedial reading, vocabulary,
and debate. But already experimental programs are being de-

veloped to help students improve their sentence structure or increase their understanding of literary selections.

Such innovations are greeted variously by English teachers. Some regard machines with such alarm that they begin to fear that they themselves are in danger of technological unemployment. Others say, in effect, "Wonderful! Now I can really teach. I can let the machines take care of the routine tasks, I can individualize assignments, and I can let each student work on a significant topic until he has mastered it. I shall have more time for conferences, for lesson preparation, and for evaluating student writing. There still isn't a machine to grade compositions!"

Related to technological changes and sometimes stemming from them are changing uses of instructional personnel. In team-teaching experiments, students meet on some days for large-group instruction, on other days for small-group or individual help; often they work independently. A combination of team teaching and teaching machines (once enough good programs become available) may well represent the instructional pattern of the future.

Finally, *The emerging English curriculum has implications for teacher education.* The two major implications can be summarized in this way: 1. Many currently employed teachers will need additional work, probably in institutes, to familiarize them with recent developments in study of the language, in composition, and in literary criticism. Supervisors, department heads, and all who work on curriculum development will need to study the workings of a spiral-cone pattern, will need to give much thought to the results that will be available from the curriculum study centers and other sources, and will need to consider how rapidly or slowly they will want to introduce team teaching, programed instruction, and other innovations into their schools. 2. Programs for future teachers need to be planned with emphasis on modern study of the English language, on composition, and on literature. These teachers, too, need to be informed of modern trends in the curriculum, and be introduced to team teaching and the use of electronic and other equipment.

It would be inaccurate to describe what is happening in the English curriculum as a breakthrough. Rather, it is another step, a big step, in a gradual evolution. The goal is simple to state, but difficult to reach: to enable each child to read, write, listen, and speak as well as he is able.

Tension on the Rope—English 1961

JAMES R. SQUIRE
Executive Secretary,
The National Council of Teachers of English

Perhaps more than any other American, Margaret Mead has made all of us realize that tension and anxiety are intricately related to the central concerns of our culture. In her studies of the South Seas, particularly in *Coming of Age in Samoa* and her more recent *New Lives for Old,*[1] she describes foreign cultures in which citizens live virtually free from the pressures that beset them in ours—societies which permit members to enjoy lives of comparative ease not unlike the fabled paradises so often depicted in motion picture travelogues. But if quiet calm and lack of concern in these societies produce a peaceful, carefree existence, the societies also produce little art, no literature, no great products of permanent human value. One of the consequences, it seems, of freedom from disquieting concern is release from feeling *deeply* enough about *anything* to strive for great achievement. No one feels anxiety because no one really cares. How different from our society, reminds Mead, where anxiety, pressure, and tension rise in direct proportion to our society's basic concern about achieving major goals. "The whole point of hitching one's wagon to a star," she writes, "lies in the tension on the rope." [2] Why else, indeed!

The "tension on the rope" is everywhere apparent in American education today. More than at any time during recent history, we seem to be approaching a consensus concerning fundamental imperatives for our schools. Today we seem more than willing to cast aside traditional ritualistic practices which have enshackled our efforts of the past. Today, for example, we are beginning to distinguish between what has been called "the strategies of subject matter" and the empty, dull traditionalism which has for so long masqueraded as academic education. Today, we are separating the educational services of the school from the community services, like health and

[1] Margaret Mead, *Coming of Age in Samoa* (New York: The New American Library, 1949); *New Lives for Old* (New York: William Morrow and Company, Inc., 1956).
[2] Mead, *New Lives* . . . , *ibid.,* p. 158.

driver training, which might be performed by other community agencies. "Some subjects are more important than
others," writes John Gardner for the President's Commission
on National Goals.[3] To what should go top priority in our
programs in English? Increasingly, we in education are finding ourselves in agreement that the fundamental content of
the school curriculum resides in a solid intellectual subject
matter. "The curriculum of a subject should be determined
by the most fundamental understanding that can be achieved
of the underlying principles that give structure to that subject," writes psychologist Jerome S. Bruner in his influential
report on *The Process of Education*,[4] a most carefully studied
document in professional education.

The arguments and debates, both bitter and insightful,
the projects and proposals—all are part of the "tension on the
rope" of American education today. If we view this tension
as reflecting the distance between our purpose and our practice
—between what we want to do and what we are able to do—
then we can see present efforts less as sources of confusion
than as signs of ultimate strength, less as a rejection of the
past than as a herald of future accomplishment. How much
worse our situation if we did not care! Despite tension created
by well-meaning, misguided people, worrying in the wrong
way about the wrong things at the wrong time, how much
worse if they did not care at all!

The focus of this paper is on the tension, on the potential
for change, on the new developments. Because the most
spectacular events are those involving experimentation with
staff utilization, we should perhaps begin with a review of
some of these new approaches as they are affecting English.
Ultimately, however, we must recognize trends within our
subject matter itself.

By now many of you have read the small paperback by
Trump and Baynham entitled *Focus on Change*,[5] a book which
summarizes the results of the National Association of Secondary School Principals' Staff Utilization Project and presents
an arresting, dramatic picture of what is repeatedly called

---

[3] John Gardner, "National Goals in Education," in *Goals for Americans*,
The Report of the President's Commission on National Goals (New York:
Prentice-Hall, Inc., A Spectrum Book, 1960), p. 86.

[4] Jerome S. Bruner, *The Process of Education* (Cambridge: The Harvard
University Press, 1961), p. 31.

[5] J. Lloyd Trump and Dorsey Baynham, *Focus on Change: A Guide to
Better Schools*. National Association of Secondary School Principals, Commission on the Experimental Study of the Utilization of the Staff of the Secondary School (Chicago: Rand McNally, 1961).

"the school of tomorrow." Team teaching, educational television, teacher aides, teaching machines, flexible scheduling —the ideas are now familiar if the practices are not. Alvin Eurich of the Ford Foundation, the agency which trumpets its contribution to the last ten years of education in a bulletin called *A Decade of Experiment*, enthusiastically supports the case of educational television.[6] Eurich's somewhat overeager acceptance of new yet-to-be-proved approaches may be regarded in part as resulting from his pride in authorship. Yet, symbolically at least, there is much in what he says.

During the past year, a special committee of the Illinois Association of Teachers of English completed an exhaustive survey of new procedures on staff utilization in English and identified four major areas of experimentation: teaching teams, lay personnel, electronic devices, and freedom from rigid patterns.

Team teaching. This is the device by which two or more regular teachers work together and plan large- and small-group instruction for classes ranging from fifty to two hundred students. It seems to be achieving results in many parts of the country. In English, the programs at Cleveland Heights, Ohio, at Bloom Township and Evanston, Illinois, and at Newton High School in Massachusetts have attracted particular attention. The program at Cleveland Heights will serve as an example. There, six teachers and 480 students have been engaged in the experiment. Three teachers teach nine English classes during the first three periods. Three teachers teach nine English classes during the last three hours. All six teachers meet in conference during the middle hours of the day, with a rotating chairman. This arrangement makes it possible for teachers to meet classes in normal discussion groups of twenty-five to thirty students in terms of special strengths or weaknesses in writing or reading, and to provide for testing or audio-visual experiences in large groups of seventy-five to eighty students so that the other teachers are freed for individual instruction or special preparation.

Similar practice is followed in the other situations. Newton High School schedules three or four classes at the same grade level to meet together for specially prepared lectures. Key teachers are designated as lecturers for this purpose and are often released from all other activity. This makes it possible not only for teachers to prepare lectures, say an examina-

[6] *Decade of Experiment: The Fund for the Advancement of Education 1951–61* (New York: The Fund for the Advancement of Education, 1961).

tion of a poem, but to work with the regular classroom teachers during the follow-through. Thus, at Newton, team teaching becomes in part a method of providing for in-service education and guidance for beginning teachers.

Certain observations may be cautiously advanced about team teaching in these and other experiments: (1) Team teaching does permit the teacher to group students more flexibly. It can give the teacher an opportunity to specialize (some on language, for example, others on composition). At the same time, teachers must make certain that what is presented in large-group lectures cannot be better taught in discussion groups. It is foolish and futile to lead a discussion or to talk about the delivery of a speech in a group of one hundred persons. What most students need is to practice their discussion and speech in the smaller classes.

(2) Team teaching can increase the opportunity for teachers to meet together to analyze common problems and goals. The opportunity for professional persons to meet in careful deliberation can do much to provide the vigorous intellectual stimulation which is all too seldom found throughout our high schools. But when adequate time is not set aside for such meetings, when the groups become less teams than leaders and followers, when the discussion leaders know little about the content of the lectures and students perceive almost no relationship between the two, then team teaching offers little more than an open invitation to chaos and confusion.

(3) Team teaching seems to offer no real solution to the problem of teacher load, despite some assertions to the contrary. While we do find in these schools classes of sixty, ninety, or even two hundred, we find others of only ten and fifteen. It is noteworthy, I think, that the addition of teacher-lecturers at Newton High School resulted in an increase in staff members rather than in a reduction. Again and again, teachers engaged in such experiences insist that team teaching becomes a real possibility only if clerical help is available, if lay assistants are provided, and if the teams have time for conference. In a few cases, where such help has not been provided, the team approach has been abandoned. Let us look to team teaching as a way of producing more efficient instruction, not as a royal road to reduction in teacher responsibility, teacher load, or teachers' work.

Use of lay personnel. Whether or not team teaching offers a permanent solution to any of our vexing problems, most would agree that the increased use of clerical aides for teachers is an exceptionally promising trend. This practice, now so widespread that one hesitates to single out any particular school, is based upon the recognition that the workload in the modern school is so great that the professionally trained teacher must have some help if he is to focus on professional tasks. More and more schools are employing general aides to perform routine duties, such as test checking, record keeping, exercise correction, study hall supervision, bus supervision, and endless other tasks. Probably the most influential feature of Diederich's "Rutgers' Plan" is its widespread use of teacher aides.

The most thoroughly tested and most promising of all the new developments in English is the use of lay readers or contract correctors. Yet again, we must emphasize that lay readers are useful not because they relieve the teacher of work (there is some indication that they add to the burden), but because they result in more efficient learning. In a properly designed lay reader program, students can write more and learn more about writing. Let it be said firmly, too, that in a properly designed program, the regular teacher does as much composition reading as she had ever done and that whatever is read by the lay reader is in addition. Evidence of pupil improvement in writing resulting from the intelligent use of lay readers has been reported by Burke.[7] Such evidence, supported by the enthusiastic comments of many teachers in Massachusetts, Wisconsin, Illinois, Texas, Iowa, and elsewhere, indicates that lay readers help if—and the "if" is thoroughly qualified—(1) if lay readers are carefully selected, usually by passing both written tests and interviews; (2) if readers receive careful preparation to grade papers, often at a two- or three-day workshop run by a specialist on composition; (3) if readers are carefully matched to the teachers with whom they will work closely during the years. Often this has meant observing the interrelationships at a day-long meeting or two; (4) if provision is made for conferences between teachers and readers to discuss the purposes of the assignments and to check each other's work; (5) if provision is made for conferences with the students, because experience shows that students tend to react unfavorably to mysterious voices from the unknown and to respond with

[7] Virginia M. Burke, "The Lay Reader Program: Backgrounds and Procedures" (Milwaukee: Wisconsin Council of Teachers of English, 1961. Available from the National Council of Teachers of English).

enthusiasm to personal comments from another reader; and (6) if the regular teacher continues to do all that she normally does, so that the addition of lay readers provides additional writing experiences for pupils.

Electronic devices and teaching machines. The revolution in electronics provides us with still a different approach to improving the efficiency of instruction. Illinois is in the four-state area over which the Purdue Air-borne Television Project hovers uncertainly, threatening on the one hand to impose an unwanted standardization of curriculum in many subject areas, and promising on the other to enrich the resources of the school. "Educational crop dusting," is the term applied by most teachers to this phenomenon. Television itself is scarcely news on the educational scene, but we have yet to determine exactly how it must best be used. Many schools have turned away from TV as a direct and total means of instruction. But as a supplementary method of instruction, it offers a potential which has yet to be realized. For example, a series of half-hour weekly programs on "The History of the English Language" presented by a scholar who can communicate with the young would offer a potential resource that few eleventh- and twelfth-grade English teachers would willingly reject.

More potentially revolutionary for our schools today are the rapidly moving developments in teaching machines and programed learning, those mechanical tutors that attempt to present subject matter in an orderly, logical way. Already spelling, certain reading skills, and aspects of English grammar have been programed with at least some slight degree of success.

Any material can be programed if it is reduced to a logically organized sequence of learnings to which students can respond with correct or incorrect reactions. Programed materials differ from other stimulus devices—from television or motion pictures, for example—because they provide practice in response. The basic psychological principles underlying the approach are rather clearly defined: (1) instruction is tutorial; (2) individuals respond at their own rates, and (3) the programs perform the task rather than the machines.

On this basis, a number of programed textbooks are being prepared, and teachers who have difficulty adjusting to mechanical devices will welcome the appearance of programs in the more traditional guise. English teachers will wish to review these new programs with care. The strong voice of the psychologist in programing *must* be tempered by that of the subject specialist. It has not always been thus. Not a few of the first materials have been built on a content in English largely rejected by our schools. And in some areas of English, notably in composition and language, we may not yet know enough about the sequence of steps leading to mastery to develop satisfactory programed instruction.

Flexible scheduling. Widespread experimentation in scheduling is being attempted to free teachers from routine responsibilities. Most attempts include one or more of the following practices: (1) variation in class size, (2) variation in the number of times a class meets, (3) utilization of several teachers in a subject area, and (4) provision of more independent study by students.

The "Rutgers' Plan" is probably well known in this area. It is noteworthy that many schools have seized upon its reading program. Suffice it to say, too, that in Detroit, the twenty-odd English teachers engaged in a modified Rutgers' Plan elected unanimously to continue the use of it.

A few other projects may also be mentioned as examples. Senn High School, Chicago, divides its eleventh-grade class into ten weeks of literature and ten of composition. While one teacher presents literature to fifty students for the ten-week period, two other teachers review composition to class groups of twenty-five each. Although the approach sacrifices the strength which emerges from a related program in literature and composition—a strength founded both on research and on sound experience—it does offer a realistic way of providing for ten weeks of intensive work on certain aspects of composition with much teacher-supervised study.

Another Chicago teacher divides her regular class of thirty-five students into three ability sections. For three days a week, the total class meets together in a teacher-controlled situation. On Tuesdays and Thursdays, however, group assignments receive priority. Thus each group in turn, on a different day, browses and reads in the school library, meets with a student leader for discussion, and meets with the teacher for discussion, planning, and special assignment.

At Stillwater, Oklahoma, a special honors program provides still another illustration of flexible scheduling. There, thirty selected students attend their regular classes only four days a week. On the fifth day, the students are released for completely independent research under the supervision of faculty members.

All these experiments seem based on the realization that we can no longer equate what is learned with the number of minutes spent in class.

Virtually all the new developments mentioned thus far deal with the form rather than the essence of English education. Many offer a better way of doing what is already being done. But there are important developments within the subject matter of English which must also be considered.

THE SUBJECT MATTER OF ENGLISH

Literature. The major concerns in literature seem to focus on the organization and sequence of classroom study. Various approaches are receiving careful scrutiny.

The historical-bibliographical-chronological approach as a way of organizing a total literature program or a total course is finding little support. Its influence is declining, and even the more conservative college instructors, who often teach this way themselves, are realizing it. Their disillusionment stems from the recognition that courses which aim for vast coverage of content necessarily sacrifice depth, that intensive textual study of a few complete selections generally proves more fruitful than the brief reading of snippets or fragments from many, and that many historical surveys of literature end in emphasizing the history at the expense of the literature. This is not to say, of course, that all authors can be divorced from their cultural settings. To try to understand Emerson or Thoreau, for example, without some conception of New England in the eighteen-thirties and forties is unthinkable, yet always the emphasis must be on "Self-Reliance" or on "Reflections beside Walden Pond" rather than on transcendentalism as an historical phenomenon.

The classic background of Western literature is experiencing a resurgence of interest. Faced with a generation of elementary and high school students who cannot tell Aeschylus from Aphrodite, college instructors are demanding more attention to myth and folklore in our programs. Elementary teachers, especially, are being asked to survey their offerings in literature to ascertain whether they should achieve a better balance between contemporary selections and the works of the past.

Topical and thematic units are receiving increasingly careful study. Where we have failed in the past to distinguish between the two, we are now beginning to see certain fundamental distinctions. Topics like "Backwoods America" or

"Westward Adventure," more penetrating themes like studies of "The Meaning of Courage," "The Nature of Justice," or "The Impact of Loneliness on the Individual" are examples. Both approaches force attention to the meaning of literature —to the content and to the communication of the author— and they seem to be becoming increasingly popular as teachers develop skill in planning and acquire sufficient grasp to break away from more conventional patterns. Increasingly we are recognizing that, in teaching literature, *at different times* we must deal in our classes with the symbolic, linguistic, historical, ideational, and other aspects.

Some critics, noting the misuses of the thematic approaches, are scorning any precise arrangements, but even they urge that high school students should concentrate on the study of ideas. In using topical or thematic approaches, we also need to satisfy ourselves that our student-readers do not emerge with superficial or simplified conceptions as a result of classroom study. *Macbeth*, for example, is about ambition, to be sure, but it is also about order and disorder, about the disintegration of the human personality, about a host of other problems. To teach it only for what it reveals about the impact of ambition is to do disservice to the tragedy and to the complexity of literature. Rich works of this kind are sometimes best taught independently. Indeed, in the junior and senior years of high school, students might well concentrate to a considerable extent on close textual analysis of a few major works.

Finally, the sequence of literary instruction is receiving definite attention; so are problems of balance and continuity. Do we spend too much time on prose fiction which teachers like to teach and students like to read? Why? Do students perhaps need less help in learning how to read novels than in reading all other forms of literature? What should we do about the reading and study of poetry? Or are we really doing anything at all? What is the role of world literature in helping us understand the hopes and aspirations of other people?

Some of these considerations are not particularly new, but they become increasingly crucial at a time when our educational system is redefining priorities in education.

Language and grammar. During the past decade, especially, the research of descriptive linguists and the success in applying linguistics to a method of classroom study have presented us with a new point of view on language. Coming first as a trickle, more recently as a deluge, the reports have had tremendous impact—how great may be estimated by the fact that, during the last year, articles on at least some phase of linguistics are contained in more than two-thirds of the affiliate publications received at the NCTE headquarters. Half of the NCTE cosponsored summer workshops dealt with the problem, and the Council appointed the fourth Commission in its history to deal with this important matter. Where five years ago the bulk of the linguists' attention was directed at freshman composition, or at least focused on advanced courses in language, a perceptible shift now finds new theorists aiming directly at the secondary and elementary curriculum itself.

How has this new grammar affected English? The effects are legion and are only just beginning to be recognized. Here are a few of the more apparent.

The developments have invested English language teaching with a tremendous excitement. Teachers are aroused, concerned, interested, reading, studying. Last fall the preconvention workshop of the NCTE was vastly oversubscribed. A similar group planned for this year's workshops dealing with linguistics is bulging with enrollments; so are conference programs scheduled on the topic. Of great value may be the impetus given to restudy, for reidentification of goals and methods, for a review of content. The College Entrance Examination Board's summer institutes will devote one-third of their time to modern language study.

The applicability of past research dealing with the methodology of teaching grammar has been questioned to a considerable degree. Possibly the new grammar will be more helpful than the old in teaching students how to write; possibly it will not. Advocates are probably justified in urging us not to assume that the new grammatical instruction will be as disappointing as the old in improving communication. Yet it is equally possible that methods proved wanting in teaching traditional grammar will serve linguistic grammar no better. One suspects, for example, that students of average and below-average ability will have as much difficulty in retaining generalizations gleaned through the new grammar as through the old, since their basic problem apparently is inability to cope with generalization, not with the accuracy of the concepts involved.

What does seem to be one sound assumption, however, is that students who are taught by teachers who know the new

grammar or grammars—who understand the distinction between writing and speech, who know how to analyze the
structure of language—may be taught more effectively than
those who do not have such instruction. Indeed, the abysmal
ignorance of many teachers of English about the nature and
structure of our language may well explain many of the
inadequacies of present instruction. Only about one-third of
the colleges preparing English majors to teach in our high
schools require these students to complete even a single
course in grammar and usage, whether the grammar be structural, traditional, or transformational. Only about half the
many elementary teachers have enough instruction in English
language, nor do they have any substantial work in language
development or how to teach language to children. Small
wonder, then, that our school programs seem so confused.

Increasingly we are finding many of the students of language urging a study of grammar for its own sake, not for its
contribution to the pupils' ability to write and speak. These
adherents are articulate, vocal, intelligent, sincere. They claim
that the process of language distinguishes man from other
animals and thus demands direct study in general education.

The emphasis on phonology and oral language embraced in
the new studies awakens us to the importance of oral pattern
practice. The Detroit and Chicago schools, faced with the
problem of teaching the standard dialect to students from
culturally deprived homes, are reporting important successes
in using tape recorders and language laboratories for oral
drill. Moreover, the study of the grammar of sound within
the English sentence, like the grammar of structure, will
probably cause thorough extension and revision in our methods
of teaching reading, once the new insights are properly understood and assimilated.

Yes, there is much new in the language study. The tension
on the rope is taut indeed.

Composition. In the teaching of composition, schools are
devoting more and more attention than before to the skills
of organization. The concern in itself is not new—attention
to ways of presenting ideas effectively is as old as the arts of
rhetoric and logic themselves. What has created "a fresh
awakening" is evidence pointing to the centrality of form and
organization in communication. In high school and college,
ability to communicate at reasonably mature levels—levels
expected for normal theme writing—appears to demand a

consciousness of form, of relationships or organizational principles more than anything else.

The University of California recently established a special faculty committee representing several departments to study the prevalence of substandard writing among undergraduates. The group was concerned because the standard introductory freshman course in English—and the remedial course known there and elsewhere as "bonehead English"—seemed not to be coping with the problem in any permanent way. The committee studied term papers and examinations of fifteen hundred undergraduates. Its most conclusive finding was that difficulties in organization and structure predominate in poor writing; proficiency in the techniques of grammatical usage seemed a corollary of general ability to organize material logically. This finding of the significance of "form consciousness" will not surprise those familiar with recent research in written composition. In short, good writers tend to be those concerned with organization, with the problems involved in forming relationships. The poor writers are those concerned primarily with mechanics. Moreover, poor writers, unlike the good, are totally unable to recognize good writing in others. One wonders whether those of us who have concentrated on spelling, punctuation, and vocabulary in our classes—that is to say, concentrated on writing rather than composition—have contributed to this disability in any way.

TRENDS IN ENGLISH TEACHING

Research in linguistics and composition is serving as impetus for change in many programs. A number of trends are apparent:

(1) Increased emphasis on organizing sequential instruction concerning specific processes and principles of composition, as contrasted with miscellaneous, unsequential programs which merely require much writing. Oakland, California, for example, has tried to identify important principles of composition to be emphasized at every cycle level. The writing begins at the primary level, continues in the upper grades and later.

(2) Greater interest in the teaching of composition in the upper elementary grades, rather than exclusive emphasis on writing experiences alone. This is not to say that creativity and fluency should not be fostered; rather it recognizes the need to detect and control some of this fluency.

(3) Greater emphasis on expository writing in the upper

secondary grades as contrasted with personal or creative writing. This is because the ability to identify and develop an expandable idea tends to be more easily taught in relation to composition based on impersonal topics. Themes dealing with personal experiences, "What I Liked on My Vacation," "When I Won the Game," and the like, are appropriate and understandable topics for many young people. But they become increasingly less appropriate if they become a regular diet. Eleventh- and twelfth-graders must be encouraged to reach somewhat beyond this level, to try coping with mature, abstract subjects, such as "The Impact of Change on Some Aspect of Society," "The Concept between Justice and Vengeance" in a play like *Medea* or *The Visit*.

(4) More frequent, brief writing assignments of paragraph length or so and a few long, infrequently assigned massive papers. Although some college students claim never to have written a theme in high school, it does seem reasonable that overworked secondary teachers of English have sometimes accepted quantity rather than quality. Unable to assign more than a paper a month, they ask for a "long one" to make the writing worth while. The folly in such an approach is evident. Most skills of organization can be taught in principle at least in relation to the paragraph—and is it not the principle of organization which is of basic concern? The person is not far wrong who said, "If a student can write a good paragraph before he enters the twelfth grade, I can teach him everything he needs to know about a long theme. If he cannot write a good paragraph by this time, there is not any point in trying to teach him anything more."

(5) Less and less emphasis in the secondary school on the long research paper. The suitability of the paper for high school students has been questioned by many college instructors. The objections have been many, but primary is the one that students who cannot organize a 500-word essay should not be expected to cope with a 5,000-word theme. This is not to say, of course, that needed library skills cannot be taught through brief research assignments.

(6) Recognition that the traditional book report violates every principle of sound composition taught elsewhere in the program, that it forces students to string together a series of virtually unrelated paragraphs (on setting, on plot, on most interesting incident, etc.), and thus seriously undercuts the composition program being developed elsewhere. In its place, more and more teachers are substituting something which

might be called a book review, where students, like professional reviewers, are asked to develop a single idea expressed in each book and to organize their comments around this theme.

(7) Increased emphasis on essay examinations as the only valid means of assessing competence in composition. The College Entrance Examination Board has reinstituted an essay examination as part of its official program. Some schools are establishing an annual essay examination for all students, perhaps one graded by special groups of readers. At Lenoir High School in North Carolina, for example, each English teacher now requires three "trial themes"—in September, January, and May. These are short papers written in class, read by outside teachers as well as by the classroom teacher, in an attempt to dramatize progress and to point up problems. Under the leadership of Marion Zollinger, high schools in Portland, Oregon, have been doing this for several years. A city-wide essay examination is held annually for all students in junior and senior high school. Papers are impromptu and written in fifty minutes. The students are even permitted to use dictionaries, since it is composition, not spelling, for which they are working. The entire set is graded by a Central Board of experienced teachers. In a recent assessment, observers found some teachers who questioned the artificiality of the testing situation and the spurious nature of the test results. However, most who have been living with the system for some time believe it contributes a certain uniformity to standards, that it has resulted in upgrading composition, and that it provides considerable continuity for pupils. The most dramatic result is a decrease in the number of students assigned to a special twelfth-grade section from 28.3 per cent in 1953 to 5.8 per cent in 1958.

All seven trends show the attention that some schools are now placing on organization of ideas. Perhaps to some extent this emphasis reflects the recent interest in form and structure of scholars in all areas of English—an interest in form shared in a different way by the structural linguists who study the ways ideas are expressed, an interest shared by those concerned with symbolic logic and aesthetic theory.

CONCLUSION

These, then, are some of the heralds of change. Let us remember, however, that any social institution as complex as our schools will change only slowly, no matter how radical the stimulation. Some developments will wither on the vine before reaching maturity; others will reach fruition and affect instruction in ways not yet even estimated. These new ideas—this tension on the rope—are to be welcomed, not to be feared, but welcomed with a hard head, albeit a sympathetic heart. They should be welcomed because they bring to our subject an excitement and a vitality, and because they force us to rethink our purpose and methods and to retain the best of the old. Above all, they should be welcomed because they demonstrate anew to us the endless fascination of our subject.

Grammar and Linguistics in the Teaching of English

ALBERT H. MARCKWARDT

Professor of English and Linguistics
Princeton University

Currently there are two attitudes toward the teaching of grammar in the schools. Possibly for quite different reasons, the lay public and those teachers who do not have to deal with it in their classes are emphatic in their demands for renewed emphasis on grammar. Many whose business it is, or could be, to teach grammar as part of a secondary school or college freshman English program maintain that it has little or no effect upon the writing of their students. There is, moreover, a considerable body of experimental data (some of it highly dubious in nature) to support these claims.

The issue is confused even more by the fact that *grammar,* as the term is employed in this running debate, has two quite different meanings. In one of its senses it refers to a body of proscribed usages characteristic of nonstandard English, combined with a complementary insistence upon the corresponding features of the standard language. The nonstandard usage may be characteristic of a social or of a regional dialect (*e.g., taken* as a preterit; *ain't*), or it may amount to nothing more than the intrusion of one of the features of standard spoken English into the written language (preverbal position of *only*).

In the second sense the term *grammar* suggests the attempt to describe the structure of language or of *a* language by means of a terminology and a series of concepts derived from the Romans and ultimately the Greeks, one which succeeded not too badly in describing a highly inflected language in terms of the philosophy and what passed for psychology prevalent at the time. From this we derive the terms we use to label the parts of speech, the elements of a sentence, and the various ways in which these elements may behave.

There is some right and some wrong on both sides of the dispute to which I have referred. It is probably true that the way in which grammar is and has been taught in thousands of American classrooms has had little or no effect upon the language of the pupils. There is an element of truth as well as irony in the story of the boy who, for corrective purposes having been made to write *I have gone* on the blackboard one hundred times, concluded his task by leaving a note for the teacher which read "I have wrote *I have gone* one hundred times and I have went home." Nor can we place any substantial degree of reliance upon the likelihood of transfer from workbook exercise sheets to student themes. Yet this by no means excludes the possibility that a language analysis which did portray accurately and cogently the structure, operation, and potentialities of the language would not have the desired effect.

As a footnote we must also account for the fact that "in the good old days" when grammar was "really taught" it was or seemed to be an efficacious corrective discipline. There are several reasons for the truth, real or apparent, of this assertion. First, the student population particularly in the secondary schools and colleges was more homogeneous, reflecting generally an upper or upper middle class background, and speaking a better facsimile of standard English than is the rule today. These same students had more experiences with other languages, both ancient and modern, than do their current counterparts. This reinforced the presentation of grammar as such to begin with, and even more important, the very contact with another language threw into bold relief the structural features and potentialities of the native tongue. Finally, such wholly artificial exercises as diagraming the first sentence of *Paradise Lost,* a time-honored staple of the English classroom at the turn of the century, whatever their defects may have been, did have the virtue of forcing close analytical attention to a highly stylized literary dialect quite different from the normal language habits of the student, one which was unusually rich in intricate developments of, and variations from, the norms of modification patterns and clausal structure.

Returning however to the dual concept of grammar presented earlier, (1) a series of recommendations prescribing a body of specific usages, and (2) an attempt at a structural description, let us ask ourselves in all candor why these well-intentioned approaches to a systematic treatment of language have failed, at least partially, in their purpose.

The first of these, English grammar in its prescriptive aspect, developed in eighteenth-century England through the work of such men as William Ward, Robert Lowth, and Dr. Johnson. As C. C. Fries, S. A. Leonard, and F. E. Bryant have shown, many of the specific recommendations made at that time and continued in American textbooks through the first three decades of the present century, had no basis even in the literary usage of the period. "Some of our most celebrated writers and such as have hitherto passed for our English classics have been guilty of great solecisms, inaccuracies, and even of grammatical improprieties, in many places of their most finished works," wrote Thomas Sheridan, father of the dramatist, in the preface to his dictionary of 1780.

We need not concern ourselves with the social and cultural circumstances which encouraged the acceptance of such an unrealistic attitude toward language, except to say that the very factors which made it seem desirable in eighteenth-century England were also present in nineteenth-century America. We are interested, however, in the net results. There were at least three. One was the adoption by many students of what may be called, for want of a better term, classroom dialect, a sapless and super-correct form of the language employed only within the hearing of the English teacher and in written work subject to her scrutiny, and for the most part, dropped like a hot-cake as soon as the hour was over. Somewhat more harmful in the long run was the fixation and perpetuation in the consciousness of many individual students of six or seven shibboleths which they carried about with them for the rest of their lives and not infrequently passed on to succeeding generations. Among these may be included the prejudice against a preposition at the end of a sentence, the avoidance of *real* as an intensive, *like* as a conjunction, *ain't* even in the first person negative interrogative, and above all the peculiar notion that "colloquial" is in some manner a term of opprobrium. Aside from the essential negativism of this attitude, there is the further complicating factor that no two people seem to carry about with them the same collection of linguistic prejudices. Finally, the whole approach has resulted in giving many products of our educational system a feeling of inferiority about the language they use which amounts almost to a guilt complex, rendering them an easy prey to the quackery of the "better English" manuals.

To some degree the most violent excesses of the prescriptive grammarians have been brought under control through the efforts of a good many linguistic scholars. Textbooks no longer tell us that "*lesser* is a barbarous corruption of *less,* formed by the vulgar from the habit of terminating comparisons in *—er,*" and some of the more advanced have even come to recognize the thousand-year-old propensity of *none* for a plural verb. The principal difficulty with the so-called *liberal* (I would prefer to term it *realistic*) attitude toward language usage is that perforce it must admit that in many instances English has no one or single established form. There are alternatives; the recognition and honest presentation of these will often result in a complexity which is likely to be pedagogically ineffective.

Nevertheless, as long as we continue to educate an ever-increasing proportion of our youth, we shall be dealing with students who come from homes where standard English is not habitually spoken. With them, part of our responsibility amounts to teaching them to substitute a particular prestige dialect of English for that which they normally employ, for Standard English is currently a social dialect and historically a regional one. Incidentally, the magnitude of this task is literally overwhelming, unequaled by anything in past educational and linguistic history. As long as we continue to attempt it, we shall have to employ prescriptive grammar to a degree. We must see to it that we use it in as enlightened a manner as possible. Among other things, we must recognize that language habits can be changed only through constant drill, and that the number of new habitual responses which can be firmly established within a given period is very small indeed. This demands careful selection and programing of what is to be taught.

Now let us consider briefly grammar as we, in the profession, usually think of it when we talk about teaching or knowing grammar. "In the usual approach to the grammatical analysis of sentences," says Charles C. Fries, "one must know the total meaning of the utterance before beginning the analysis. The process of analysis consists almost wholly of giving technical names to portions of this total meaning. . . . 'Knowing grammar' has thus meant primarily the ability to apply and react to a technical terminology consisting of approximately seventy items." [1]

Unquestionably many teachers would be quite happy if their students were able to recognize and apply a grammatical terminology of considerably less than seventy items. There are some I know who would almost settle for the eight parts of speech. Unfortunately, however, as Robert Pooley has pointed out in his most recent book, "a great number of elementary school children are taught a large number of formal grammatical concepts . . . these same materials are begun again in the junior high school and carried a little farther . . . and still the same materials are begun again in the ninth grade of senior high school, and are repeated year after year through the twelfth grade. The results do not in any way justify the time and effort apparently put forth in this endless repetition." [2]

There are some, no doubt, who will maintain that the present-day school does not spend this much time and effort on grammar. The only answer that can be given to them is that Pooley bases his conclusion upon the best available evidence, including published courses of study, current textbooks, the estimates of experienced teachers, and the content of articles in the pedagogical journals.

This leads us next to ask why grammar teaching has not been more effective. The following explanation by Paul Roberts sounds somewhat polemic, but it has the virtue of being brief and to the point. "In one sense," he says, "the descriptions of language found in English grammars *are* true. They deal—in part, at least—with real phenomena existing in the language. . . . Sometimes, to be sure, the grammarians describe categories which do not exist . . . But for the most part, English grammars discuss real things. They do not, however, discuss them truly. The reasoning on which the descriptions rest is a nightmare of confusion, contradiction, circular argument, jumbling of principles, and plain foolishness. . . . When we try to find logic in the proceedings, we are forced to conclude that English grammar doesn't have any. Intellectually it can only be described as a mess." [3]

[1] *Structure of English*, Harcourt, Brace and Co., New York, 1952, p. 55.
[2] *Teaching English Grammar*, Appleton-Century-Crofts, New York, 1957, p. 55.
[3] *Understanding Grammar*, Harper & Brothers, New York, 1958, p. 139.

This is a strong statement. Nevertheless, it is all too easy to document the charges of circularity, contradiction, and confusion. This is not to say that a wise and intelligent teacher cannot work with the system; many have done so. The difficulty is that the system has too many flaws to assure even a reasonable chance of success at the hands of the less wise and the less intelligent.

There are many reasons for the shortcomings in the system, but one in particular is worth pointing out, since it will help us to understand the possible role of present-day linguistics in this connection. It is well known that the apparatus of traditional English grammar goes back ultimately to the Greek analogist Dionysius Thrax, through the Latin works of Donatus and Priscian. As a language analyst, Dionysius performed reasonably well. The categories and concepts which he developed were well adapted to a description of Greek, a language which depended heavily upon inflection as a device for signaling meaning. In other words, Dionysian grammar did for its time and its subject just about what a competent language description should do today. The machinery worked somewhat less successfully with Latin, but no major shortcomings were apparent.

The attempt to apply this particular analysis to English ran into severe difficulties. Here, after all, was a language with really a minimum of inflection, depending largely upon word order and function or structure words as signaling devices. Consequently the basic categories and concepts which had been worked out for the inflectional languages could no longer be identified or recognized in terms of form but had to be defined in terms of meaning, thus reversing the normal procedure of any descriptive science. Largely because of this do we find the circularity, contradiction, and confusion that Roberts complains about.

This brings us to the role of linguistics. Let us consider first the kind of description of English (call it grammar, if you will) that the linguistic scientist would like to develop, next the extent to which such a description has been achieved, and finally, how it may be put to effective use in the English curriculum.

To begin with, the linguist recognizes that English employs numerous contrastive patterns of arrangement, as well as certain other patterns of form, and that these patterns constitute parts of a structural whole. Our procedure, then, is to describe these patterns first, and only *after* they have been adequately described are we ready to ask just what meanings are signaled by these formally identified structures. Observe that this is precisely the reverse of the process that defines a noun as the name of something, or the subject of the sentence as the actor of an initial step.

Thus the question of "knowing" or "learning" such a grammar does not arise. It is obvious that each of us has "learned" this grammar by the age of four, since we have all been unconsciously reacting to and employing these signaling devices from that time on. School grammar would then consist of making the individual fully conscious of the operational structure of the language, in the faith that an awareness of its mechanisms, including both the potentialities and shortcomings of the machinery, would enable him to manipulate it that much more effectively. The linguist assumes, in addition, that a scientifically defensible description of the language is a better tool for the job than one which is full of contradiction and confusion.

So much for the underlying theory and approach of the linguist. We must now ask to what extent a workable and applicable description of the language has emerged. A candid reply to this question must recognize that the two principal approaches to the problem, one by Charles C. Fries, set forth in his *Structure of English*, and the other by Henry Lee Smith, Jr. and George L. Trager, available now only in the highly condensed *Outline of English Structure*,[4] do differ on such matters as terminology, the extent to which phonological evidence is employed, the order of analysis, and certain other less fundamental matters. The differences between them are very fully described by James Sledd in a review in the journal *Language*.[5] Still, we must not overlook the fact that compared with the traditional old-line grammatical analyses, the features that Fries and Smith-Trager have in common are far greater in number and more important than the ways in which they differ. Recently a more extended presentation of what is in essence a Smith-Trager type of analysis has made its appearance. A. A. Hill's *Introduction to Linguistic Structures* bears the significant subtitle, "From Sound to Sentence in English."[6]

A fair appraisal would recognize that these two analyses do provide us with a basic framework that can be employed

[4] Studies in Linguistics: Occasional Papers, No. 3. Battenburg Press, Norman, Oklahoma, 1951.

[5] Vol. 31, No. 2 (1955): 312–345.

[6] Harcourt, Brace and Company. New York, 1958.

in school texts, that to a degree both of them follow some false scents, and that in other minor matters all the details necessary to a completely satisfactory description of the language have not yet been worked out. Unfortunately the least has been done in what for our purposes is the most critical area, namely syntax. Moreover, thus far the scientific description has been virtually limited to the single sentence. Utterance sequences larger than this still remain to be dealt with. Yet despite these shortcomings, there is enough to provide a foundation for able teachers and textbook writers —and also enough to mislead and mystify the less perspicacious.

During the past four years four textbooks have appeared, all prepared by authors who know something of linguistic science, who have tried to apply it in the books they have written, and who have recognized their indebtedness to it. They are:

H. W. Whitehall, *Structural Essentials of English*. Harcourt, Brace, 1954, 1956.

D. Lloyd and H. Warfel, *American English in Its Cultural Setting*. Knopf, 1956.

Paul Roberts, *Patterns of English*. Harcourt, Brace, 1956.

Paul Roberts, *Understanding English*. Harper and Brothers, 1958.

At least two others are in preparation. Only Roberts' *Patterns of English* is designed for the high school student; the others are intended chiefly for college use.

These books do have in common certain features which distinguish them from other texts, features which may point the directions that grammars of the future may conceivably take. They all use the suprasegmental features of the spoken language (stress, intonation, and juncture) to help segment and identify language units. Not one of them begins with the parts of speech and other conventional definitions—in fact, not one of them even uses the term "part of speech." Instead, they speak of "form classes" or "word classes," and arrive at these only after some examination of how the language operates. They all recognize the distinction between lexical and structural meaning, and then focus their attention upon the major devices which English employs to signal structural meaning, including word order, structure words as markers, as well as inflection. From such an analysis, four major form classes (noun, verb, adjective, and adverb) usually emerge, defined in terms of form and behavior rather than meaning. In addition, certain groups of structure words are recognized, some of which are the leftover parts of speech; others reflect such concepts and functions as determination and intensification.

Though small, this is a beginning. Thus far there is no experimental evidence on how well it works. We have only the testimony of enthusiasts and the doubts of the skeptics. If this is indeed the right track, the immediate tasks are three in number:

1) To improve the present descriptions of English, *i.e.*, to push forward on the scientific front.

2) To extend the application of linguistics through the preparation of more and better textbooks, reaching down into the junior high school and the elementary grades. Irrespective of the age at which abstractions can be grasped, children can observe language *behavior* as successfully as they can observe nature or any other phenomenon.

3) To train or retrain teachers to employ and apply this kind of language analysis. Professor Waldo E. Sweet of the University of Michigan wisely refused to release his linguistically oriented Latin materials to teachers who had not had some training in their use or in linguistics generally. We shall do well to proceed with similar caution.

These three steps will not be achieved overnight, and if we are to move toward them with deliberate speed, I would be inclined to place the major stress upon deliberation. I should prefer to see the movement as a progression rather than a revolution, emphasizing always the virtues of painstaking and rigorous observation of the language, an open-minded but nevertheless critical examination of the analyses which result, and a constant evaluation of the teaching devices which must be designed to make the presentation of the language structure functional and operative.

What Have We Accomplished in Reading?— A Review of the Past Fifty Years

NILA BANTON SMITH
Professor of Education,
New York University

This last half-century stands out as a truly golden period in the progress of reading instruction. More innovations have been effected in reading during the last fifty years than during the entire three hundred years antedating this period of American history. I am sure that progress has been equally notable in the other phases of the language arts constellation. It is most appropriate that accomplishments in all of the language arts areas be reviewed upon this momentous occasion—the Golden Anniversary of The National Council of Teachers of English!

Progress in reading instruction has been marked by a succession of turning points. For a period of years reading methods and materials all over the country are quite similar —so similar, in fact, that an unbiased examiner might arrive at the conclusion that all had been turned out of the same mold, with just a slightly different crimp here and there in the contour of the pan. Then, rather suddenly, a new plan becomes popular, and we teach reading in this manner until another turning point arrives. Thus, epoch after epoch of reading instruction passes (26).

Fortunately printed records are available to which we can turn in delineating these epochs and ascertaining their characteristics. In attempting to obtain information to bring to you about reading epochs during our recent half-century the following source materials, published between 1910 and 1960, were explored: prominent educational magazines that usually contain reading articles, yearbooks of learned societies, summaries of published investigations in reading, lists of unpublished masters' and doctoral researches completed or under way. More than 300 pieces of materials were surveyed for the purpose of picking up the sequence of events and trends which marked the pilgrimage of reading in its upward march from 1910 to the present time. This information will be presented to you by decades.

ACCOMPLISHMENTS FROM 1910 TO 1920

The dramatic decade beginning with 1910 ushered in the first truly great breakthrough in reading progress. This was the birth of the scientific movement in education. In 1909 Thorndike made the initial presentation of his handwriting scale before a meeting of the American Association for the Advancement of Science, and in 1910 it was published (29). Generally speaking, the publication of the Thorndike scale has been recognized as the beginning of the contemporary movement for measuring educational products scientifically. In the immediately ensuing years, scales and tests appeared rapidly: Courtis arithmetic tests, Hilligas' Composition Scale, Buckingham Spelling Scale—and then a reading test—The Gray Standardized Oral Reading Paragraphs (13). This test was published in 1915. Other reading tests followed shortly.

As a result of the strong new surge of interest in placing education on a scientific basis together with its correlative motives for developing instruments of measurement, we would naturally expect that the scientific study of reading problems would take a vigorous spurt. And this it did.

Through all the years up to 1910 only 34 studies had been reported in reading. During the 1910–20 decade, 200 accounts appeared, about six times as many as had been reported during the entire history of reading preceding this time. These studies had to do mostly with tests and school surveys as would be expected.

As for method: the most revolutionary thing happened that had happened since clergy began to teach reading in churches, and dames began to teach reading in kitchens. "For hundreds of years oral reading had maintained a supreme and undisputed claim on teaching methods" (25). During this decade, however, the concept of teaching *silent* reading burst into our slumbering complacency like a bombshell. It came suddenly and in the midst of a period in which school people were serenely content in the use of sentence-story methods applied to the oral reading of selections in literary readers. For the most part they continued to use these practices to the end of the decade but the startling new idea was at least launched. Discussions of the advantages of silent reading appeared for the first time in the Sixteenth (16) and in the Eighteenth (17) Yearbooks of the National Society for the Study of Education. Speakers at educational conventions began to talk about it, magazine articles began to discuss it. The idea had been born.

To sum up: developing the concept of applying scientific techniques to the study of reading, devising standardized instruments to measure reading achievement, increasing the number of studies tremendously, initiating the silent reading idea. These seem to have been the major accomplishments from 1910 to 1920.

ACCOMPLISHMENTS FROM 1920 TO 1930

The period extending from 1920 to 1930 is perhaps the most golden decade in this golden era of progress in so far as fundamental changes in reading practices are concerned.

These changes were largely due to the scientific movement which had shaped up during the preceding period and which now was opening up fresh wells of information with improved and extended applications.

The new studies conducted during this decade carried with them three distinct earmarks of progress: the number increased tremendously; they covered a wider scope of problems; many of them were conducted in classrooms by teachers and other school personnel, rather than being confined to the laboratory.

As to the number of investigations: Gray's summaries reveal that 763 were reported as compared with 200 during the preceding decade. This unprecedented increase reflected the zeal and enthusiasm with which school people were searching for more information about the important subject of reading.

The studies of this period probed a variety of problems, but there were three problem areas which were most highly significant. They were significant because they resulted in sweeping changes in practice. These three areas were: (1) silent reading, (2) individual differences, and (3) remedial reading.

The first half of this decade might well be called "The Age of Silent Reading." "These years were marked with an exaggerated, often exclusive emphasis on silent reading as opposed to the traditional oral reading techniques" (25). As previously mentioned, the concept of teaching silent reading was initiated during the latter part of the preceding period, but it didn't really take hold as a nation-wide classroom practice until during the years of 1920 to 1925. This sudden and widespread reversal in practice was largely due to two influences: the development of tests which revealed that silent reading was superior to oral reading in speed and comprehension; and the publication of The Yearbooks of the National Society for the Study of Education. As already indicated, one article each appeared in the Sixteenth (16) and the Eighteenth (17) Yearbooks. The climax, however, came with the publication of the Twentieth Yearbook, Part II (19) of which was devoted entirely to the report of the "Society's Committee on Silent Reading." Following the appearance of this Yearbook, "textbook writers began to produce readers based on silent reading procedures; other authors prepared professional books on silent reading; teachers busied themselves in preparing exercises that would check comprehension of silent reading by means of drawings, true-false statements or completion sentences and so forth. The whole country for a time seemed to be obsessed with the idea of teaching silent reading" (25).

This extreme emphasis, however, was soon balanced with other factors. By 1925 the novelty of the new idea had worn off, somewhat; investigations revealed some unique uses of oral reading, school people discovered that there still were some special needs for oral reading in the school program. Perhaps, the culminating influence came with the publication of the Twenty-Fourth Yearbook, Part I (20) which appeared in 1925. This Yearbook advocated a broader program of reading instruction which among other things recognized both oral and silent reading. New courses of study, professional books and readers immediately reflected the broadened objectives of this Yearbook and methods during the years 1925–1930 were shaped largely by its contents. So during the first two decades of the last fifty years we progressed from extreme oral reading to extreme silent reading to a broader program which recognized both. In my opinion, this was an indication of real accomplishment.

As for individual differences: with the administration of the newly developed tests, a very great fundamental truth became apparent with a violent impact—the realization that there were wide individual differences in the reading achievement of children, in the same grade and in the same classroom. This discovery spurred school people to experiment with a variety of adjustments in classroom organization and instruction, designed to cope with this newly revealed variation in the learning rate of children.

There were reports of adjustments made in classrooms which maintained the regular organization such as ability grouping, flexible promotions, and differentiated assignments. But the pulsating new idea was that of breaking up class organization entirely to permit of individual progression. This plan of organization received as much attention at this time as it is receiving at the present moment. Speeches, articles, and Yearbooks dealt with the subject. San Francisco; Los Angeles; Detroit; Winnetka; Madison, Wisconsin; and other school systems reported (21) results they had obtained by individual instruction. The states of Connecticut and Illinois reported (21) experiments in individualizing instruction in rural schools.

The various plans, on the whole, were patterned after

the Winnetka or the Dalton ideas, in both of which individual progression in reading and other subjects was made possible by means of assignments in which the child worked through subject material that increased in small increments of difficulty. The important point to note is that attention to individual differences in reading received its first great impetus during this decade of remarkable progress.

The concept of *remedial* reading was launched from its small island of study during this period and sent out over unexplored seas in quest of answers to disability problems. The movement was spurred on by the use of standardized tests. These tests revealed that thousands of boys and girls were failing each year to make normal progress in reading. Published reports of work in the reading disability field indicate that the chief interest at this time was in diagnosing individual cases. As for method, it was during this period that Fernald evolved her kinesthetic method, and that Orton expounded his theory on mixed dominance and the treatment that accompanied it. Remedial reading did get under way during this period.

In the beginning reading there also were innovations. Experience charts first came into use. The Nineteenth Yearbook (18), published in 1920, dealt with reading materials. In it examples were given of charts based on children's experiences, and the practice of introducing children to beginning reading through the use of such material was advocated. This practice was not widely accepted until much later, but progress had been made in evolving the idea.

And last but not least, mention must be made of another mark of progress which clearly stamped itself into the later annals of this decade. The reading readiness concept began to take shape at this time.

In 1926 The International Kindergarten Union in co-operation with the United States Bureau of Education conducted an investigation on "Pupils' Readiness for Reading Instruction upon Entrance to First Grade." The first articles on this subject were published in Childhood Education in January, 1927. Two of these articles used the term "reading readiness." In so far as I am aware, this was the first time that this phrase crept into our reading vocabulary (27). In Gray's summaries published in 1928, he reported for the first time three studies on reading readiness. A few masters' theses and a trickling of articles on this subject also appeared before the close of the decade. The new concept, however, was still in the formative stage, and little was done about it in a practical way until the following period, but the movement was on its way.

Much more could be said about the accomplishments made during this unprecedented period. I should like to dwell longer on the accumulation of information gathered about reading and the auspicious innovations in classroom practice that were inaugurated at this time, but I must pass on to other conquests and other days.

ACCOMPLISHMENTS FROM 1930 TO 1940

This period may be characterized largely as one of extension and application rather than one of revelation and initiation.

Investigations continued at an accelerated pace. In round figures about 1200 studies were reported between 1930 and 1940. Not only were these studies greater in number, but they were superior in isolation of problems, in designs, and in controls.

Some of the embryo ideas that had sprouted in the preceding decade came into full bloom and fruited profusely at this time. For example: the reading readiness interest reached its zenith in this period (27). Published investigations on this topic increased steadily during each successive year of this decade (9), reaching their climax of frequency in 1940 when Gray reported 22 studies relating to this topic in one year. Since that time the number has decreased steadily.

Turning to unpublished research, this was the hey-day of aspiring masters and doctors in finding problems for research in the readiness area. The first doctoral dissertation on readiness was reported in 1927. From that time on, the number of master and doctoral studies increased, reaching its peak in the years 1937 to 1940. Fourteen such studies were completed in 1937, 15 in 1938, 14 in 1939, and 12 in 1940. Since that time only 2 or 3 academic studies on readiness have been reported each year.

A similar trend is seen in published articles on reading readiness. Periodicals abounded with discussions on readiness topics from 1930 to 1940. Articles on this subject rarely appear in present-day literature.

In the light of this evidence, it may be concluded that this was the period of most vigorous emphasis, both on investigations of reading readiness and applications of the readiness theory. The concept has been accepted now and we hear little about it at the present time.

Remedial reading, which had experienced a touch-and-go recognition during the preceding period, now became established and gained stature. Many significant studies were conducted in the remedial reading areas: causes of difficulties, diagnosis, and corrective procedures. Professional books devoted exclusively to remedial reading were first published. Some laboratory studies were still made but the majority of studies now were conducted in schools. Remedial reading, which had started in laboratories, now became a topic for practical experimentation in the public schools themselves.

A new trend that began to emerge was that of giving beginning attention to high school, college, and adult reading. Studies made at these levels, however, were mostly concerned with interests in, and uses of reading, rather than with reading achievement and teaching procedure.

Every decade reviewed so far has been characterized by one or two events of great distinction. In the 1910–1920 decade, it was the application of scientific measurement and investigation to reading, in the 1920–1930 era, it was the startling innovations of silent reading and of individual progression. What was the spectacular event in the nineteen-thirties?

The Activity Movement swept the country during these years, and the startling new idea in reading was to teach this skill as a part of the Activity Program. In such a program children worked freely and spontaneously and actively in following their own interests; and teachers were intrigued with the new "game" of trying to get all of their subject matter across through "Units of Work."

In so far as reading was concerned, pupils had access to a considerable number of books bearing largely on the topic of their "Unit of Work." This was the first big impetus for bringing a quantity of books into the classroom for reading. There was a profusion of charts and school-made booklets growing out of children's interests. Pupils read functionally from their co-operatively prepared materials and out of many books in doing research in connection with their Units. In a word, this was how reading proceeded in the Activity Program in the thirties.

We no longer hear of the Activity Program at this time nor of the teaching of reading in connection with this program. The Activity Movement, however, made a vigorous impact on the teaching of reading and other subjects at this time—an impact so strong that its influence still continues. The Activity

Movement distracted the school public from its age-old concept of schools centered almost exclusively on subject-matter goals to schools in which consideration is given to the child, himself, his stage of development, his interests, his activities, his choices and his decisions.

In summary, we may say that progress in this decade was characterized by continuing investigations, greater in number, higher in quality than in the preceding decade; intensive application of the readiness concept; transfer of remedial activities from laboratory to classroom; beginning attention to reading at higher levels; and widespread interest in teaching reading as an integral part of the Activity Program.

ACCOMPLISHMENTS FROM 1940 TO 1950

An event resulting from progress in science overshadowed all other indications of progress during this period. The "birthday of the atomic age" is officially set as December 2, 1942, when Dr. Enrico Fermi turned on the first successful nuclear energy machine in Chicago. The first atomic bomb destroyed Hiroshima on August 6, 1945. On the face of things this terrifying discovery with its possibilities for good or for evil reduced to comparative insignificance our little scientific achievements in reading. Yet, could this achievement have been possible without reading? Can we cope adequately with its future destructive or beneficent effects, as the case may be, without more efficient reading skill and a wider-reading citizenry? The atomic age and reading immediately become interactive.

But we didn't realize this at the time. We were too close to this earth-shaking event to sense its import for reading instruction. The war probably only had two *immediate* effects on reading. One of these was a diminution in the number of reading investigations. This was probably due to the fact that many of the psychologists and educators who conducted research in reading, or stimulated others to do so, were in the armed services.

The other major effect of the war was the shocking discovery that at this day and age thousands of young men in the military service could not read well enough to follow the simple printed instructions for camp life. Coupled with this discovery was the revelation that reading could be taught to these young men in army camps in an amazingly short time. Concurrently, several new investigations disclosed reading deficiencies in large numbers of high school and college students. These several influences combined to produce a spurt in attention to reading at these higher levels. Immediately following the war, a great deal of professional literature on reading emerged and among these publications several bulletins and one Yearbook appeared dealing with high school and college reading. Chief among these publications was a bulletin of the National Education Association titled *Reading Instruction in Secondary Schools* (15), and the Forty-Eighth Yearbook, Part II of The National Society for the Study of Reading, titled *Reading in High School and College* (24). The actual teaching of reading at these levels had not progressed far at this time but the idea was vigorously expanding.

During this period, reading in the content subjects also became a matter of wide discussion and the subject of a few investigations. The studies at this time pointed to the general conclusion that while good readers can read well in all subject fields, special practice in reading in particular subject areas is helpful to average and poor readers.

In the forties, wide recognition was given to the interrelationships amongst the language arts. Studies, articles, speeches were concerned with the relationship of reading to spelling, handwriting, vocabulary, and composition. As a result we came to recognize that reading was not an isolated skill independent of other skills used in the interchange of ideas, but that it was just one aspect of the total language arts constellation mutually dependent upon and interactive with all other skills in the communication dimension.

A strong new concern also sprang up in regard to the effects of three of the newer media for mass communication: comics, movies and radio. Television did not come in for much attention until the next decade but during this period wide dissemination of entertainment through the first named agencies stirred up worry on the part of school people and parents. They feared that interest in listening to radio, looking at comics, viewing movies would reduce interest in reading and thus decrease the amount of reading done. Numerous popular articles bemoaned the situation and pointed out its dangers. Several studies were conducted directed toward the exploration of students' interests in this area and finding out how much time they devoted to the offerings of these types. Thus initial steps were taken in obtaining information to combat what was thought to be the first threat to reading.

Remedial diagnosis and treatment continued to claim a large segment of the spotlight. Mechanical instruments and devices which had been introduced during the preceding period increased in numbers and use. There were fewer studies reported on psychological factors such as dominance, handedness, eyedness, and reversals. An increasing number were devoted to personal factors as related to reading: personal interests and attitudes, personal status in social, emotional, and experimental maturity. This attention to other growth and development factors as related to reading was certainly one of the most notable advances made during this period.

To sum up: the chief points of progress during this decade were increased attention to teaching reading at the higher levels; growing attention to reading in the content subjects; concerns about mass communications; attempts to find relationships between reading and handwriting, spelling, vocabulary and composition; and perhaps, most important of all, a growing consciousness of the profound truth that reading doesn't develop in a vacuum by itself, but that it is part and parcel of general child development and is affected by all other aspects of child growth.

ACCOMPLISHMENTS FROM 1950 TO 1960

A most exciting decade! For one thing, interest in reading instruction became almost universal during this period. There was a time when primary teachers were the only people interested in the teaching of reading. Now teachers of all subjects and at all levels want to know more about reading. Parents are asking questions, pursuing books and articles on reading. Students at high school and college levels and adults beyond college are flocking to reading centers. Slick magazines and laymen are discussing reading freely. A great conflagration of interest has been ignited amongst teachers and students, and more especially amongst the lay public. And this is good.

During this period, however, for the first time in history, reading instruction in American schools underwent harsh and severe criticism by laymen. School people maintained that the criticisms were unfair and rose to the defense of their methods through articles, speeches, discussions, and investigations. Several comparative studies of "Then and Now" were made. These studies, on the whole, showed that we were teaching reading as well as or better than in preceding years.

Insofar as progress is concerned the criticism by laymen probably had three good effects: it caused school people to examine their present methods more carefully; it stimulated the interest of parents and other laymen in reading instruction; it offered motives and opportunities to school people to explain the research, psychology, and philosophy on which present methods are based. So in this situation, as is often the case in other situations, even criticism caused reading to move forward.

Perhaps as an offshoot of interest and criticism, coupled with a growing awareness of the complexity of the reading process, there has been a spurt of activity in the reinstatement and increase of reading courses in the curriculums of teacher-training institutions. Concurrently with this interest in adding more courses, standards are being raised in regard to the qualifications of teachers of reading and of reading specialists. This movement toward better-trained teachers in reading is a big step forward.

As for the number of investigations: studies during this period reached incredible proportions. Gray reported over 1,000 studies in his 1960 summary, but in his introduction he said for the first time in his thirty-five years of annual summarizing, "The number of studies are increasing so rapidly that it is no longer possible to report all of them in this annual summary. Those referred to this year represent either a new or distinctive approach to a problem or suggest significant issues in need of further study." Not only was this increase apparent in the published reports of reading investigations, but it also was reflected in the reports of dissertations completed or in progress which soared to new numerical heights, the number reported averaging about 90 per year as compared with about 50 in the preceding decade.

Advance is shown in the subjects of investigation. Reading in the content fields, adult reading deficiencies, and television as related to reading came in for strong additional attention. The most gratifying trend revealed, however, is that we are at present delving more deeply into the reading process and more broadly into the factors that affect it. The former popular topic of phonics now seems to have been replaced with studies of perception. Comprehension is no longer treated as a lump sum; the emphasis at present is upon the higher thinking processes of interpretation and critical reading. The old readiness studies are replaced with investigations of prediction and expectancy. Remedial reading is not so much concerned now with studies of gadgets and specific teaching remedies as it is with organismic and personality factors. Parental personality, attitudes, and interactions with the child as related to reading entered the research scene for the first time during this period, and many reading investigations concerned with parents and their children are now being reported. Studies are made in regard to the climate of the classroom and its effect on reading. This mere glimpse at some of the subjects of the most recent studies is indicative of a trend toward probing to greater depths and in wider breadths than was evident in most of the studies preceding this period.

Special mention should be made of a clearly discernible advance in regard to reading and the other language arts. In the preceding decade we became strongly concerned about the relationships of reading to the subjects of spelling, handwriting, vocabulary, and composition. During this decade we have moved on to a concern about aspects of the language arts which perhaps are less tangible than the subject-matter areas but more inclusive in their application to the entire block of communication skills. Listening studies have increased by leaps and bounds. Some of the most recent dissertation topics have to do with semantic studies of reading content, multiple meanings, figures of speech in reading, and the linguistic approach to reading. Is it not an accomplishment to have moved on from subject interrelationships to relationships dealing with listening and the various aspects of linguistics?

The innovation in reading method which has loomed large on the horizon of late is the plan known as *individualized instruction.* The amount of attention given to this plan in this decade is comparable to that given to individual instruction in the nineteen-twenties. It probably is the most popular topic of discussion at present in educational magazines and often at teacher gatherings.

This individualized plan of the present is different from individual instruction which was popular in the twenties. The earlier plan was subject-matter oriented. Each child was given subject-matter assignments divided into small increments of difficulty and he was permitted to progress as fast as he, personally, could complete each successive increment. The present plan is child-psychology-oriented utilizing particularly Dr. Willard Olsen's theory of *seeking, self-selection,* and *pacing,* in that the child seeks that which stimulates him, selects the book he desires to read, and proceeds at his own rate.

This plan has been used too recently for research reports to have crept into published summaries of investigations. Most of the research on this topic at present falls into the unpublished category of theses, dissertations, or mimeographed reports of experiments carried on in certain school systems. An examination of the most recent sources listing dissertations completed or under way indicates that a quantity of research is now taking place in regard to this topic. Much of it will undoubtedly find its way into print in the near future.

Much more could be said about this period, but because of lack of time we now shall let the curtain fall over the last scene in fifty years of reading accomplishment. As we review the stirring events of the past, we have a right to feel cheered, grateful, proud. In looking back in retrospect we might wonder whether another fifty years could possibly bring about so many changes. This was the first period in which experimentation could be conducted scientifically. In consideration of the newly developed tools, our eagerness to learn, and studies conducted, we might reason that practically all facets of reading instruction have been explored and thus another era could never be so great as this.

If we do reason to this conclusion, we probably are wrong. We pioneered during this period in unexplored territory. We chopped down and cleared away the large virgin trees, but perhaps some of the humble shrubs or creeping vines or fragile mosses may hold even more significance for us than the strikingly obvious, first-sight timbers. But these more obscure growths won't yield their significance with the use of heavy saws and axes. We shall need fresh, piercing insights in choosing which of these to select for dislodgment, and then we shall need unique, delicate tools to pry them loose from their tangled environment and to test the potency of their effect.

What I am trying to say is that while our accomplishments have been very great, indeed, it may be that we have only penetrated the first layer, the troposphere, so to speak. Undoubtedly, brilliant new insights will be revealed, ingenious new techniques of experimentation will be evolved. Possibilities of such developments portend opportunities for unlimited achievement in the future.

Most assuredly, we shall not rest complacently in the glory of achievement during this past golden age. Rather shall we look forward to still greater accomplishments in reading. Let us push on and on with more and more vigor in the next decade and the next decade, and in all of the other decades ahead!

REFERENCES

This bibliography would be too voluminous if each separate piece of material examined were listed. In case of educational journals, yearbooks, and summaries of investigations, each successive issue or publication was examined during the period of years indicated by dates accompanying the general reference. In cases in which a specific reference was made, or a quotation was stated from one particular publication, that publication is listed. Professional books on reading were examined but the titles are too numerous to include in this list.

1. Betts, Emmett Albert, and Betts, Thelma Marshall. *An Index of Professional Literature on Reading and Topics.* American Book Company, New York: 1945.

2. *Childhood Education,* 1–37, 1924–1960.

3. *College English,* 1–22, 1939–1960.

4. *Doctoral Dissertations Accepted by American Universities,* H. W. Wilson Co., New York: 1934, 1955.

5. *Educational Index,* 1–31, H. W. Wilson Co., New York: 1930–1960.

6. *Elementary School Journal,* 10–60, 1910–1960.

7. *Elementary English,* 1–37, 1924–1960.

8. *English Journal,* 1–49, 1911–1960.

9. Good, Carter V. "Doctoral Studies Completed or Under Way," *Phi Delta Kappan,* 1923–1953; (Separate publications) Lyda, Mary Louise; Jenson, Glenn; Brown, Stanley; Anderson, Harold. Phi Delta Kappa, Bloomington, Ind. 1954–1959.

10. Gray, William S. *Summary of Investigations Relating to Reading.* University of Chicago Supplementary Monograph, No. 28, Chicago: 1925.

11. Gray, William S. "Summary of Investigations Relating to Reading," *Elementary School Journal,* 26–32, 1925–1932.

12. Gray, William S. "Summary of Investigations Relating to Reading," *Journal of Educational Research,* 5–54, 1932–1960.

13. Gray, William S. *Oral Reading Paragraphs Test,* Public School Publishing Co., Bloomington, Indiana: 1915.

14. National Education Association, "Newer Practices in Reading in the Elementary School," *The National Elementary Principal,* Seventeenth Yearbook, 1938.

15. National Education Association, *Reading Instruction in Secondary Schools,* Research Bulletin, Vol. 22, No. 1, 1942.

16. National Society for the Study of Education: *Sixteenth Yearbook, Part I,* 1917.

17. *Eighteenth Yearbook, Part II,* 1919.

18. *Nineteenth Yearbook, Part I,* 1920.

19. *Twentieth Yearbook, Part II,* 1921.

20. *Twenty-Fourth Yearbook, Part I,* 1925.

21. *Twenty-Fourth Yearbook, Part II,* 1925.

22. *Thirty-Sixth Yearbook, Part I,* 1937.

23. *Forty-Eighth Yearbook, Part I,* 1949.

24. *Forty-Eighth Yearbook, Part II,* 1949.

25. Smith, Nila Banton. *American Reading Instruction,* Silver Burdett, New York: 1937.

26. Smith, Nila Banton. "Historical Turning Points in Reading," *National Education Association Journal* (May, 1952), 280–282.

27. Smith, Nila Banton. *Readiness for Reading and Related Language Arts.* National Council of Teachers of English, 1950.

28. *The Reading Teacher,* International Reading Association, 1–14, 1947–1960.

29. Thorndike, E. L. *The Thorndike Scale for Handwriting of Children,* Bureau of Publications, Teachers College, Columbia University, New York: 1910.

30. Traxler, Arthur E. Educational Records Bureau, New York: *Ten Years of Research in Reading* (with Seder, Margaret), 1941. *Another Five Years of Research in Reading* (with Townsend), 1946. *Eight More Years of Research in Reading* (with Townsend), 1955. *Research in Reading During Another Four Years* (with Jungeblut).

31. U. S. Library of Congress, Catalog Division, *American Doctoral Dissertations* Lists, Government Printing Office, Washington: 1913–1940.

Social Science and the New Curriculum

FRANKLIN PATTERSON

Lincoln Filene Professor of Citizenship and Public Affairs at Tufts University and Director of the Lincoln Filene Center

AN IRONY AND A NEED

It is a curious irony that the curriculum of American schools has remained so little touched by the social sciences in an age when the chief remaining enemy of man is man himself. This irony is compounded by the growth of the social sciences and by their great impact on aspects of our society other than the formal program of the schools.

The impact of the behavioral sciences is certainly widespread, as a report prepared for the President's Science Advisory Committee recently noted.[1] Among other effects, these sciences are changing our society's fundamental ideas about human desires and possibilities. Through the filter of popularization, the social sciences in the past few generations have altered the beliefs that many people have about intelligence, child rearing, sex, public opinion, organizational management, and other matters. It is not uncommon even for unproved behavioral hypotheses to find widespread, casual acceptance, a fact which underlines the need for better education about what the social sciences are and are not.[2]

The society's need for what these sciences may be able to offer, however, goes far beyond the question of accurate translation. It includes a need for policy scientists to give leadership, as de Grazia has put it, in "the posing and staffing of solutions to the great problems . . . that remain with modern man."[3] But since we are concerned, despite nearly overwhelming social change, to reconcile social order with individual freedom and initiative and keep the immediate power of those who rule subject to the ultimate power of the ruled, our need is even broader, involving the competence of the general citizenry. The social studies are needed to impart a body of factual knowledge, a theoretical apparatus for supplying this knowledge with order and significance, a methodology of inquiry and verification, and an appreciation of the range of values reflected in the study of man. Long has commented that this mixed enterprise needs to be concerned on one hand with the pursuit of scientific knowledge and on the other with the "humanistic and philosophical task of entering the student into an informed and critically intelligent appreciation of his cultural inheritance and even of the broader milieu in which the educated and responsible citizen of today must function."[4] It is in the arena of competing social values, conflicting policy choices, and difficult decisions that people generally must be prepared to operate, today and for the indefinite tomorrow.

One would not suspect the dimensions of this need from what is currently offered in the way of social studies in American schools. For the most part, the present social studies curriculum is simply obsolescent. It has remained essentially unchanged for forty years or more. Immense changes in human society and knowledge, in the nature of social responsibility and character, have occurred without compensatory development in the social studies curriculum. The most recent significant change in the social studies offering came as a result of a national commission statement in 1917 and 1918. Since then little new of value has been added and little old dropped. The social studies in elementary and secondary schools, as a result, are not geared to the swiftly changing social, economic, and political world in which we and our children live. The curriculum in most schools still disregards the non-Western world. Areas of public policy that are difficult and controversial are principally avoided. The social sciences other than history (and government, presented as a mechanical system) are largely ignored. As far as the majority of our schools are concerned, it is as though the tremendous development of the sciences of man in the past half-century has not occurred. Economics gets short shrift— and mainly as mythology. The findings of anthropology, sociology, social psychology and related fields get little attention. The subject matter that comprises today's social studies in the schools is presented in highly sanitized mass production textbooks intended to offend no conceivable interest group, and is dealt with chiefly in a read-recite-quiz manner which would seem almost calculated to reinforce both its inanity and its short-term retention. It is hardly remarkable that students characteristically regard social studies as a crashing bore. The irony of all this is that the need for a wide and deep literacy in the studies of man is so critically urgent.

WHY SOCIAL SCIENCE LAGS

The backwardness of social studies in our schools is partially a function of the state of the social sciences themselves. Not only are these fields "new" as disciplines and therefore late-comers to the academic table, but they suffer other disabilities. Their growth in this century has proceeded at a constantly accelerating rate, in a kind of metastatic way. Today, the social sciences seen from the middle distance seem extraordinarily diverse, sprawling, complex, and often either portentously tentative about the obvious, or given, as Ann Roe once said, to better and better research designs about matters of less and less importance. As an influence upon the schools, they are handicapped by their lack of anything resembling a unified body of social science theory. Despite the efforts of a few men like Tyler to reflect multi-disciplinary generalizations to the schools, there has been little substantial or co-ordinated endeavor in this direction, and the school social studies curriculum shows it.[5]

Another, perhaps more serious, obstacle to the modernization of the social studies curriculum arises out of the forbidding nature of the problems that social science may deal with. As Havighurst has pointed out, the chief limitations that the schools have as agents of social change are in the realms of social taboo and controversial social values.[6] In these realms, where social science is accustomed to move with relative freedom, school curriculum is most unresponsive or hostile to change. Here are what Hunt and Metcalf call "areas of belief and behavior characterized by a relatively large amount of irrationality, prejudice, inconsistency, confusion, and taboo."[7] And these areas (e.g., economics, race relations, social class, sex, religion, nationalism, and patriotism) tend to be "closed," in the sense that investigation of materials and reflective treatment of problems are largely inhibited or excluded in contemporary schools.

The dominant role that one discipline, history, plays in the existing social studies curriculum makes the lag in developing a broader base in the new social sciences even more understandable. Feldmesser, in his recent paper for the American Sociological Association, has summed up ably the static reliance of schools on standardized course work in history.[8] His grievance is not only that such offerings are limited and out of date but that, as taught, they are bad social science for the most part. In a 1962 summer conference, Feldmesser was even more direct, saying ". . . in the strongest possible terms: we shall make no progress in transforming the social studies into social science until we slaughter the sacred cow of history."[9] Be this as it may, the cow is tough as well as venerable and may take more than a sociologist's words to slay. Whatever else school history instruction today is, it is *safe;* tiresome, mechanical, and shallow, perhaps, but wonderfully inoffensive, except to social scientists and a few other students of society.

Other factors in lag may be added. At least one has been dealt with by de Grazia, "the hatred of new social science." Distrust, if not hatred, is easy to find. Auden's commandment

Thou shalt not sit with statisticians
Or commit a social science

is repeated in less interesting language and at more length by a wide range of scholars and laymen, not all of whom are poets or classicists. At its best, outside skepticism about social science can be as helpful as it is keen, deflating the turgidity with which we sometimes describe self-evident discoveries. The humanist Fiedler's penetrating critique of voting studies in particular and political sociology in general is a case in point.[10] But the skepticism of the informed and sympathetic critic is less common than the blank hostility of the proudly ignorant. The latter include at least some academics and laymen whose personal anxieties are heightened by the thought that social science deals with phenomena that should not be looked into, at least not with an objective eye.

Another very real reason why the new social science has not been taken up in a new social studies curriculum lies in the teaching manpower available. With notable exceptions that prove the rule, school teachers in the social studies are not characteristically well prepared even in history or the older social sciences (e.g., economics, geography), to say nothing of the newer fields. Nor do the extreme pressures of day-to-day teaching allow them time in which to read or study to raise their level of scholarly competence, assuming that motivation to do so might be present. By their lack of broad or special preparation in the disciplines and their demolishing schedules, social studies teachers are driven to the easy way out: reliance on a standardized text in history or civics for most of what they try to teach. To expect such hardpressed people to innovate, especially in a curriculum area as sensitive and inchoate as "the new social studies," would be naïve.

SIGNS OF CHANGE

At present and in the recent past, signs have appeared that may signal substantial moves to modernize the social studies. Many of these signs have been raised by leaders in the social disciplines and associations, but there has been complementary activity by certain individuals, groups, and agencies speaking for the school social studies.

In 1958 a special commission of the National Council for the Social Studies, headed by Howard E. Wilson, called for new educational programs responsive to social change and the funded insights of the social and behavioral sciences.[11] This report was followed by the establishment of a joint *ad hoc* committee by the Council and the American Council of

Learned Societies, seeking a vehicle for school teachers and social scientists to join forces for curriculum reform. In 1960, the NCSS–ACLS group commissioned a series of papers in which scholars were asked to present the social science concepts and generalizations that high school students should be expected to have learned by the time of graduation. These papers were presented to the annual meeting of the NCSS in November, 1961; their publication is scheduled for the current academic year.

In December, 1961, the School and University Program for Research and Development (SUPRAD) of the Harvard Graduate School of Education conducted a two-day conference, chaired by Feldmesser, on the Behavioral Sciences in the Secondary School. Some thirty-five sociologists, anthropologists, psychologists, and education specialists took part, concluding (a) that more behavioral science should be taught in secondary schools; (b) that teaching methods and the variability of cultures were important considerations; and (c) that a variety of curriculum innovations should be tried and evaluated.[12]

In the same period at the end of the 1950's, scholarly associations were moving hopefully towards the provision of curriculum leadership for the schools. Thus today all of the social science professional societies have established committees to forward the cause of their several disciplines in the schools of America. All well intentioned, these committees vary greatly in their sophistication about the conditions and needs of American schools, teachers, and children. The best-known of efforts by these committees has been the work of the Task Force in Economic Education, which produced a report and recommendations in 1961 reflecting the joint conclusions of professional economists, teachers, and the Committee on Economic Development.

In addition, certain school systems (e.g., Newton, Massachusetts, and others) have undertaken social studies curriculum revision on their own. In these efforts, history has tended to be the dominant orientation, with the new social science getting little play. Here and there, individual social scientists have experimented with the teaching of their disciplines at the high school level, but these are isolated undertakings.

Easily the most comprehensive and potentially the most influential current development in school social studies curriculum reform is a proposal of the American Council of Learned Societies and Educational Services, Incorporated. This proposal grew out of a two-week conference in June, 1962, held at Endicott House, the M.I.T. facility at Dedham, Massachusetts. The conference dealt with the relationship of the social sciences *and* the humanities to the school curriculum from kindergarten through secondary school. Some forty scholars from various universities, and school people from several parts of the nation participated. Frederick L. Burkhardt, President of ACLS, and Jerrold R. Zacharias of M.I.T. were cochairmen of the conference, and the principal general model of curriculum revision considered was the massive program of the Physical Science Study Committee (PSSC) in which Zacharias has been the moving force.

The Endicott House conference relied heavily for its instructional orientation on Jerome S. Bruner, and the nondidactic, inductive approach which characterizes the PSSC program and much of the new teaching in mathematics. For some specialists, e.g., those in anthropology and political science, this orientation was easier to accommodate to and use in thinking about curriculum design than it was for others, notably in economics. The conference group rejected the idea of reproducing in small at the school level separate courses in the several disciplines, except as electives. Instead, the Endicott group saw the long-run task as one of creating *integrated social science* sequences for the lower and secondary schools, related to comparable sequences in the humanities, and geared to varieties of individual development, intellectual growth, and responsible citizenship.

Two forms of follow-up have resulted from the conference. One is experimentation with integrated social science sequences, including the development of a framework of concepts, new materials, and instructional techniques. Douglas Oliver of Harvard is working in this regard with a small group of scholars who are concerned with kindergarten through sixth grade. Richard Douglas of M.I.T. is doing the same thing with another team interested in the senior high school years, and I am working with a group on the junior high school social studies curriculum. The second form of follow-up is the projection of a major effort to program the new social studies in relation to the new social science on a comprehensive scale over a period of time. This large-scale undertaking is in a formative stage, but envisions a modernization comparable to that provided by PSSC, with various new units, courses of study, films, artifacts and other materials, texts, teacher's guides, and the like. The designation of this project at present is the Curriculum Development Program in the Humanities and Social Sciences, and its joint sponsors are the ACLS and Educational Services, Inc. (which now handles the PSSC program).*

REQUIREMENTS AND OUTLOOK

Recent and current activity should not be mistaken for solid achievement. Whether papers, pronouncements, and projects are the prelude to genuine modernization of the social studies in a significant way will turn on a number of factors.

One of these is money. To get some idea of how much would be needed in social science-social studies curriculum revision from kindergarten through high school, consider the fact that the successful PSSC program has required approximately a million dollars a year for the past six years to upgrade one course in high school physics alone. Thus far no foundation, agency or group has shown either the wit or courage to venture the level of support that a major across-the-board reorganization of social education would require. Instead, monumental caution and lack of imagination have been displayed by the National Science Foundation and other potential sources of leverage. The NSF, for example, appears committed only to exceedingly modest, tentative, and piece-meal support of "course-improvement" in such areas as the introduction of anthropology at the high school level. One is reminded of Gardner's comment that "our thinking about the aims of education has too often been shallow, constricted, and lacking in reach or perspective." [13] Or his suggestion that in American education all along we have had the blueprints for a cathedral, but that we have insisted on referring to it as a toolshed. Whether a cathedral or toolshed approach is taken to the building of a new social studies program remains to be seen.

Much depends, too, on the degree to which scholars who are accustomed to working only in their special fields can learn their way into the situation and needs of our vast school enterprise and contrive to see its social studies problem as a whole. Disciplinary parochialism, piecemeal tinkering, or enthusiastic spinning of wheels in isolated special projects are not apt to do the curriculum much good.

At present, there is a crucial, basic need for elucidating

* The Steering Committee of the Project are Frederick Burkhardt, Jerrold Zacharias, Elting Morison, Robert Bishop, Henry Bragdon, Charles Brown, Jerome Bruner, Howard Mumford Jones, James R. Killian, Henry Levy, Robert Merton, Douglas Oliver, and this writer.

an intellectually viable structure for unified social studies as a school field of learning. What exists currently in our schools is a *mélange* which is mostly dysfunctional in terms of process, substance, and the needs and capabilities of individual learners. Achieving a functional structure of knowledge for the schools, given the diffuse state of the contemporary social sciences, will not be easy; it will involve hard choices and risk, but it is essential. Only scholars in the social disciplines can meet this need. The schools cannot do it alone.

Certain conceptions of the task may assist in developing structure for a new unified social studies approach in the schools. One of these is to conceive social education as being concerned essentially with studying causation and valuation in human experience. Another is to conceive social studies in American schools as contributing to the education of individuals who will be competent citizens in a constitutional democracy faced with rapid change, who will make informed choices among alternatives, basing their choices on values that are critically examined rather than accepted haphazardly and unconsciously. An additional conception is that social studies should contribute to the continuous reorganization of perception, the enhancement of communication, the understanding of group relationships, the capacity for problem-solving, and the development of self and social identity. Closely related is the conception of social studies as operationally introducing students to the methods of the social sciences, their strategies of inquiry.

The new social studies hopefully will be designed for individuals who are seen as *both* learners and citizens. Thus there will be a need to involve students in efforts to deal rationally with fundamental social issues: opening "closed areas," using problem-solving procedures in case materials, gaming, simulation, and other ways.[14] There will be a need, too, as Rokeach, Kemp, and others made clear, to see learning and critical thinking in the social studies as including questions of emotion and personality in addition to the problems presented by an intellectualized body of subject matter.[15] And university scholars will need to remember that every child is not a graduate student, that each goes through developmental stages about which we are only learning, that all come from socio-cultural situations that condition their behavior, that they have widely varying natural endowments, and that while less than half of them will go beyond high school, all of them will be potential voters.

The outlook, then, may be determined less by money-support than by the intellectual breadth, social vision, and creative educational inventiveness of those who are willing to set their hands seriously to constructing a new social studies based in the social sciences and closely related to the humanities.

REFERENCES

1. *Strengthening the Behavioral Sciences,* Statement by the Behavioral Sciences Subpanel, The Life Sciences Panel, President's Science Advisory Committee, The White House, Washington, D. C., April 20, 1962 (Washington, D. C.: U. S. Government Printing Office, 1962), 19 pp.

2. *Ibid.,* p. 2.

3. Alfred de Grazia, "The Hatred of New Social Science," *The American Behavioral Scientist,* Vol. V, No. 2, October, 1961, p. 13.

4. Norton E. Long, "Political Science in the Schools," mimeographed working paper prepared for the American Council of Learned Societies, 1962, p. 2.

5. Ralph W. Tyler, "Human Behavior: What Are the Implications for Education?" *The National Education Association Journal,* October, 1955, pp. 426–429.

6. Robert J. Havighurst, "How Education Changes Society," *Confluence: An International Forum,* No. 1, Spring, 1957, pp. 85–96.

7. Maurice P. Hunt and Lawrence E. Metcalf, *Teaching High School Social Studies: Problems in Reflective Thinking and Social Understanding.* New York: Harper Brothers, 1955, p. 230.

8. Robert A. Feldmesser, "Sociology and the Social-Studies Curriculum of the American High School." Duplicated paper prepared for delivery at the meeting of the American Sociological Association, Washington, D. C., August 31, 1962.

9. *Report,* Conference of the Social Studies and Humanities Curriculum Program, at Endicott House of the Massachusetts Institute of Technology, Dedham, Massachusetts, June 9–23, 1962. Mimeographed, p. 4.

10. Leslie A. Fiedler, "Voting and Voting Studies," Chap. 9 in *American Voting Behavior,* Eugene Burdick and Arthur J. Brodbeck, editors. Glencoe, Illinois: The Free Press, 1959, pp. 184–196.

11. "Curriculum Planning in American Schools: The Social Studies." A Draft Report of the Commission on the Social Studies of the National Council for the Social Studies. Wash-

ington, D. C.: The Council, November, 1958. Mimeographed, 26 pp.

12. Feldmesser, *op. cit.*, p. 11.

13. John W. Gardner, "The Servant of All Our Purposes." Reprinted from the 1958 *Annual Report,* Carnegie Corporation of New York. White Plains, New York: Fund for Adult Education, 1958, p. 1.

14. Cf., for example, Franklin Patterson, *Public Affairs and the High School: A Summer Pilot Program.* Medford, Massachusetts: The Lincoln Filene Center, Tufts University, 1962, 43 pp.

15. Cf., C. Gratton Kemp, "Critical Thinking: Open and Closed Minds," *The American Behavioral Scientist,* Vol. V, No. 5, January, 1962, pp. 10–15.

The New Curricula in Social Studies
with Emphasis on History

HENRY W. BRAGDON
*Formerly Instructor of Social Studies
at Phillips Exeter Academy*

Two decades ago the authors of *Reorganizing Secondary Education* could find little good to say about the conventional academic disciplines. They branded traditional subjects such as algebra, physics, and grammar as "a real hindrance" in equipping the child with the intellectual tools he needed for "independent participation in a democratic society." [1]

Three years later the authors of one of the volumes describing the famous Eight-year Study could find no more reason for the presence of foreign languages and abstract mathematics in the curriculum than that "they have always been taught." [2]

And so languages went by the board, mathematics was replaced by consumer arithmetic, and English gave way to "language arts." Somehow composition was not considered a language art, since in the world of tomorrow all communication was to be by the spoken word. So training in writing was abandoned, along with written examinations of every sort.

[1] Thayer, Zachary, Kotinsky, *Reorganizing Secondary Education* (New York: Appleton-Century-Crofts, 1939), pp. 421–27.
[2] Giles, McCutchen, Vekiel, *Exploring the Curriculum* (New York: Harper Bros., 1942), p. 100.

Now the pendulum swings the other way. Subject matter and the subject-centered teacher are again becoming respectable. Instead of merely wringing their hands, university scholars have begun to act in concert with school teachers and educators, and the result has been an extraordinary outburst of pedagogical activity. The Physical Science Study Committee, for instance, under the aegis of the National Science Foundation, created a brand-new physics course, emphasizing active, heuristic learning instead of rote. Modern languages have entered elementary school, and methods of teaching have been revolutionized so that students learn to think in an alien tongue. The teaching of mathematics has moved so far and so fast that second graders are dealing with number theory.

Perhaps never before in history has there been such an attempt to reduce the gap between the cutting edge of scholarship and what is taught in the classroom. Different as the disciplines are, their rapid progress has been characterized by certain common phenomena:

(1) College teachers work long and hard to sharpen means of communicating their discipline to others.

(2) Partnerships are created among professors, school administrators, classroom teachers, and professional educators in developing new materials and trying them out in schools.

(3) Teachers are "re-tooled" through sabbaticals, seminars, and summer institutes.

I have before me a list of more than a dozen organizations working on a national scale to improve the teaching of particular disciplines, such as the Commission on English of the College Entrance Examination Board, the Biological Sciences Study Committee, and the School Mathematics Study Group. But up to now improvements in the teaching of the social studies have been unco-ordinated and piecemeal. The American Historical Association established a Service Center for Teachers, but its activities have been limited to publishing pamphlets discussing recent interpretations and bibliography in special areas of history.

One impact on history teaching has come from the Advanced Placement Program. The materials and techniques it has devised for the able can be adapted for the less able and for younger students, so that the benefits of the program reach out and down. Perhaps its greatest benefit has been to open channels of communication between teachers in high schools and colleges all over the country. The result has been a general raising of sights. Teachers have discovered, for instance, that boys and girls of reasonable ability can go to the frontier of scholarship, dig up their own materials, assess them objectively, set them forth with order and grace, and mature rapidly in the process. The Advanced Placement Program has operated mostly with highly gifted students taught by unusually well-trained teachers. More is needed.

TODAY'S CURRICULUM

For the present history curriculum satisfies neither teachers, administrators, social scientists, historians, nor the needs of society. It lacks rigor, coherence, or underlying philosophy. Teachers too often lack training in their disciplines, and courses are too often taught simply because they are difficult to displace. At the junior and senior high school level there is much variety between school systems, but one is apt to find something like this:

Seventh grade: Geography, which consists in coloring maps and learning inert facts about climate, topography, and resources.

Eighth grade: American History, usually with special emphasis on the Colonial period and a strong dose of patriotic indoctrination.

Ninth grade: Local History and/or Civics, the latter dealing with the structure of government and very little with process.

Tenth grade: World History—cave man to Khrushchev (said one teacher: "I have them study Greece and Rome for the first night, but I don't hold them for it").

Eleventh grade: American History, often with a strongly contemporaneous slant.

Twelfth grade: Problems of Democracy, which may include anything from predriving instruction to the United Nations.

Except for the fact that most of the time is devoted to the American scene, as though we were living in 1890, there is nothing inherently wrong with this common pattern. More serious is the way social studies are taught in practice. History is too often simply a matter of studying a single text, with the aid of a workbook furnished by the publisher, and taking pre-canned objective tests. The courses in contemporary society have recently been characterized as follows:

> [The social studies are generally] a series of *ad hoc* explanations (often in terms of the greed or irrationality of other people), exhortations to be a "good citizen," and advice on how to use his personality and his budget in "getting along with

others." It is patently obvious that these do not constitute the rational and intelligent approach which is needed to cope with vast and urgent questions.[3]

But the difficulties of effecting fundamental change in the social studies are enormous. Self-dubbed patriotic societies are constantly combing textbooks for anything they consider subversive, and the teacher is hedged about with an elaborate series of taboos. A recent book on the social studies mentions six "closed areas" where scientific analysis in the school classroom is forbidden: economics; race and minority group relations; social class; sex, courtship, and marriage; religion and morality; nationalism and patriotism. This may seem ridiculous, but the introduction of fearlessly objective social science into school courses is not something to be taken lightly. As sociologist Robert Feldmesser has frankly conceded, scientific objectivity may seem to the layman and the school child like the abdication of ethical standards.

In the introduction to their basic textbooks, the Physical Science Study Committee wrote, "Throughout the student is led to realize that physics is a single subject of study." That can hardly be said of the social studies. The geographers, political scientists, anthropologists, psychologists, and sociologists share a tendency to classify, to quantify, and to look for universals, but they work apart from each other and speak different languages. In any case, there is a profound philosophical cleavage between them and the historians, who tend to distrust any suggestion that there is reality beyond the discrete individual and the unique event. And when the historians are left to themselves, they disagree about such matters as whether there is a pattern to history, what makes for historical change, and whether the lessons of the past can be applied to the present.

But whatever their differences, the practitioners of the social studies will all agree, and society will support them, that "the proper study of mankind is man." We know no final answers either in scholarship or pedagogy, but we can certainly develop a social studies curriculum far less trivial than that which now obtains in most of our schools, one far more likely to help the child to find identity in the world of today and to help him to deal with the world of tomorrow. We must

[3] Lundberg, Needham, Feldmesser, *Foundations of Human Behavior: A Teachers' Guide for an Initial Unit of a Course in Behavioral Sciences* (School and University Program for Research and Development, Behavioral Sciences Curriculum Project, Concord, Mass., 1961), Introduction.

subject the social studies to the same kind of rigorous analysis and re-creation that has been undertaken in other disciplines. The difficulty of the task does not minimize its importance.

An attempt to institute a reform of the entire social studies curriculum was begun in the Summer of 1962. Under the leadership of Jerrold Zacharias of M.I.T., Vice-President of Educational Services, Inc., and Frederick Burkhardt, President of the American Council of Learned Societies, some 40 scholars representing various disciplines, along with educators, authors, and school teachers, met at Endicott House, outside Boston, for a fortnight to consider whether it would be possible to devise "a unifying approach . . . that would provide guidelines for the structuring of a humanities and social studies curriculum running through the entire elementary and secondary sequence."

NEW APPROACHES

The dominant philosophy of the Endicott House conference was that expressed by one of its occasional members, Jerome Bruner—that students will learn effectively, and will be equipped for further learning, if they are introduced to the real structure of a field of study. History so taught should be genuine investigation of the past, not pious indoctrination or mere memorization and regurgitation. Social sciences must deal objectively and rigorously with real situations, not with predigested formulae. As the report of the conference put it, "The way a problem is attacked, the tools and techniques employed, the awareness of relevance in the chaos of detail —these as *things experienced*, rather than inert knowledge *about*, were to be the substance of the teaching-learning process." The conference generally accepted Charles Keller's belief that curriculum builders in the social studies must "posthole" (go deeply into certain topics) and have "the courage to exclude."

One group worked on the notion of a year's course on the North Atlantic Community in the seventeenth and eighteenth centuries, which might perhaps replace the present unreflective, insulated, genuflective narrative history of the United States now commonly taught in the eighth grade. The principal structural idea was "to treat the history of England—and to some extent of Western Europe—and the American colonies as that of one Atlantic community." The course would carry through chronologically a few major topics—the transplantation of English institutions and political ideas and how they were modified; the struggle between King and Parliament in the seventeenth century and between the colonies and mother country in the eighteenth, with the concomitant shift from the concept of "subject" to that of "citizen"; the web of ocean trade in terms of space, time, ships and navigation, climate, national rivalries, mercantilism, natural resources. It was agreed that there should be "intensive study of certain key events, periods, and themes." Every effort would be made to project the student imaginatively into the past. To get the "feel" of a period, and to provide materials for investigation, the classroom should be equipped with facsimile maps and documents; artifacts, tools, and scientific instruments; bulletin board displays, slides, and films, and a classroom library. There should be both individual and group projects for students of different interests and different levels of ability. There is as much reason to spend at least a quarter as much money on a laboratory for history or social science as is spent on one for chemistry or physics.

Such a course may be labeled history for convenience, but it is a history designed both to train children in scientific method and to introduce certain concepts of the social sciences. Ideally, it should mesh with earlier courses—building on skills and insights acquired in other years and looking ahead to later courses. We may in this particular course be aiming over the heads of eighth graders; we can find out only by working it out in detail with junior high school teachers and then trying it out in schools.

One last disturbing thought: Just as in the world, where today the rich nations are getting richer faster than the undeveloped ones, so the better schools are improving their instruction faster than the rest. Independent schools, suburban high schools, and specialized urban schools can command the services of the best-trained teachers and usually have a relatively homogeneous middle class or upwardly mobile student body. Meanwhile, rural or small-town schools, those in the great urban sprawl, and those under the iron discipline of state-imposed curricula which discouraged teacher initiative lag farther and farther behind.

Furthermore, the curricular improvements described in this article have mostly affected the academically oriented students. What about the rest? As things are, they will be farther behind than ever. In an automated America where there will be less need for unskilled labor, this means that doors will be shut permanently to them before they reach maturity.

Many low-IQ children are simply culturally deprived. Coming from families where they hear a foreign language, or where there are no books, they are not unintelligent so much as unequipped with the verbal symbols they must manipulate to handle academic disciplines. Unless we can devise means of tapping the immense reservoirs of intelligence now hidden by cultural deprivation, the exciting curricular progress described here may prove only to be a means of promoting the haves at the expense of the have-nots.

Geography in the High School

WILLIAM D. PATTISON

Professor of Geography,
University of California at Los Angeles
and Director, The High School Geography Project,
Sponsored by The Joint Committee on Education of
American Association of Geographers and the
National Council of Geographic Education

The American public high school of today is without counterpart in any other country. Aiming to provide education for all American youth, the high school has assumed its present form, to quote James B. Conant, "because of our economic history and our devotion to the ideals of equality of opportunity and equality of status." [1]

There are about twenty thousand high schools in the United States, of three years' and four years' educational span. One may say, accepting any current definition of geography, that probably in all of them some geographic instruction takes place. But only a minority of these institutions offers clearly identifiable geography courses. Of these courses relatively few are believed to reflect our field's current trends of thought.

For many years past professional geography has had slight contact with secondary education. We professional geographers, by and large, hold opinions on the high school that arise from individual experience with isolated schools, and from an awareness of a lack of geographic background on the part of college students. We tend to deplore what we hear about the school social studies program; we tend to regret

[1] James Bryant Conant, *The American High School Today: A First Report to Interested Citizens* (New York: McGraw-Hill Book Company, 1959), p. 8.

that something like 80 per cent of social studies teachers were history majors in college; and we tend to take heart whenever yet *another* test is publicized in the newspapers demonstrating the "geographic illiteracy" of American youth. But the high school has remained, for most of us, somebody else's business.

Still, there are signs of a change in attitude—a change for which we owe thanks, in large part, to the efforts in recent years of members of the Joint Committee on Education of this Association and of the National Council for Geographic Education. The present paper is offered in support of those efforts.

My argument, in what follows, reduces to the following few propositions: that the general thinking of high school leadership has drastically changed in the past; that opportunities for high school geography have been shaped by such changes; that today a new phase of change has begun; and that this new phase brings with it a chance for professional geography to act on behalf of high school geography, possibly with dramatic results.

QUICK SUCCESS AND SUBSEQUENT RECONSIDERATION

Let us turn our attention, to begin, to the celebrated Report of the Committee of Ten on Secondary School Studies, of 1893.[2] That report issuing from a committee chaired by the president of Harvard University, provided basic organization for thought concerning high school policy. Its effects were felt throughout the United States. The report declared intellectual discipline to be the chief goal of secondary education, and developed this view into curricular recommendations by drawing upon the written advice of nine subsidiary conferences, one of which was on geography.

The conference on geography of 1893, for its part, spoke out against any further pursuit of a survey type of world geography then in fashion, and recommended in its stead one or more courses in earth science, embracing physiography, geology, and meteorology. In consequence, new textbooks came forth—the first of them by Tarr of Cornell—and around these texts new courses were constructed. In reality, any single high school during the ensuing years was likely to offer

[2] *Report of the Committee of Ten on Secondary School Studies, with the Reports of the Conferences Arranged by the Committee* (American Book Co., 1894). Also published as Chapter 2 of *Report of the Commissioner of Education for the Year 1892–93*, Vol. 2 (1895).

but one earth science course. By 1900, in any event, earth science, weighted heavily in favor of physiography, had become the leading science course in the American high school. It was spoken of as "the New Geography." And it had attained pre-eminence within a high school rationale stipulated by the Committee of Ten.

Some readers will perhaps be acquainted with earth science courses that survive from this era, but such courses—true survivors—are relatively rare. Their popularity began to falter during the first decade of the twentieth century as high schools grew away from the academic ideals of the Committee of Ten. School administrators found general science increasingly attractive as a course that would meet broad citizenship needs. Existing earth science courses proved to be rather easy to convert into general science through curtailment of outdoor observation, through general simplification, and through an increase in the amount of attention given to the elements of physics and chemistry.

Geography teachers, in the same decade, sensed a "socializing of the curriculum," with which they appear to have been sympathetic. They also noted with hopefulness a quickening of interest that occurred in the earth science classroom whenever suggestions were made that earth conditions might somehow exercise a kind of "control" over the affairs of men. These observations, combining with dissatisfaction among geographers in teachers colleges and universities, produced a sharp reaction. A new view of high school geography rapidly developed, finding clear expression in a committee statement of 1909.[3] The authors turned their backs upon college entrance requirements (which had dominated the thinking of the conference on geography of 1893), they reasserted the value of a broadly informational geography, and they staked the future of their field in the high school on "a concrete study of human response to the environment." This view, too, became known as "the New Geography"; new books appeared in its support; much was expected of it; but, except in relatively few school districts, it succeeded neither in checking the decline of earth science nor in opening the way for geography as an independent study of society.

[3] James F. Chamberlain, *et al.*, "Report of the Committee on Secondary School Geography," *Journal of Geography*, Vol. 8 (September, 1909), pp. 1–9. Compare this paper, read before the National Education Association, with another, read by Richard E. Dodge before the Association of American Geographers, "Report of Committee on Geography for Secondary Schools," *ibid.*, Vol. 13 (March, 1910), pp. 159–165.

PROFESSIONAL EDUCATORS TO THE FORE

Meantime, general school leadership was passing to persons whose profession was education. By 1915, professional educators felt ready to assume responsibility for fashioning a new, broad high school ideology. It emerged in the following few years through reports by which nearly every secondary educator is guided today, to some extent—reports of the National Commission on the Reorganization of Secondary Education.[4]

The Commission officially defined an environment of educational thought which, spreading among the high schools of the nation, conditioned the life of all subjects of instruction. In Commission reports one finds, among other things, the following: (1) seven "cardinal principles of secondary education," bearing slight resemblance to the principles of the Committee of Ten; (2) sanction of the junior high school movement, which was already well begun; (3) support of vocational training as a specialized part of high school education; and (4) emphatic authorization of a social studies program involving at some grade levels a fusion of traditional subjects.

What, one asks, were the consequences for geography arising in later years from the Commission's pronouncements? In vocational training, or more exactly, business education, various forms of economic geography fared very well. After earlier trials in business colleges, economic geography was ready to serve in the high school, and it did so conspicuously in the 1920's and 1930's—in the company of business law, business English, and business arithmetic. Economic geography served worthily, but speaking generally economic geography took a position *outside the realm of recognized academic subject matter*. And there it stands today.

What can be said of the fate of geography among the social studies, pursuant to the Commission reports? It was a fate which, though deeply disappointing to proponents of independent geography, was in no way surprising. Social studies curriculum planners, freed to range over the six full years of junior and senior high school, took geography where they found it as a study pertaining to man, that is, in the seventh and eighth grades; and holding it there, they brought

---

[4] Particular reference is made here to Commission on the Reorganization of Secondary Education, *Report of the Subcommittee on Social Studies in Secondary Education* (Bureau of Education Bulletin No. 28, 1916) and *idem, Cardinal Principles of Secondary Education* (*ibid.*, No. 35, 1918).

it into line with dominant educational thought. At higher levels of schooling geography waited literally for decades for anything approaching national recognition. When it came, it came tentatively, and in a form answerable to the educator's sense of social need: as the educator's response to air transport and war. It came in the form of world geography, during World War II.

World geography courses brought geography back into the *academic* life of the high school proper (that is, of grades 9 through 12), but the re-entry proved to be less than triumphant. Enrollments then and in the years thereafter made no strong showing. They stayed at what might be called a respectful distance below those of another course no less world-minded and much more amenable to the prevailing social studies point of view. That course was world history.

RENEWED INITIATIVE FROM THE DISCIPLINES

Today, for the third time in seventy years, the thinking behind American public high school policy is undergoing fundamental change. The origins of pressure inducing reform are diverse, ranging from concern over national security to the demands of individual careers. Among the aspects of resultant change it is especially fitting that the attention of the Association be drawn to one. It is this: whereas the Commission on Secondary Education maintained, in its day, that schooling should be determined by (1) the needs of the society to be served, (2) the character of the individuals to be educated, and (3) the knowledge of educational theory and practice available, *now* educators are welcoming assistance from a fourth source: the disciplines of higher education and research.

Let there be no mistake: this is not 1893. There is little reason to expect that a new Committee of Ten, with its conference on geography, will proceed to reimpose upon the schools an outsider's point of view. The educator, professionalized and responsible for the school domain, is here to stay. But the disciplines, co-operating with educators, can be expected to respond to their newly opened high school opportunities with increasing force and effectiveness. Indeed, disciplinary endeavors, well financed and capably organized into various projects, are already influential on the high school scene.

Identification of three of these projects will serve to suggest the character of the disciplinary undertakings in general.

The National Task Force on Economic Education. This unit has set forth for high school guidance an extended statement on economic understanding, developed around key institutions in the American economy and key concepts employed by the economist in normal economic analysis.[5]

The Commission on English, of the College Entrance Examination Board. The Commission, intent upon establishing standards for language, literature, and composition, as the three major components of high school English instruction, is preparing volumes on all three subjects for the four high school years.[6]

The Physical Science Study Committee. At a cost in excess of three million dollars, to date, this project is making it possible for high schools to place in their science curricula a beautifully redesigned physics course, which puts to integrated use a laboratory guide, teachers' guide, library of paperbound books, demonstration films, tests, and newly marketed apparatus.[7]

Additionally, anthropology and history are inaugurating projects, biology is making itself felt through the already well-developed program of the Biological Sciences Study Committee, chemistry is represented by both the Chemical Educational Materials Study and the Chemical Bond Approach Project, and mathematics is taking initiative through the School Mathematics Study Group and seven other projects.[8] Interdisciplinary competition for high school time is becoming intense.

Geography, I am happy to be able to report, has been reacting positively to the challenge of the high school in several ways. Included in the reaction has been the organizing of a project through which geography can test its capacity for competitive constructiveness. This is the High School Geography Project, whose aim is to serve teachers by making the findings of professional geography available for classroom

[5] *Economic Education in the Schools,* Report of the National Task Force on Economic Education (Committee for Economic Development, 1961). See also *Study Materials for Economic Education in the Schools,* Report of Materials Evaluation Committee (Committee for Economic Development, 1961).

[6] *Preparation in English for College-Bound Students,* Statement by Commission on English (College Entrance Examination Board, 1960).

[7] Stephen White, "The Physical Science Study Committee (3) The Planning and Structure of the Course," *Contemporary Physics,* Vol. 2 (October, 1960), pp. 39–54.

[8] The best single source on projects that aim at revision of the instructional program in American public schools is Dorothy M. Frazer, *Current Curriculum Studies in Academic Subjects,* Report prepared for the Project on Instruction (National Education Association, 1962).

use.[9] Project efforts are being directed toward creation of a one-year demonstration course.

Four principal contemporary high school courses have attracted the attention of representatives of the High School Geography Project: earth science, economic geography, world geography, and a certain social studies elective.

Earth science. This is our old course, now making a comeback under new management. Due to the stimulus of the International Geophysical Year and for other reasons earth science is gaining favor rapidly, behind the hard-driving leadership of geology in co-operation, principally, with meteorology and oceanography. Nation-wide promotion of this course has already proceeded far. A few geographers are acutely aware of the challenge to geography that the course involves. More, it is believed, will become so.

Economic geography. In support of this course we find an unbroken record of contribution from individual geographers, acting as textbook authors, of more than forty years' duration. Economic geography now appears to be at a crossroads, where it could, by taking a wrong turn, travel toward extinction. Assistance is called for.

World geography. World geography, as a ninth- or tenth-grade course, has been doing well. A recent survey of city school systems shows that.[10] The fact that at least six high school world geography texts are now in print or soon to be published shows that, too. But in enrollment the course still trails world history by a wide margin. World geography takes many forms in high schools today, practically all of them reflecting the position of the course, deeply embedded in a social studies structure. Encouragingly, a national leader in education recently has asked that geography *as a discipline* assist in the improvement of this type of instruction.[11] The request is not expected to go unanswered.

Senior year elective course in geography. This is the least-taught course of all, but one with a virtue inherent in its position. It stands on the "growing edge" of the social studies

[9] See "A Joint Effort to Improve High School Geography," *Journal of Geography,* Vol. 60 (November, 1961), pp. 357–360, and "High School Geography Newsletter," *ibid.,* Vol. 61 (March, 1962), p. 132.

[10] Willis D. Moreland, "Curriculum Trends in the Social Studies," *Social Education,* Vol. 26 (February, 1962), pp. 73–76, 112.

[11] Arthur W. Foshay, "A Modest Proposal," *Educational Leadership,* Vol. 18 (May, 1961), pp. 506–511, 528. The author, not confining his attention to geography, proposes an increased participation of scholarship generally in education, as does William H. Cartwright, "The Social Studies: Scholarship and Pedagogy," *Social Education,* Vol. 22 (May, 1958), pp. 228–232.

program, the edge where courses are being tried that clearly and emphatically express the disciplines from which they derive. There is no assurance that the High School Geography Project will create its course for this place in the curriculum, but if it should do so, it will bring within the reach of possibility, for the first time since the days of physiography's success, general recognition of high school geography as a step to higher education.

In closing, I respectfully suggest, on behalf of the High School Geography Project, and of all persons active in the improvement of high school geography, that the high school today is "on the move" in a general direction which professional geography should be proud to promote. I also suggest that a favorable outcome of this movement, so far as geography is concerned, should not be taken for granted. The future attitude of Association members, in this connection, may be decisive in its effect.

BANTAM CLASSICS

BRAVE NEW WORLD Aldous Huxley................HC206 60¢

THE IDIOT Fyodor Dostoevsky.........................SC179 75¢

SISTER CARRIE Theodore Dreiser....................HC207 60¢

LORD JIM Joseph Conrad.............................FC201 50¢

OF MICE AND MEN John Steinbeck................FC240 50¢

HERMAN MELVILLE FOUR SHORT NOVELS...SC226 75¢

CANNERY ROW Jonn Steinbeck......................FC196 50¢

ANNA KARENINA Leo Tolstoy.......................NC180 95¢
    (Translated by Joel Carmichael—Introduction by Malcolm Cowley)

ARMS AND THE MAN George Bernard Shaw........FC256 50¢
    (Introduction by Louis Kronenberger)

CRIME AND PUNISHMENT Fyodor Dostoevsky.....HC140 60¢

ALL THE KING'S MEN Robert Penn Warren.........SC202 75¢

WASHINGTON SQUARE Henry James.............FC258 50¢

THE RED AND THE BLACK Stendhal.............SC40 75¢
    (Translated by Lowell Bair—Introduction by Clifton Fadiman)

THE DARING YOUNG MAN ON THE FLYING
    TRAPEZE William Saroyan.........................FC105 50¢

THE AENEID Vergil.................................HC193 60¢
    (Edited and with an Introduction by Moses Hadas)

EYELESS IN GAZA Aldous Huxley..................SC93 75¢

HENRY ESMOND William Makepeace Thackeray.........FC90 50¢
    (Introduction by Lionel Stevenson)

SWEET THURSDAY John Steinbeck................SC273 75¢

FIVE SHORT NOVELS Ivan Turgenev...............SC92 75¢
    (Translated and with an Introduction by Franklin Reeve)

REFLECTIONS IN A GOLDEN EYE Carson McCullers FC100 50¢

FOR A COMPLETE LISTING OF BANTAM CLASSICS WRITE TO: Sales Department; Bantam Books, Inc.; 271 Madison Avenue; New York 16, N. Y.

Look for Bantam Classics at local newsstands and bookstores. If your dealer does not carry these books, they may be ordered by sending the price of the book plus 10¢ postage and handling charge for each copy to: Dept. BC; Bantam Books, Inc.; 414 E. Golf Rd., Des Plaines, Ill. (On orders for 5 or more books there is no postage charge.) Sorry, no C.O.D.'s. Send check or money order. No currency please. Allow three weeks for delivery.   1 BC-10-64